The Disney+ Kingdom

Also of Interest
and from McFarland

Popular Music in the Classroom: Essays for Instructors (edited by David Whitt, 2020)

Myth in the Modern World: Essays on Intersections with Ideology and Culture (edited by David Whitt and John Perlich, 2014)

Millennial Mythmaking: Essays on the Power of Science Fiction and Fantasy Literature, Films and Games (edited by John Perlich and David Whitt, 2010)

The Disney+ Kingdom

Essays on Nostalgia, Representation and Branding

Edited by David Whitt *and* John Perlich

McFarland & Company, Inc., Publishers
Jefferson, North Carolina

This book has undergone peer review.

Library of Congress Cataloging-in-Publication Data

Names: Whitt, David, editor. | Perlich, John R., editor.
Title: The Disney+ kingdom : essays on nostalgia, representation and branding / edited by David Whitt and John Perlich.
Description: Jefferson, North Carolina : McFarland & Company, Inc., Publishers, 2024. | Includes bibliographical references and index.
Identifiers: LCCN 2024013785 | ISBN 9781476690056 (paperback : acid free paper) ∞ ISBN 9781476653310 (ebook)
Subjects: LCSH: Disney+ (Firm) | Walt Disney Company. | Video-on-demand—United States. | Streaming video—United States. | LCGFT: Essays.
Classification: LCC HD9697.V544 D57625 2024 | DDC 384.55/540973—dc23/eng/20230224
LC record available at https://lccn.loc.gov/2024013785

British Library cataloguing data are available

ISBN (print) 978-1-4766-9005-6
ISBN (ebook) 978-1-4766-5331-0

Printed in the United States of America

McFarland & Company, Inc., Publishers
Box 611, Jefferson, North Carolina 28640
www.mcfarlandpub.com

For Weston, Lena, Rowan and Rhodes. I hope someday
we can all experience Disney World together.
—Dave

For Caiden and Kelyn. Use your voices
to change the world!
—John

Acknowledgments

Dave would like to thank Nebraska Wesleyan University for awarding him with an Ameritas Faculty Fellowship to pay for his entire trip to Disney World. He is thankful to teach at an institution that supports faculty research interests, particularly those that require riding Pirates of the Caribbean, Space Mountain, and Dumbo the Flying Elephant, along with eating Mickey Mouse–shaped pretzels and ice cream sandwiches. He would also like to thank his NWU Communication Studies colleagues for their support, particularly Dr. Rachel Pokora, for reading his essay and providing valuable feedback. Finally, Dave would like to thank Johnny P. for also reading his essay, but more importantly, being coeditor on yet another book adventure.

John would like to thank his colleagues at Bemidji State University for their unwavering support. He is blessed to participate in conversations with amazing scholars (and nerd out with fellow fans, e.g., Andy Bartlett). There are too many colleagues to acknowledge, but friends in the offices of Academic Affairs, Accessibility Services, Communications & Marketing, DEI, CICH, Sociology & Communication Studies, Student Activities, Student Life/Success, and Sattgast Hall have been integral in helping us produce this book. Donna, Tim, and Cindy were unbelievably supportive throughout the writing process. Caiden (John's daughter) provided an invaluable editorial eye.

Finally, John would like to thank the Lando to his Nien Nunb. See you *At the Parthenon*, Dave!

Table of Contents

Introduction

John Perlich *and* David Whitt

Netflix. Amazon Prime Video. Max. Hulu. Paramount+. Peacock. Apple TV+. The streaming wars are here. According to Judy Berman of *Time.com*, this entertainment arms race began in the 2010s, quickly putting pressure on media companies to "launch in-house streaming platforms and grow their audiences through massive original-content spends" (2023, para. 5). On November 12, 2019, Disney Entertainment entered the fray, launching their Disney+ streaming service offering original films and television programming for not only Disney but also for Pixar, Marvel, Star Wars and National Geographic. Over the next several years, Disney+ subscribers would quickly grow to more than 221 million worldwide, even passing Netflix subscriber numbers in 2022 (Forbes.com, 2022).

However, despite the popularity of the Disney brand, its movies, television programs, Broadway musicals, and theme parks have long been a focal point for cultural critics. Years before the streaming wars began, Giroux and Pollock (2010) argued Disney "reconstructs" identities through entertainment. Disney has shaped, and continues to shape, ideas about "gender, race, education, the family, community, education, place, and globalization" (Inman & Sellers, 2016, p. 39). Disney has endured longstanding criticisms for the use of historical revisionism, tired tropes, and reductionistic archetypes; Disney+ provides the "Mouse House" with an opportunity to challenge conventional narratives through their new streaming platform. In other words, criticisms of past Disney programming can be revisited and potentially undone through this new steaming service. However, have new programs been successful in reshaping the Disney brand and image? Has the new content on Disney+ been a plus or a minus? These are questions this collection seeks to answer.

When viewing the table of contents, astute readers will notice an implicit structure behind the order of the essays. Beyond this introduction, the first and last essays constitute bookends for the volume. Working within a similar framework, both White and Whitt document the process of media-induced nostalgia. White views Disney+ nostalgia as allowing for escape from turbulent times. Using an autoethnographic approach, Whitt applies the concept of intertextuality to demonstrate a layering of significance between Disney+ shows like *The Imagineering Story* and *Behind the Attraction* and his own lived experience. Together, these essays demonstrate the transformative power of Disney+ programming at both the cultural and individual level.

As previously noted, Disney+, as a streaming platform, provides the "Mouse House" an opportunity to address well-known criticisms in the area of cultural representation. Central to our next three essays is the revision of representation. Extending White's analysis of nostalgia, Gatto documents the manner in which *The Mighty Ducks* film franchise revisits the past through its series *Game Changers*, yet provides new direction for the future—one example is by adding "warrior princesses" to the Mighty Ducks hockey team. Following Gatto's essay, Thomas and Burnett deconstruct the changing nature and significance of the Disney Princess trope—clearly showing how Disney has challenged cultural understanding of feminine identity. Tecson highlights a blind spot when it comes to representation, holding Disney accountable through her critique of *Doogie Kameāloha, M.D.*

We feature two essays covering the *High School Musical* phenomena, both of which highlight Disney's journey toward the revision of representation, particularly in regard to queer identities. While Bindig Yousman and Hester seemingly contradict each other, we believe there is value in differing perspectives. Ultimately, the reader is allowed to decide which argument seems most persuasive in their analysis of Disney+ programming.

The final four essays of this volume by Paul and Nisbett, Sánchez-Rodríguez, Blanton, and Perlich and Baird represent some of the most lucrative and high-profile programs in the Disney+ lineup by focusing on the Marvel and Star Wars universes, respectively. In sum, these essays illustrate the degrees of revision in representation achieved by Disney since launching the streaming service in 2019. Previously invisible groups and identities have become profoundly more visible because of shows like *Moon Knight*, *She-Hulk*, *The Mandalorian*, and *Andor*. These essays highlight counter-hegemonic messages and new faces within two blockbuster franchises.

Ultimately, it would be wrong of us to contend that we have been able to cover the entire spectrum of change in Disney programming since 2019. One of our reviewers (who is greatly appreciated) believed "it's an oversight to not include *WandaVision*, especially as one of the foundational series to Disney+, and also because Wanda does something uncharacteristic of the rest of the superheroes … providing a meta-narrative of [Disney Corporation].” Rather than spoil the fun by explaining their insight, we call you—the reader—to action. Future volumes will allow for additional perspectives and deconstructions. Join us in our analysis of these artifacts. Finally, we hope you will heed our call to action, particularly after reading the final essay in this book, by considering (plus or minus), how Disney+ has transformed you.

References

Disney surpasses Netflix subscriber count: What does that mean for investors? (2022, September 27). *Forbes.com*. Retrieved from https://www.forbes.com/sites/qai/2022/09/27/disney-surpasses-netflix-subscriber-count-what-does-that-means-for-investors/?sh=72d7aacf5e0b.

Giroux, H.A., & Pollock, G. (2010). *The mouse that roared: Disney and the end of innocence*. Rowman & Littlefield.

Inman, J.O., & Sellers, K.M. (2016). The Disney princess dilemma: Constructing, composing, and combatting gendered narratives. *Counterpoints, 477*, 39–50.

Navigating the Worst of Times

Nostalgia on Disney+

Rhema F. White

Introduction

Though there was no way for Disney to know that a global pandemic was imminent, the release of the Disney+ streaming service on November 12, 2019, was timely. Since its launch, subscribers have taken to blogs, social media, and everyday conversations to discuss the platform's nostalgic elements. With the availability of classic titles such as *Snow White and the Seven Dwarfs* (1937), and newer retellings like *Maleficent* (2014), Disney+ is using nostalgia to construct reality in a moment largely characterized by Covid-19 and inflation-fueled anxiety. It is also arguable that despite the financial intentions of the corporation, users—conceivably aware of the organization's bottom line—are engaging with the content on their own terms. Specifically, Disney+ subscribers are actively analyzing the platform's nostalgic content, as evidenced by their varied responses on social media celebrating, critiquing, and comparing Disney's slate of original programming.

Generally, nostalgia is thought of as a sentimental feeling brought on by memories of the past (Sedikides et al., 2008). In the present digital age, however, it has taken on a new dimension with its distinct connection to media products. Wulf, Rieger and Schmitt (2018) define media-induced nostalgia as a "bittersweet and fundamentally social emotion ... elicited by remembering or re-experiencing media content and technologies from the past" (p. 70). As suggested, the state of contemporary society is a reason for why products that induce nostalgic feelings are so popular. Ewen (2020) notes, for instance, that the present moment is characterized by fear and anxiety, and subtly inquires that when the world one lives in is in turmoil, who among us would not wish to escape to more pleasant days, such as childhood? Hence, as society continues to navigate a global pandemic, war, and other pressing challenges like climate change and increased crime, a strong reason for the astronomical success of Disney+ makes itself readily apparent: nostalgia as escapism from a turbulent present. This essay seeks to explore this phenomenon further, with an emphasis on audience reception, in the context of the Disney+ platform.

Background

The following sections situate the 1990s, and the 2000s, by proximity, as popular periods for contemporary mass media to revisit, and delineates the main routes taken by Disney to implement nostalgia on the Disney+ platform.

Locating the 1990s as a Preferred Site for Revisitation

Known as the Disney Renaissance, 1989–1999 was a productive and profitable time for Walt Disney Studios (Sundleaf, 2020). The output of commercially successful feature films released during this period, such as *The Little Mermaid* (1989), *The Lion King* (1994), and *Tarzan* (1999), mirror that of Disney's Golden Age: the 1930s to the 1960s (Kothenschulte, 2016). It becomes simple, then, to locate the 1990s and early 2000s as premier periods of revisitation for modern audiences. In addition to Disney's grasp on the construction of childhoods in the 1990s, this decade also sets itself apart for alternate reasons. Ewen (2020) explains that the '90s constituted a peaceful and ideal era before the September 11 attacks in the following decade, and was the last era in history during which smart phones and social media sites were virtually non-existent. The impact of the latter has, further, arguably facilitated contemporary feelings about the ways in which social media has "ruined" how we interact with one other, and aides in constructing the 1990s and early 2000s as years during which relationships and social interactions were viewed as more "authentic" than today.

Main Routes for the Nostalgic Audience on Disney+: Classic Films and Original Reboots

In all, Disney+ appears to engage nostalgia in two distinct ways: by the availability of classic titles on its platform, as well as through reboots and remakes of some of those same films. The primary intent of Disney is clear: to reach their financial bottom line. It cannot be overlooked, however, that in this capitalistic enterprise—which most critics will agree reeks of nostalgic exploitation—audience members are using nostalgia for their own purposes and ascribing their own meanings to it. Consider the following tweet from a Disney+ user:

> I've been doing some self therapy [*sic*] by watching movies today that I last saw as a child. Nostalgia is an amazing feeling, reconnecting with my younger self but also understanding the stories as an adult. Disney Plus therapy for less than $10 a month.

Despite this, it must be noted that while the previous tweet was made in reference to the general availability of childhood classics on Disney+, the reception to original Disney+ remakes appear mixed. Some users give the impression that they appreciate the reimagining of classics and the opportunities they offer for being re-enchanted by the past, but others question their authenticity and wonder if the financial bottom line is impeding the perceived quality of Disney's media products. The following section illuminates this mixed reception by using two 1990s influenced shows on Disney+, and one from the early 2000s, as examples.

Nostalgia for the 1990s and Early 2000s in Disney+ Original Content

Disney+ programming, namely *The Mighty Ducks: Game Changers* (2021–2022), *Home Sweet Home Alone* (2021), and *The Proud Family: Louder and Prouder* (2022), constitute compelling examples of the modern media landscape's 1990s/2000s nostalgia trend. As discussed previously, the '90s and the early years of the '00s include pop culture moments that modern films and television shows frequently revisit. As new additions to Disney+, the abovementioned shows account for a fresh slate of programming not yet studied at length by pop culture historians and nostalgia scholars.

***The Mighty Ducks: Game Changers* (2021–2022)**

The Mighty Ducks: Game Changers (2021–2022) is an original series on Disney+ that was released as a continuation of the 1990s *Mighty Ducks* film trilogy. The Ducks are a youth hockey team who, in the original movies, were not the most skilled group of youngsters. In the newer version, the once-despondent Ducks are now a powerhouse, and with this redistribution of power emerges a new team of underdogs: the Don't Bothers. Gordon Bombay (Emilio Estevez), coach of the Ducks in the original film, becomes assistant coach—and head coach, briefly—for the Don't Bothers in the 2021 revival. Other characters return as well, such as Marguerite Moreau's character Connie Moreau, and Justin Wong's Kenny Wu, among other fan favorites. The series has received generally positive reviews—Rotten Tomatoes presently shows an 87 percent critic score, and 67 percent audience score (Rotten Tomatoes, n.d.)—with additional feedback on Twitter conveying audience reactions as follows (tweets have been transcribed verbatim):

> "I've seen the first 3 episodes of The Mighty Ducks: Game Changers & while it's not quite that, it made me beyond happy. As a fan of the franchise, sports movies, and nostalgia, it does an excellent job of evolving while paying homage to the OG. Cobra Kai-lite. Cant wait for more."
>
> "Watching the Mighty Ducks Game Changers, experiencing peak millennial nostalgia. A+."
>
> "The new mighty ducks on Disney plus is corny and cheesy but it brings back the nostalgia and I gotta say it was pretty well done."

Responses such as these suggest critical engagement on behalf of audience members as they acknowledge that while the show may not quite grasp the particular magic of its original form, newer versions, when constructed mindfully, are able to capture a bit of its essence. As it pertains to *The Mighty Ducks: Game Changers* (2021–2022), specifically, a large number of Disney+ subscribers on Twitter seem to feel that the new series holds its own weight while incorporating pleasant, but not incessant, callbacks to its admired 1990s predecessors.

Home Sweet Home Alone (2021)

Home Sweet Home Alone (2021) is the sixth installment in the *Home Alone* franchise. It was recently produced as an original title for Disney+ and, unlike *Game Changers*, released to overwhelmingly poor reviews: per Rotten Tomatoes (n.d.), critics have given the film an average score of 15 percent, and audiences, 12 percent. Critiques heavily focused on bungled attempts to recreate specific scenes from the original 1990 film. Sebren (2021), in fact, found that if set side-by-side, scenes from the original film and the reboot are synchronized almost perfectly throughout the trailer. Additionally, in the 2021 version, character names have changed, but each person's persona makes them easily identifiable to anyone who watched the original 1990s films.

There are further callbacks to the original movies as the main characters' home has "McAllister Security" installed, and Buzz, Kevin's older brother, has become a police officer. In an interview with Jason Guerrasio (2020) of *Insider*, Chris Columbus, director of the first two *Home Alone* films, denounced the remake with the following statement and question: "I'm a firm believer that you don't remake films that have had the longevity of Home Alone. You're not going to create lightning in a bottle again. So why do it?" (para. 25). Feedback on Twitter, similarly, shows audience members' reactions as follows:

> "Home Sweet Home Alone is a 3/10. A soulless cash grab with little to offer, that desperately tries to invoke feelings of nostalgia through constant cheap callbacks to the original."
>
> "It [*Home Sweet Home Alone*] is, in no small dose, utterly, utterly appalling."
>
> "I watched sweet home home [*sic*] alone on Disney plus yesterday! It was an alright movie! I like the original home alone better!"

Additional comments found on Twitter are, for the most part, consistent with what is included here: generally positive feelings towards the *Mighty Ducks*, and overwhelming disappointment with *Home Sweet Home Alone*. This disparity suggests that there may exist a preferred way to incorporate nostalgia into newer works without cheapening the experience. What *is* for sure, however, is that audiences are unquestionably exhibiting their ability to mindfully engage with this content.

The Proud Family: Louder and Prouder (2022)

In line with the revitalization of select shows from the 1990s, programs from the early 2000s such as *The Proud Family: Louder and Prouder*, have also found themselves returning to production on Disney+. The original series, concisely titled *The Proud Family*, ran on Disney from 2001 to 2005 and was disruptive in that it introduced one of television's first animated Black families to the masses (Sandoval, 2022). Though the original was not exempt from critique—e.g., allegations of negative stereotypes pertaining to the very people it was meant to positively represent (Steele, 2016)—its cultural impact has been undeniable, with advocates hailing the show as "groundbreaking" and "educational" (Jackson, 2022).

The original animated series follows a 14-year-old Penny Proud and her teenage exploits, and in the 2022 revival that premise remains pretty much the same. There are storylines navigating adolescent friendships, romantic relationships, and family life, but updated to uniquely mirror life for present-day teens. Specifically, the newest iteration explores racism, queerness, and children on the spectrum, to name a few. Just as the original show was watched and appreciated by a plethora of young viewers of all races across America—many of whom were young African Americans—the 2022 *Proud Family* reignited excitement of those same audience members, whilst targeting a new generation. Here's what a fraction of those familiar with the initial show had to say about the revival on Twitter:

> "The Proud Family Louder and Prouder is a masterclass on how to reboot a show. Bring back the original cast, add a couple new characters to keep it interesting, and modernize the world without losing the nostalgia from the original"
>
> "the proud family reboot is saur good. i wonder if children enjoy it as much as my grown self"
>
> "the proud family reboot is hilarious. is it good? debatable but it is so funny omg"

Overall, the disparate nature of responses to each of the above-mentioned Disney+ original reboots, both separately and collectively, allude to an audience who is actively consuming, interpreting, and communicating what comes across their screens independent of, in concert with, and at times wholly against, what Disney executives and show writers intend. The following section delves deeper into this concept with a discussion of active audience theory.

The Active Audience: Consumption and Interpretation

Active audience perspectives shift the focus from corporations and their motives to audiences and *their* active engagement with commodities. This viewpoint ultimately rejects the once-popularly held perception of audiences as people who passively consume media content, instead regarding them as a dynamic group with the ability to choose media for their own purposes, independent of what media executives intend. As Willis (2015) makes clear:

> Our basic point is that human consumption does not simply repeat the relations of production—and whatever cynical motives lie behind them. Interpretation, symbolic action, and creativity are part of consumption. They're involved in the whole realm of necessary symbolic work [p. 244].

This further suggests that though pessimistic perspectives abound concerning media consumption in a capitalist culture, these practices by powerful corporations do not negate the value of their products. The value is instead found in the meaning derived from them, by the audience. From uses and gratifications—e.g., the possible use of nostalgic content for escape—to Stuart Hall's encoding/decoding model (exploring the preferred, negotiated, and oppositional readings of nostalgia on Disney+), active audience frameworks reject the oversimplified notion of "consumption"—considering it instead a complex site of negotiation, indicating that multiple, competing interpretations are possible, and, often, present.

This shift in perspective has uncovered an arena for audience research that highlights essential implications for media industries and consumers alike. One such example, as previously mentioned, and that will be discussed here in terms of Disney+ content, is Stuart Hall's encoding and decoding model of communication.

Theoretical Perspectives: Stuart Hall's Encoding/ Decoding Model in a Disney+ Context

Hall's encoding/decoding model was developed and refined between the 1970s and 1980s. These were years characterized by the field of Cultural Studies' deep interest in television and audiences (Corner, 2004), and just prior to the more disruptive era of social media. The latter period, which has come to frame much of how we discuss mass media today, and which has also been increasingly characterized by an abundance of streaming platforms, has been found to mesh well with analyses using Hall's model (Palmer, 2020; Shaw, 2017). Platforms like Disney+, which are uniquely infused with features of traditional television *and* socially mediated (or disruptive) elements, are therefore advantageously positioned to be studied by media scholars.

In his view, Hall (1980) notes that media texts are inscribed with messages by media producers, and that audiences typically deconstruct these texts according to one of three distinct positions: the preferred, oppositional, or negotiated reading. If an audience member decodes a message given exactly as the media producer intends, then they are said to have adopted the preferred reading. Contrastingly, if an audience member completely rejects the message-as-intended, they are thought to be espousing an oppositional reading. In a negotiated reading, the audience member dually rejects some parts of the message, while accepting others.

Based on the nature of media cultural industries, it can be assumed that creators, producers, and writers of the three Disney+ originals mentioned in this essay, sought to use nostalgia to relate to past audiences, thereby increasing viewership for the revitalized shows, and engendering positive sentiment from the start. Contrarily, as Hall would expect, and as evidenced from Disney+ subscribers on Twitter, viewers adopted various readings: some in support of the new shows, some not, and some in the middle. Three examples using each of the shows/films noted here, which illustrate this are as follows:

- **Preferred Reading for *The Mighty Ducks: Game Changers***

"This 90s kid is loving The Mighty Ducks show on Disney Plus." This user reacts positively to the series, drawing from their background of having grown up in the 90s, just as show executives intended.

- **Oppositional Reading for *Home Sweet Home Alone***

"Watching Home Sweet Home Alone on Disney+ and my lord, it's infuriating. Why would they do this? [facepalm emoji, exploding head emoji, crying emoji]." This user not only appears to reject the remake, but is angered by what they consider to be the daring nature of Disney to take this project on. It can be presumed that this audience member did not feel the remake measured up to the original.

- **Negotiated Reading for *The Proud Family: Louder and Prouder***

"The Proud Family Reboot isn't bad ... but it's missing a little something that I can't put my finger on." This user neither wholly accepts nor rejects this reboot, landing in the middle with their analysis. They acknowledge that while the show is not bad, it could also be better. Continued engagement with the series, and adjustments by Disney, could lead them further in either direction.

The reason for this myriad of interpretations comes down to one reality: regardless of what media conglomerates, producers, and writers intend, audience members hail from vastly different walks of life. As a result, their experiences inform the ways in which they "read" the respective shows they watch. In the examples mentioned above, and as stated, media producers sought to use nostalgia to connect with past audiences to generate viewership and facilitate positive attitudes towards the shows. However, audiences responded in several ways. An extensive review would likely uncover additional examples of each type of reading as labeled by Hall's model—a model which does well to lead us into healthy inquiry regarding what works in these shows, what does not, and why.

The Role of Nostalgia in Encoding and Decoding Media Messages

Interestingly, in a BBC article discussing Disney and nostalgia in the Covid age, Rahman-Jones (2020) highlights the social aspect of nostalgia by quoting Dr. Wijnand van Tilburg, University of Essex psychology lecturer and nostalgia expert, who notes that part of nostalgia's usefulness is due to its "strong social elements" (para. 20). Nostalgia has the ability to aide us in feeling more connected to others who have some of the same shared experiences—and in the midst of an ongoing pandemic, cultural texts able to give that feeling of connection to people are vital. Though Disney's intention is clearly to make money, and consumers' consistent engagement with their products guarantee them said money, in the end, true power lies with the audience. Regardless of what Disney aims to do, their products are meaningless until consumers give them meaning.

Discussion

It is apparent that feelings of nostalgia are often capitalized on during uncertain times for monetary gain, and the Disney corporation is not exempt from this money-making practice. While profit is the end goal for Disney, the opportunities Disney+ offers its subscribers to make its media work for their own purposes, as well as the varying meanings they derive from it, are not to be overlooked. As the Mouse House makes their vault of classics more widely available and offers new "original" content, a good bit of which plays off past successes, Disney is arguably giving some consumers exactly what they want: an escape route to happier times. As noted, however, the blowback Disney receives in lieu of its remakes brings up questions: is there a limit to nostalgia's effectiveness? Is it simple access to past titles that subscribers want, as opposed to modern remakes of those same films? Is there a "wrong" way to incorporate nostalgia into a contemporary cultural product?

Considered collectively, the nostalgia on Disney+ outlined in this essay, though certainly not exhaustive, is indicative of a heightened interest in revisiting the past to escape a tumultuous present. More than being simplified as a cash grab by Disney, this moment can also be regarded as one that personifies the agency that exists in consumption. In the words of Gilroy (2015) as he analogously speaks about music:

> Consumption is a vague word that trips far too easily off the dismissive tongue. People use these images and the [music] that they enclose for a variety of reasons ... the presence of the extra cultural resource does not, of course negate or deny the act of capitalistic exchange through which the record is usually acquired. But the guidance, solace, and pleasures which the commodity may impart cannot be understood as an incidental adjunct to the sometimes solitary act of purchasing it [p. 503].

In other words, consumption itself is also a site of cultural production. True, people may purchase a product, but what they do with it, as well as the meanings they ascribe to it, are further essential junctions to consider in the act of media engagement.

Toward a Formula for a Successful Reboot

In the end, it cannot be denied that in a period characterized by as much loss as the present moment, numerous subscribers find solace in Disney+. When considering the platform's ability to link people who are physically apart by shared interests and memories, as well as its power to mentally transport people to "better eras," Disney+, in these turbulent times, *is* a plus. Nonetheless, the Mouse House would do well to listen to those who critique its recent string of reboots.

Here, a question naturally presents itself: what makes a successful reboot? Why do some, like *The Mighty Ducks: Game Changers* and *The Proud Family*, generally score more positive feedback from critics and audiences alike, while others, like *Home Sweet Home Alone*, do not? Initial glances at audience sentiment suggest two main things as a precursor to reboot success: (1) the newest form need not be a modern shot-by-shot recreation of the original (like *Home Sweet Home Alone* was purported to be), but must be able to stand on its own. This helps to capture the attention of new viewing publics. However, for the viewing pleasure of audiences familiar with the original, it may help to (2) include at least a few aesthetic callbacks to the first version, like *The Mighty Ducks* and *The Proud Family* did. A few examples of this implemented successfully elsewhere are Peacock's *Bel-Air* (2022–), a dramatic reimagining of the beloved 1990s sitcom *The Fresh Prince of Bel-Air* (1990–1996), and *Saved by the Bell* (2020), a revitalization of its popular 1990s teen-centered predecessor. Both employ nostalgia in different ways, with the former opting for a reconstructed and more dramatized world with characters of the same name and a few familiar storylines, while the latter implements past characters into a contemporary context with new protagonists and narratives.

Future systematic and long-term studies are needed to demonstrate relationships, and more definitively provide explanations for audience reactions. As a result, media corporations would be provided with a working formula that functions for their own goals, but also—and most importantly—is amenable to the attitudes and values of audience members watching their shows. To that end, there remains the necessity of not insulting the intellect of the audience when creating content for them. It is important to remember that viewers are not a monolith and bring varied life experiences to the media content they consume. Though Gen Xers and millennials constitute the bulk of the target audience for these revitalizations, this does not mean that nostalgic content geared toward their coming-of-age periods will automatically foster their positive regard. It is in this vein that highlighting active audience perspectives, especially in the work of increased nostalgic media content, is vital.

Conclusion

The purpose of this essay was to explore media-induced nostalgia on Disney+ by historically contextualizing the nostalgic elements of the platform and locating the 1990s and early 2000s as a preferred site of revisitation. Three distinct examples of '90s and '00s influenced Disney+ original content were explored, and the phenomenon situated within a discussion of active audience theory. Ultimately, there is value in exploring the potential that exists in the consumption of Disney's nostalgic commodities, as opposed to a sole focus on the exploitation of fond memories. While millions flock to the streaming service to re-watch childhood classics, the critique of select Disney reboots cannot be ignored. Despite valid criticisms, Disney, a corporation that has aided childhood identity construction and shaped society over the decades (Binkley, 2016), has seemingly struck gold with Disney+ in these trying times.

References

Binkley, M. (2016). An argument on Disney and psychological development. *URJ-UCCS: Undergraduate Research Journal at UCCS, 10*(1), 11–18.

Corner, J. (2004). Television studies: Plural contexts, singular ambitions? *Journal of British Cinema and Television, 1*(1), 6–13.

Ewen, N. (2020). "Talk to each other like it's 1995": Mapping nostalgia for the 1990s in contemporary media culture. *Television & New Media, 21*(6), 574–580.

Gilroy, P. (2015). Wearing your art on your sleeve: Notes towards a diaspora history of black ephemera. In R. Guins & O.Z. Cruz (Eds.), *Popular culture: A reader* (pp. 495–503). Sage. (Original work published 1993.)

Guerrasio, J. (2020, December 24). *"Home Alone" at 30: Director Chris Columbus talks Trump "bullying his way" into a cameo and more never-before-told stories.* Business Insider. https://www.businessinsider.com/home-alone-30-anniversary-chris-columbus-trump-cameo-2020-11.

Hall, S. (1980). Coding/decoding. In S. Hall, D. Hobson, A. Lowe, & P. Willis (Eds.), *Culture, media, and language* (pp. 63–87). Routledge.

Jackson, L. (2022, February 23). A groundbreaking cartoon family returns, "Louder and Prouder." *New York Times.* https://www.nytimes.com/2022/02/23/arts/television/proud-family-returns.html.

Kothenschulte, D. (2016). *The Walt Disney film archives: The animated movies 1921–1968.* Taschen.

Palmer, M. (2020). *Facebook as a meta-ideological apparatus: Reassessing the encoding/decoding model in the context of social media.* [Doctoral dissertation, University of Technology Sydney.]

Rahman-Jones, I. (2020, September 2). Mulan: Disney remakes and the power of nostalgia during coronavirus. BBC. Retrieved from https://www.bbc.com/news/newsbeat-47696220.

Rotten Tomatoes (n.d). *Home Sweet Home Alone.* https://www.rottentomatoes.com/m/home_sweet_home_alone.

Rotten Tomatoes (n.d). *The Mighty Ducks: Game Changers.* https://www.rottentomatoes.com/m/home_sweet_home_alone.

Sandoval, L. (2022, March 10). "The Proud Family: Louder and Prouder." *Los Angeles Sentinel.* https://lasentinel.net/the-proud-family-louder-and-prouder.html.

Sebren, B.L. (2021, October 13). *Home Sweet Home Alone trailer is a shot-for-shot remake of the original Home Alone trailer.* MovieWeb. https://movieweb.com/home-sweet-home-alone-trailer-side-by-side-comparison/.

Sedikides, C., Wildschut, T., Arndt, J., & Routledge, C. (2008). Nostalgia: Past, present, and future. *Current Directions in Psychological Science, 17*(5), 304–307.

Shaw, A. (2017). Encoding and decoding affordances: Stuart Hall and interactive media technologies. *Media, Culture & Society, 39*(4), 592–602.
Steele, C.K. (2016). Pride and prejudice: Pervasiveness of colorism and the animated series *Proud Family. The Howard Journal of Communications, 27*(1), 53–67. https://doi.org/10.1080/10646175.2015.1117028.
Sundleaf, V. (2020). *The Disney renaissance historical influences, the films, and the lasting impacts (1989–1999).* [Doctoral dissertation, University of Nebraska at Omaha.]
Willis, P. (2015). Symbolic creativity. In R. Guins & O.Z. Cruz (Eds.), *Popular culture: A reader* (pp. 495–503). Sage. (Original work published 1990.)
Wulf, T., Rieger, D., & Schmitt, J.B. (2018). Blissed by the past: Theorizing media-induced nostalgia as an audience response factor for entertainment and well-being. *Poetics, 69*, 70–80.

Ducks Fly Together

A Look at Disney+ as a Facilitator of Nostalgia and Transportation

Kristi Gatto

Since 1923, the Walt Disney Company has captivated the masses through their films, TV shows, and theme park experiences. On November 12, 2019, Walt Disney joined the streaming wars with Disney+ and by the end of its first day had 10 million-plus subscribers (Alexander, 2019). CEO Bob Iger declared, "the launch of Disney+ [as] a historic moment for our company that marks a new era of innovation and creativity" (Disney Media & Entertainment Distribution, 2019). With the introduction of Disney+, a plethora of media content was suddenly available for streaming and binge-watching. Fans were able to watch Disney classics like *Steamboat Willie* (1928), *Tugboat Mickey* (1940), and *Chip an' Dale* (1947) along with Disney Channel Original Movies including *Cadet Kelly* (2002) and *Double Teamed* (2002)—all of these programs were previously unavailable for decades.

Disney+ is the home of popular nostalgic content, but it has also become a production house, releasing new television shows and films that align with its treasured content. For example, all three *High School Musical* films were released in conjunction with the premiere of a new Disney+ original *High School Musical: The Musical: The Series* (2019–). Disney+ premiere day was also highly sentimental for *Star Wars* fans, who woke up on release day to a surplus of content including Episodes I–VIII. Additionally, these fans were able to create new Star Wars memories through *The Mandalorian* (2019–), a Disney+ Original series. Disney+ continues to benefit the Walt Disney model of innovation and creativity as fan favorite films and television shows are not only readily accessible across electronic devices, but new content is being released with nostalgic and transportive elements.

Lost in Our Own Memories

Nostalgia has been a concept whose meaning has evolved over time. The derivation of "nostalgia" comes from the Greek words "nostos" and "algai" which refers to returning home and pain, respectively (Wildschut et al., 2008). However, new research techniques (Batcho, 2013) allowed scholars to examine the phenomenon more closely, and position it as a cognitive emotion (Marchegiani & Phau, 2010). Now, it is situated as a yearning for the past (Sedikides et al., 2008). According to Natterer (2014) one type of yearning is personal nostalgia, which examines the longing to relive one's own past experiences or recreate memories. Mechanisms of personal nostalgia can include self-referencing and forms of autobiographical memories (Bernsten, 1996; Tchernev et al., 2021) which, in turn, allows us to compare our experiences with those characters, animated or real, as we view them on the screen (Oatley, 1999).

Narrative transportation explains the ability to lose oneself in a story world (Green & Brock, 2000). Originally derived from Gerrig's (1993) conceptualization of transportation in relation to moving from one world to the other, Green and Brock (2000) furthered this notion by introducing it as a persuasive technique of narratives. van Laer et al. (2014) discusses the antecedents that help facilitate narrative transportation. These antecedents, broken down by storyteller and story-receiver, highlight the importance of identifiable characters, imaginable plot, and verisimilitude, as well as familiarity, attention, transportability, age, education, and sex (van Laer et al., 2014). A crucial part of narrative transportation is character development as identification with characters often leads to adopting their beliefs (Cohen, 2001). With proper character development, the audience cultivates sympathy towards them (Tal-Or & Cohen, 2010). Narrative transportation is furthered by the mental imagery that is created through video content (Green, 2021) which helps trigger our own memories.

Nostalgia has been shown to be the precursor to initiating transportive experiences. Evans et al. (2021) describes the process as an individual activating an experience from their past. As the memory progresses, the individual goes deeper into the memory through transportation as the imagining is relived. For instance, if a memory of a trip to Walt Disney World is triggered watching the opening credits of a Disney film (i.e., usually Cinderella's castle), the more the individual relives that experience, the more "lost" they become. Additional research has shown that personal nostalgia from events generates a greater level of positive affect (Muehling and Sprott, 2004) and improved well-being (Wildschut et al., 2010). Evans et al. (2021) found that mental transportation can heighten nostalgia's positive, psychological benefits; specifically, nostalgic recall and its linkage to mental transportation elicited "social, existential, and self-oriented psychological benefits" (p. 84).

While Disney's vast collection of films provokes personal nostalgia, a recent trend has been their live-action remakes of beloved classics designed to tap into personal nostalgia. In the early 1990s, Boomers and Generation X parents enjoyed some Walt Disney classics such as *Beauty and the Beast* (1991), *Cool Runnings* (1993), and *The Parent Trap* (1998) with their children. Today, those same kids are now parents and can relive these film memories with their own children in features such as the live-action *Beauty and the Beast* (2017), Disney+'s *High School Musical: The Musical: The Series* and the focus of this essay, *The Mighty Ducks: Game Changers* (2021–2022). Sperb (2015) states, "nostalgia may be especially crucial today in part because of the necessary fan investment needed to maintain both brand recognition and deeper affective loyalty that is key to anchoring these larger transmedia worlds" (p. 124). Disney+ helps facilitate these forms of nostalgia by providing content from different generations.

"Gotta go for the 'W' every time": How Disney+ Revitalized the Mighty Ducks *Franchise*

The *Mighty Ducks* franchise began in 1992 with the release of *The Mighty Ducks*. This film introduced Gordon Bombay (Emilio Estevez), a reckless lawyer who believed that you must win every case, saying, "losing fair is still losing." However, reality gets in the way of Bombay's career as he is arrested for drunk driving. His community service task is coaching a youth hockey team, but he has disdain for the sport as he used to be a prominent hockey player.

The Mighty Ducks (1992) had a budget of $10 million and went on to gross over $50 million worldwide (Box Office Mojo, 2022). The film and its themes of overcoming challenges and building camaraderie were a surprising success that led to the release of two sequels, *D2: The Mighty Ducks* (1994) and *D3: The Mighty Ducks* (1996). These sequels would continue the story of the resilient hockey team that went from no-names to state champions. The three films in the franchise created a cult-like following, becoming Disney classics showcasing children who were highly relatable and experienced real-world problems.

The Ducks starting lineup, and other players featured throughout the franchise, include Charlie Conway (Joshua Jackson), Connie "the Velvet Hammer" Moreau (Marguerite Moreau), Fulton Reed (Elden Henson), Lester Averman (Matt Doherty), Greg Goldberg (Shaun Weiss), and Adam Banks (Vincent Larusso). These characters, like Coach Bombay, go through lifechanging moments and their development is crucial to the success of the film trilogy.

Developing Everyone's Favorite Team

At the beginning of *The Mighty Ducks*, the young hockey players are not the most welcoming toward their new coach. For example, upon first meeting Coach Bombay, they talk back and grumble over his decisions, with Lester Averman telling him, "You really suck." However, despite this rocky beginning, the team slowly embraces Bombay when they start winning.

Known as the leader of the pack, Charlie Conway is always seen keeping his friend group together through tough times. However, he has some of his own problems including anger issues that surround his single-parent household. The interactions between Charlie and Bombay in the first film helps develop their surrogate-father relationship. On the other hand, Connie "the Velvet Hammer" Moreau is the sole female hockey player, and represents elegance and friendship as she is seen standing up for her team in various situations. Additionally, she signifies adolescent love as she dates Guy Germaine throughout the franchise.

Another instrumental player for the Ducks is Adam Banks, who begins as a player for a rival hockey team, the Hawks, but must transfer to the Ducks due to residential boundaries. Banks becomes a star for the Ducks, but is injured and later benched when competing in an international hockey competition (*D2*). However, he experiences a miraculous recovery and Charlie benches himself to allow Banks to play in the final game.

Afraid of the hockey puck, Greg Goldberg is the perfect choice for goalie. His fear is overcome through Bombay's unconventional practice strategies. While tied to the net, teammates unleash their fury on Goldberg, sending pucks at him left and right. This builds Goldberg's confidence as his stick skills are involuntarily activated.

Lester Averman comes to the Ducks as comedic relief. Initially a prankster, this character tries to come up with ways to avoid playing as he is smaller than most of the other players and oftentimes gets knocked down by competitors. With help from Coach Bombay, Averman's skills improve, and he becomes more proficient handling the puck.

Finally, Fulton Reed, one of the "Bash Brothers," is the outsider of the community. His introduction to the Ducks comes when he accidentally hits a hockey puck straight through a window of Bombay's car. Instead of reprimanding the boy, Bombay asks him to repeat the maneuver and ultimately invites him to join the team.

All these characters experience different journeys through their relationship with Coach Bombay. By the film's end, Bombay's personality as a devious lawyer has also taken a complete 180 degree turn as he grows through his interactions and experiences with the Ducks. Additionally, Bombay sees through the children that his struggles from the past are not as bad as he makes them seem. This is evidenced in a conversation between Charlie and Bombay when Coach brings up the moment that turned his life around:

> BOMBAY: It was the last game of the state finals. We were tied in the end of the third period. I get a penalty shot. I go in, I triple deke. I fake the goalie right out of his pads. The puck's headed in, and then.... Clang! Hits the post. We lost in overtime. A quarter of an inch this way and it would have gone in. A quarter of an inch, Charlie.
>
> CHARLIE: Yeah, but a quarter inch the other way and you'd have missed completely.
>
> BOMBAY: I never thought of it that way.

At the start of the hockey season, Bombay cannot stand the sight of his players; it reminds him of his past and what could have been of his future. However, his character develops into a father-like figure who looks out for his team and revels in their successes. Not only does he influence these kids, but he learns from them as well.

With the way the characters are developed, it is natural that conflict would follow. Coach Bombay faces his first challenge inside of the rink when he must contend with his former coach, Jack Reilly, now coaching the Ducks main rival, the Hawks. This issue intensifies when Hawks player Adam Banks transfers to the Ducks due to a town boundary. Similarly, in *D2* the big rival is Wolf Stansson, the coach of Team Iceland. From the first appearance of Stansson, audiences are introduced to a character who has a "winning is everything" attitude, similar to that of Bombay at the beginning of *The Mighty Ducks*.

In *D3*, Bombay is off coaching at the Junior Goodwill Games and the Ducks are at a new prestigious, private school, Eden Hall. Much of the conflict that arises in *D3* stems from Bombay's absence. The players are not happy with Coach Orion (Jeffrey Nordling), do not fit in at Eden Hall, and come close to losing their scholarships. However, Bombay returns in the role of the Ducks "lawyer" and successfully argues for maintaining their scholarships. At this point, the players are more aligned with Coach Orion, and are brought together at the end with the return of their favorite jersey; the green, yellow, and purple District 5 Ducks jersey.

Much of the conflict in the *Mighty Ducks* franchise stems from, or is resolved by, the Ducks' fearless leader, Gordon Bombay. He plays an instrumental role in developing these kids not only a hockey players, but also serves as a role model into their adolescence.

The Legacy of the Ducks: Nostalgia in the Twenty-First Century

The success of *The Mighty Ducks* franchise was not only financially lucrative for Disney, but the sport of hockey as well. In the early 1990s, hockey in the United States was less popular than other sports like football or baseball (CBC Radio, 2021). Following the surprise success of the first *Ducks* film, the National Hockey League awarded the Walt Disney Company with a professional team, the Mighty Ducks of Anaheim (Sell, 1992) who wore jerseys reminiscent of the jerseys in the original film. The Walt Disney Company's marketing strategy brought the Mighty Ducks from being a relatively unknown franchise, to having one of the most beloved logos in the NHL. However, the team would undergo a complete rebranding when they transitioned to the Anaheim Ducks in 2005.

The Walt Disney Company's synergistic strategy allowed for a continuation of the *Ducks* franchise past *D3*'s release in 1996. Between the Mighty Ducks of Anaheim, a short-lived animated series (*Mighty Ducks: The Animated Series*, 1996–1997), and merchandise sales, *The Mighty Ducks* film franchise has earned over $200M (Box Office Mojo, the Associated Press, 2005). For those children, now adults, who grew up following Coach Bombay, Charlie, Goldberg, and the others, the Ducks brand had obvious potential for Disney's new streaming service.

The Return of a Classic: Game Changers

Disney+'s release of *The Mighty Ducks: Game Changers* in 2021 was a power play for the streaming service. As one of their new series, the title of the show created a sense of nostalgia for adults (Vick, 2018), and was developed as a continuation of the original hit films. *Game Changers* follows the story of the Don't Bothers, a hockey team of misfits who do not necessarily fit the role of hockey players. The first season of ten episodes chronicles how the Don't Bothers become a hockey team and the relationships built amongst the teammates. The teammates' bonds are tested as the Don't Bothers come face-to-face with their major rival, the Mighty Ducks. With the return of Gordon Bombay in *Game Changers*, fans of the original films can reflect on the decisions he makes as coach of the Don't Bothers compared to his previous ones as coach of the Ducks.

Bombay's Return

Season 1 of *Game Changers* follows protagonist Evan (Brady Noon) who is cut from the Ducks during the first episode. Following this experience, Evan and his mother Alex (Lauren Graham) attempt to create their own hockey team. As the team develops over the next several episodes, audiences see the "reckless" nature of the Don't Bothers. Alex is coaching the Don't Bothers, but her tactics are ineffective. One of the first notes of nostalgia is the introduction of Gordon Bombay, coach of the original Mighty Ducks. Emilio Estevez reprises his role as Gordon Bombay and starts with an unenthused attitude, like in *The Mighty Ducks* (1992). Bombay reluctantly helps Alex coach the team and introduces a few nostalgic surprises of his own, which include the return of some of the original Ducks. This example of personal nostalgia, Bombay's return to hockey, takes place during the first episode, and is instrumental for Disney+'s marketing strategy (Natterer, 2014) to attract viewers to the new series.

Quack, Quack, Quack: Building a Team

When Evan and Alex are building their team, it is a challenge to find players. While this contrasts with the original Ducks films, the new players fall into place identically to the films. Evan Morrow is the leader of his team, similar to how Charlie was in the original *Ducks*. Evan's character develops in the same fashion to Charlie's as his father is not seen until later in the season. Similarly, Evan (and his mother) bond with Coach Bombay who helps guide Evan through different challenges. For example, in Episode 1, Evan is tasked with recruiting players for the Don't Bothers, which is a nostalgic twist as the new Don't Bothers players match up with the original Mighty Ducks players.

Lauren Gibby (Bella Higginbotham) and Maya Kasper (Taegen Burns) are introduced as the only two girls on the team. Gibby has a free spirit but lacks coordination on the ice. Maya's personality is a little rougher around the edges and has undertones of Connie Moreau. Gibby is known for her warrior princess attire while Maya is part of the popular clique in school. Later in the series, another female player joins the Don't Bothers, Sofi Hanson-Bhatt (Swayam Bhatia). Again, similar to the original *Mighty Ducks*, Evan pulls Sofi from the rival Ducks team to play on the Don't Bothers. Sofi's character continues playing for the Ducks to please her over-achieving parents, but secretly starts practicing with the Don't Bothers.

Like Goldberg in *The Mighty Ducks*, *Game Changers* incorporates humorous characters best exemplified by Nick Ganz (Maxwell Simkins). Nick does not really know why he is playing hockey. As Evan's next-door neighbor, he prefers being a hockey podcaster, but joins the Don't Bothers to help Evan get momentum going building a team. Nick's character is nostalgic of Les Averman as both represent the team goofballs. Koob (Luke Islam), the goalie of the Don't Bothers, is recruited by Evan and Nick because of his impressive hand-eye coordination video game skills, a nostalgic callback to the first *Ducks* film. His appearance to Goldberg in the *Mighty Ducks* films is also uncanny. Finally, Logan LaRue (Kiefer O'Reilly) moves into Evan's neighborhood and is easily recruited by him. Impressed by his expensive ice skates, Evan and Nick believe he is an excellent hockey player; however, Logan is initially not that impressive on the ice. However, his dexterity on the ice grows, and he later learns to flip the hockey puck with his stick, like the pancakes he is seen cooking.

The starting line-up of both *The Mighty Ducks* and *Game Changers* are nearly identical in terms of characters and personalities. The combination of cohesion in character development, and story structure are instrumental in helping transport audiences to the past (Sestir et al., 2020), which Disney does with *Game Changers.*

Bombay as Father Figure

In both the *Ducks* films and TV series Coach Bombay takes on the reluctant role of a father figure for both Charlie Conway (*The Mighty Ducks*) and Evan Morrow (*Game Changers).* Bombay also gives advice to Charlie throughout the films. When Charlie struggles with fitting in at his new school in *D3*, Bombay says:

> I was like you Charlie. When I played hockey, I was a total hotshot, tried to take control of every game.... You gave me life, Charlie and I want to say thank you. I told Orion about all of this when I talked to him about taking over. I told him that you were the heart of the team and that you would learn something from each other. I told him you were the real Minnesota Miracle Man.... So be that man, Charlie.

In this moment, Bombay is telling Charlie he is the real champion; the one who should take control and be what others expect him to be. Charlie's reaction during this scene is one of astonishment as he struggles to believe in himself. Not surprisingly, Bombay has a special relationship with Charlie compared with the other characters.

In *Game Changers*, a similar story takes place. Evan's deadbeat dad shows up at one point and promises to see him in a game. However, his father fails to show, and Bombay is there picking up the pieces. Due to his absence, Evan becomes easily bothered when an opposing player antagonizes him. This leads Evan to knock him to the ground which results in a penalty prior to the first faceoff. Ultimately, Bombay saves the day by volunteering to drive Evan's father to the airport but instead, brings him to the game. Immediately following the game, Evan's father leaves and Bombay tells Alex that he plans to take Evan to a Minnesota Wild game. This episode reflects nostalgia in the *Mighty Ducks* franchise as Bombay is caught up consoling Charlie in the original films and now Evan in *Game Changers*.

Once a Duck, Always a Duck: Reunions, Moves, Jerseys, and Rivalries

With its focus on attracting a multi-generational audience, *Game Changers* taps into nostalgia at every turn. Halfway through the first season, the nostalgia factor ramps up with the return of some of the original Mighty Ducks. A reunion with characters Connie "the Velvet Hammer" (Marguerite Moreau), Fulton Reed (Elden Henson), Adam Banks (Vincent LaRusso), Guy Germaine (Garette Ratliff Henson), Les Averman (Matt Doherty), and Kenny Wu (Justin Wong) helps transport original Ducks fans to the world they left behind thirty years ago. However, Joshua Jackson (Charlie) was missing from the reunion due to Covid-19 protocols and scheduling constraints.

The nostalgia generated by the return of the original Ducks is powerful. While the show is aimed at the Gen Z demographic, Disney+ also targets the parents of these children who grew up with the original films. Critic Alison Herman supports this contention declaring actress Lauren Graham, who plays Evan's mother Alex Morrow, as the "audience surrogate" for the older generations (Herman, 2021). Morrow plays a key role in the series as the coach of her son's new team. The inclusion of Coach Bombay and new protagonist, Alex Morrow, keep the adult audience satisfied through memories of their past (Watts et al., 2020) whether that be from the original *Ducks* films, or in the case of Lauren Graham, starring on the popular television series *Gilmore Girls* (2000–2007).

Narrative transportation in *Game Changers* is also reflected through the usage of the "Flying V." With five players forming the letter "V," they approach the goalie and make it difficult to keep track of the puck. While the "Flying V" has been repudiated by hockey critics as a feasible strategy (Baumann, 2021), it is seen as one of the most iconic parts of the original film series (Ocal, 2021). In *Game Changers*, the Don't Bothers end up using the famous move, another nod to *Ducks* nostalgia.

Nothing is more iconic than the original District 5 jerseys that the Mighty Ducks wear in the original film. The final episode of *Game Changers* Season 1 sees the Don't Bothers reclaiming the team's name of Mighty Ducks after defeating their rival, the current Ducks. While this name-change is crucial for the series to move forward, this episode highlighted a type of nostalgic content that could induce transportation through artifacts, in this case the well-known Mighty Ducks jersey. In the middle of the rematch, the Don't Bothers switch into the original, District 5 jerseys. With Disney's highly synergistic business model (Kalb, 2015), they most likely had some type of Ducks memorabilia planned, such as the green, yellow, and purple District 5 jersey that symbolized the team since the early 90s. Essentially, this jersey was worn for two decades by the NHL's Anaheim Ducks, but was not primarily green like the District 5 film jersey. However, it incorporated a teal color and purple stripe on a white jersey. The duck on the NHL jersey was more reminiscent of a duck's bill in contrast to the film's more animated duck. Thus, they were readily accessible and most likely obtained by not only fans of the Ducks of Anaheim, but fans of the series as well.

Finally, like the original film franchise, the Don't Bothers have a rival team in the Ducks. This rivalry follows along the first film as the Ducks are despised the Hawks. Coach T (Dylan Playfair), the head coach of the Ducks, is even fashioned similarly to Wolf Stannson of Team Iceland (*D2*). His attitude and slicked back hair are very reminiscent of the television series and film franchise.

Season 2's Game Plan Deviation

The release of *The Mighty Ducks: Game Changers* was a successful move on the part of Disney+. However, Season 2 removed some of the nostalgic content from the previous season, perhaps threatening transportation for the viewer. Prior to the release of Season 2, there were reports that Emilio Estevez would not be returning to *Game Changers* due in part to the actor's decision regarding Covid-19 filming protocols (Bucksbaum, 2021). The unintended loss of Coach Bombay could have harmed the nostalgic energy that surrounded the series. Returning characters included most of the Ducks and Alex Morrow. While Lauren Graham's character might attract an older demographic, Coach Bombay was an essential part of the franchise's nostalgic appeal and success. Season 2 of *Game Changers* presents a different underdog story due to the absence of Coach Bombay. The "new" Ducks, formerly the Don't Bothers, go to EPIC hockey training camp over the summer. This camp is led by former NHL player Colin Cole (Josh Duhamel), but it is a brutal environment which reminds some of the characters of their past with the former Ducks. For example, players are required to wear wristbands that track different physical activity levels and ultimately, ranks them in real-time on a big screen.

Drama quickly enters the scene when Evan becomes focused on doing whatever he can to succeed and gain attention from college scouts. All of this would create tension with his relationship with Sofi as she does not want to return to her past of practicing hockey 24/7. Another character who experiences personal growth in Season 2 is Nick. With the introduction of very talented hockey players, and the loss of the level of friendship he had with Evan, Nick struggles throughout the season. Ultimately, Nick's passion for broadcasting shines through with him announcing the final game. The other returning characters are not as developed as Evan, Sofi, and Nick and are more secondary to the story. Additionally, the introduction of Jace Cole (Naveen Paddock), Coach Cole's son, throws a twist in this season. In the past Jace scored an "own goal" (scoring in your team's goal) and now freezes when he needs to shoot the puck. Sofi and Alex help Jace overcome his fears as his father struggles to understand his anxiety playing hockey.

Game Changers Season 2 has similar themes to *D3* as the film features the players attending a private school and competing with other players to prove their hockey skills. Initially, the hockey camp pits the players against each other, but then creates eight teams to battle it out for one spot to play against Team Canada in the Summer Showcase. A divide between the characters is formed as most of the Ducks and Jace end up being drafted onto Alex's team, whereas Evan is drafted by Coach Cole. Alex and Coach Cole become close throughout the second half of the season as they contemplate ways to trade Evan and Jace.

While Season 2 has remnants of *D3*, it begins to branch off from the nostalgia of the original *Mighty Ducks*. For example, the head coach of Team Canada is Coach T, the original Ducks coach from *Game Changers* Season 1. Similarly, at a low moment for Alex's team, she brings the players to visit the NHL's Anaheim Ducks. During the last episode, the Ducks are gifted Anaheim Ducks jerseys. While the Walt Disney Company no longer owns the Anaheim Ducks, this scene pays homage to the team they helped create. The only truly nostalgic moment in *Game Changers* Season 2 is the return of the Bash Brothers (Dean Portman and Fulton Reed) in Episode 1. These factors could be seen as a way for producers to usher in the next generation of Ducks fans with something that gives them their own memories (*Game Changers*) and the need for nostalgic references (*Ducks* trilogy) would not be required. However, this did not play out as *Game Changers* was cancelled following the end of Season 2. Perhaps the dearth of nostalgic elements ran out the clock for *Game Changers*.

Discussion

The debut of Disney+ in 2019 created generational nostalgia and transportation where fans of *The Mighty Ducks* franchise could develop identification with characters and cultivate new fandom, making it a bridge between generations. In terms of *Game Changers*, an overlaying nostalgic element comes in the form of similarity. The original Mighty Ducks (1992) and the Don't Bothers (2021) face the same struggles and camaraderie amongst teammates. Disney+ included additional narrative parallels that might not be noticeable by this new audience, such as storylines and character personalities. However, previous generations, familiar with Ducks lore, are more likely to pick up on these nuances. The memory recollection in the older generations may enable bonding through positive viewing experiences with their children due to the similarity in story structure and character development that provides for easier transportive experiences.

Showrunner Steve Brill (who wrote the original three *Mighty Ducks* films) emphasized that "*The Mighty Ducks* was always something that they needed to get back and recover and restore and recreate" (Hatchett, 2021). The terms "back," "recover," "restore," and "recreate" all suggest this series was meant to be a nostalgic venture by Disney+. Previous research has shown nostalgia's link to feelings of positive affect which, in turn, induce positive memories (Wildschut et al., 2006). Disney+ fosters this by encouraging audiences to experience some of their fondest memories of the Ducks in a familial setting. Initial audiences of *The Mighty Ducks* were younger Gen X/early Millennial children watching with their Boomer parents. With the original film becoming a cult classic and producing two sequels, additional generations were able to enjoy the Ducks on VHS and DVD. The Mighty Ducks became a household name and was successfully promoted through synergistic purchases for hockey and non-hockey fans alike (Vick, 2018).

With the loss of Emilio Estevez in Season 2 of *Game Changers*, Disney+ may have lost additional fans due to a decrease in nostalgia. With Season 2 standing more on its own in terms of storyline and characters, a simple cameo by the Bash Brothers was not enough to hold those audiences. However, the popularity of Disney+ worldwide may suggest absent characters, no matter their iconic status, might not matter. For example, despite Olivia Rodrigo, who played Nini in *High School Musical: The Musical: The Series* (*HSMTMTS*), leaving the show after Season 3, Disney+ renewed it for a fourth season. However, *Game Changers* Season 1 did not fare well in relation to the cost of production (O'Rourke, 2023), but was still renewed for a second season. The notion of continuing a series instead of remaking it, as in *Game Changers* and *HSMTMTS*, is not enough to attract an audience and secure their fandom.

Disney+ has utilized nostalgia and transportation to facilitate familial bonding and fandom across generations. *The Mighty Ducks: Game*

Changers reflects the power of personal nostalgia through a tracking of the original films' storyline and characters, attracting new fans to the show (Gen Z, Gen Alpha) while maintaining a loyal fanbase from parents (Gen X and Millennials). *Game Changers* provides a bridge between generations by creating new, and thus, shared memories for parents and their kids.

References

Alexander, J. (2019, November 13). *Disney+ surpasses 10 million subscribers on first day.* The Verge. https://www.theverge.com/2019/11/13/20963172/disney-plus-subscribers-10-million-star-wars-marvel-pixar-launch.

Anderton, E. (2022, September 26). *The Mighty Ducks: Game Changers season 2 review: New Ducks fly on their own, but nostalgia's shadow still looms.* Slash Film. https://www.slashfilm.com/1024777/the-mighty-ducks-game-changers-season-2-review-new-ducks-fly-on-their-own-but-nostalgias-shadow-still-looms/.

Associated Press. (2005, February 26). Disney finds buyer for the Ducks. *New York Times.* https://www.nytimes.com/2005/02/26/sports/disney-finds-buyer-for-the-ducks.html.

Associated Press. (2005, June 16). NHL approves sale of Mighty Ducks. Associated Press. https://apnews.com/article/274628f73856d03195057b5837dd856b.

Ball, C.T., & Little, J.C. (2006). A comparison of involuntary autobiographical memory retrievals. *Applied Cognitive Psychology, 20*(9), 1167–1179. https://doi.org/10.1002/acp.1264.

Bancroft, T., & Cook, B. (Director). (1998). *Mulan* [Motion picture]. United States: Buena Vista Pictures.

Batcho, K.I. (2013). Nostalgia: The bittersweet history of a psychological concept. *History of Psychology, 16*(3), 165–176. https://doi.org/10.1037/a0032427.

Baumann, M. (2021, March 24). *Which Mighty Ducks tactics are genius, and which are just unreal?* The Ringer. https://www.theringer.com/movies/2021/3/24/22346733/mighty-ducks-triple-deke-flying-v-knucklepuck-bash-brothers.

Berntsen, D. (1996). Involuntary autobiographical memories. *Applied Cognitive Psychology, 10*(5), 435–454. https://doi.org/10.1002/(sici)1099-0720(199610)10:5%3C435::aid-acp408%3E3.0.co;2-l.

Box Office Mojo. (2022). *Franchise: The Mighty Ducks.* IMDbPro. https://www.boxofficemojo.com/franchise/fr2470940421/?ref_=bo_frs_table_208.

Bucksbaum, S. (2021, November 8). Emilio Estevez not returning for The Mighty Ducks: Game Changers season 2 due to vaccine requirement. *Entertainment Weekly.* https://ew.com/tv/emilio-estevez-out-mighty-ducks-game-changers-season-2-vaccine-requirement/.

CBC Radio. (2021, March 26). Why Disney turned the Mighty Ducks movie into an actual NHL team. CBC. https://www.cbc.ca/radio/day6/astrazeneca-s-vaccine-mishaps-the-mighty-ducks-nhl-history-ryan-mcmahon-the-barbizon-hotel-and-more-1.5964106/why-disney-turned-the-mighty-ducks-movie-into-an-actual-nhl-team-1.5964113.

Chen, T. (2014). The persuasive effectiveness of mini-films: Narrative transportation and fantasy proneness. *Journal of Consumer Behaviour, 14*(1), 21–27. https://doi.org/10.1002/cb.1494.

Chen, T. & Chang, H. (2017). The effect of narrative transportation in mini-film advertising on reducing counterarguing. *International Journal of Electronic Commerce Studies, 8*(1), 25–46. http://www.academic-pub.org/ojs/index.php/IJCSE/index.

Cohen, J. (2001). Defining identification: A theoretical look at the identification of audiences with media characters. *Mass Communication and Society, 4*(3), 245–264. https://doi.org/10.1207/S15327825MCS0403_01.

Condon, B. (Director). (2017). *Beauty and the Beast* [Motion picture]. United States: Walt Disney Studios Motion Pictures.

Disney+. (2023). *Choose your plan*. Disney+. https://www.disneyplus.com.
Disney, W., & Disney, R.O. (Producer), & Disney, W., & Iwerks, U. (Director). (1928). *Steamboat Willie* [Motion picture]. United States: Celebrity Productions.
Disney Media and Entertainment Distribution. (2019). *Disney+*. Disney Media & Entertainment Distribution. https://dmedmedia.disney.com/about-disney-plus.
Dunham, D. (Director). (2002). *Double Teamed* [Motion picture]. United States: Disney Channel.
Escalas, J. (2004). Imagine yourself in the product: Mental simulation, narrative transportation and persuasion. *Journal of Advertising, 33*(2), 37–48. https://www.jstor.org/stable/4189256.
Evans, N.D., Reyes, J., Wildschut, T., Sedikides, C., & Fetterman, A.K. (2021). Mental transportation mediates nostalgia's psychological benefits. *Cognition and Emotion, 35*(1), 84–95. https://doi.org/10.1080/02699931.2020.1806788.
Federle, T. (Producer). (2019). *High School Musical: The Musical: The Series* [Television series]. United States: Disney Platform Distribution.
Gelman, V. (2019, April 11). *Disney+'s upcoming shows*. TV Line. https://tvline.com/gallery/disney-streaming-service-shows-preview-list-comedy-drama-photos/43rd-annual-peoples-choice-awards-arrivals-los-angeles-usa-18-jan-2017-3/.
Geronimi, C. (Director). (1940). *Tugboat Mickey* [Motion picture]. United States: Walt Disney Productions.
Gerrig, R.J. (1993). *Experiencing narrative worlds*. Yale University Press.
Green, M.C. (2021). Transportation into narrative worlds. In L.B. Frank & P. Falzone (Eds.), *Entertainment-education behind the scenes* (pp. 87–101). Springer International. https://doi.org/10.1007/978-3-030-63614-2_6.
Green, M.C., & Brock, T.C. (2002). In the mind's eye: Transportation imagery model of narrative persuasion. In M.C. Green, J.J. Strange, & T.C. Brock (Eds.), *Narrative impact* (pp. 315–341). Psychology Press. https://doi.org/10.4324/9781410606648-22.
Green, M.C., & Brock, T.C. (2000). The role of transportation in the persuasiveness of public narratives. *Journal of Personality and Social Psychology, 79*(5), 701–721. https://doi.org/10.1037/0022-3514.79.5.701.
Green, M.C., Brock, T.C., & Kaufman, G.F. (2004). Understanding media enjoyment: The role of transportation into narrative worlds. *Communication Theory, 14*(4), 311–327. https://doi.org/10.1111/j.1468-2885.2004.tb00317.x.
Greene, A. (2015, August 18). *The nostalgia machine: How Disney keeps roping you in*. Complex. https://www.complex.com/pop-culture/2015/08/disneys-forever-nostalgic-appeal.
Hannah, J. (Director). (1947). *Chip an' Dale* [Motion picture]. United States: Walt Disney Productions.
Hatchett, K. (2021, May 28). *The Mighty Ducks: Game Changers boss talks finale twist, Kenan Thompson agreeing to appear in season 2*. TV Line. https://tvline.com/2021/05/28/the-mighty-ducks-game-changers-recap-finale-season-2-kenan-thompson-joshua-jackson/.
Herman, A. (2021, March 29). *"Mighty Ducks: Game Changers" is a return to form for Lauren Graham*. The Ringer. https://www.theringer.com/tv/2021/3/29/22355524/lauren-graham-mighty-ducks-game-changers-disney-plus.
Isberner, M., Richter, T., Schreiner, C., Eisenbach, Y., Sommer, C., & Appel, M. (2018). Empowering stories: Transportation into narratives with strong protagonists increases self-related control beliefs. *Discourse Processes, 56*(8), 575–598. https://doi.org/10.1080/0163853x.2018.1526032.
Kalb, I. (2015, December 10). *The Disney synergy machine: What businesses can learn*. HuffPost. https://www.huffpost.com/entry/the-disney-synergy-machin_b_8776952.
Kreuter, M.W., Green, M.C., Cappella, J.N., Slater, M.D., Wise, M.E., Storey, D., Clark, E.M., O'Keefe, D.J., Erwin, D.O., Holmes, K., Hinyard, L.J., Houston, T., & Woolley, S. (2007). Narrative communication in cancer prevention and control: A framework to guide research and application. *Annals of Behavioral Medicine 33*, 221–235. https://doi.org/10.1007/bf02879904.
Kvavilashvili, L., & Mandler, G. (2004). Out of one's mind: A study of involuntary semantic

memories. *Cognitive Psychology, 48*(1), 47–94. https://doi.org/10.1016/s0010-0285(03)00115-4.

Lieberman, R. (Director). (1996). *D3: The Mighty Ducks* [Motion picture]. United States: Walt Disney Pictures.

Marchegiani, C. & Phau, I. (2010). Away from "unified nostalgia": Conceptual differences of personal and historical nostalgia appeals in advertising. *Journal of Promotion Management, 16* (1–2), 80–95. https://doi.org/10.1080/10496490903572991.

McDonald, D.G., Sarge, M.A., Lin, S., Collier, J.G., Potocki, B. (2015). A role for the self: Media content as triggers for involuntary autobiographical memories. *Communication Research, 42*(1), 3–29. https://doi.org/10.1177/0093650212464771.

Meyers, N. (Director). (1998). *The Parent Trap* [Motion picture]. United States: Walt Disney Pictures.

Muehling, D.D. & Pascal, V.J. (2012). An involvement explanation for nostalgia advertising effects. *Journal of Promotion Management, 18*(1), 100–118. https://doi.org/10.1080/10496491.2012.646222

Muehling, D.D., & Sprott, D.E. (2004). The power of reflection: An empirical examination of nostalgia advertising effects. *Journal of Advertising, 33*(3), 25–35. https://doi.org/10.1080/00913367.2004.10639165.

Natterer, K. (2014). How and why to measure personal and historical nostalgic responses through entertainment media. *The International Journal on Media Management, 16*, 161–180. https://doi.org/10.1080/14241277.2014.989567.

Ngan, N., & Zhang, S. (1998). *The Ballad of Mulan.* Pan Asian Publications.

Oatley, K. (1999). Meetings of the minds: Dialogue, sympathy, and identification, in reading fiction. *Poetics, 26*(5–6), 439–454. https://doi.org/10.1016/S0304-422X(99)00011-X.

Ocal, A. (2021, January 29). How the Flying V can be improved for the new Mighty Ducks in "Game Changers." ESPN. https://www.espn.com/nhl/story/_/id/30788280/how-flying-v-improved-new-mighty-ducks-game-changers.

O'Rourke, R. (2023, February 18). *"The Mighty Ducks: Game Changers" cancelled after 2 seasons at Disney+.* Collider. https://collider.com/the-mighty-ducks-season-3-cancelled/.

Pallotta, F. (2019, November 13). Disney+ has hit 10 million subscribers since launching on Tuesday. CNN Business. https://www.cnn.com/2019/11/13/media/disney-subscribers.

Peters, B., Squillace, F., & Barruso, J. (Executive Producer). (1996–1997). *Mighty Ducks: The Animated Series* [Television series]. Walt Disney Television.

Phillips, B.J., & McQuarrie, E.F. (2010). Narrative and persuasion in fashion advertising. *Journal of Consumer Research, 37*(3), 368–392. https://doi.org/10.1086/653087.

Pollock, T. (2022, September 3). *What to watch on your next Disney+ family movie night.* Disney. https://news.disney.com/disney-plus-family-classics.

Sedikides, C., Wildschut, T., Arndt, J., & Routledge, C. (2008). Nostalgia: Past, present, and future. *Current Directions in Psychological Science, 17*(5), 304–307. https://doi.org/10.1111/j.1467-8721.2008.00595.x

Sell, D. (1992, December 11). NHL expands to Miami and Anaheim in entertaining twist. *Washington Post.* https://www.washingtonpost.com/archive/sports/1992/12/11/nhl-expands-to-miami-and-anaheim-in-entertaining-twist/7afdf139-1ef7-4b5b-9e9d-ded84ba3fc7c/.

Sestir, M., & Green, M.C. (2010). You are who you watch: Identification and transportation effects on temporary self-concept. *Social Influence, 5*(4), 272–288. https://doi.org/10.1080/15534510.2010.490672

Shaw, L. (Director). (2002). *Cadet Kelly* [Motion picture]. United States: Disney Channel.

Sperb, J. (2015). *Flickers of film: Nostalgia in the time of digital cinema.* Rutgers University Press.

Tal-Or, N., & Cohen, J. (2010). Understanding audience involvement: Conceptualizing and manipulating identification and transportation. *Poetics, 38*(4), 402–418. https://www.doi.org/10.1016/j.poetic.2010.05.004.

Tchernev, J.M., Collier, J., & Wang, Z. (2021). There and back again? Exploring the real-time cognitive journey of narrative transportation. *Communication Research, 50*(3), 1–26. https://doi.org/10.1177/00936502211018577.

Thompson, M. (2022, September 22). *Here are 35 side-by-sides of animated Disney movies and their live-action remakes.* BuzzFeed. https://www.buzzfeed.com/mychalthompson/disney-live-action-side-by-side-comparison.
Turteltaub, J. (Director). (1993). *Cool Runnings* [Motion picture]. United States: Walt Disney Pictures.
van Laer, T., de Ruyter, K., Visconti, L.M., & Wetzels, M. (2014). The extended-transportation imagery model: A meta-analysis of the antecedents and consequences of consumers' narrative transportation. *Journal of Consumer Research, 40*(5), 797–817. https://doi.org/10.1086/673383.
Vick, M. (2018, January 22). A Mighty Ducks TV show is in the works! *TV Guide.* https://www.tvguide.com/news/mighty-ducks-tv-show-development/.
Walt Disney Company. (n.d.). *1923.* The Walt Disney Company. https://thewaltdisneycompany.com/history/1923-2/.
Weisman, S. (Director). (1994). *D2: The Mighty Ducks* [Motion picture]. United States: Walt Disney Pictures.
Wildschut, T., Sedikides, C., Arndt, J., & Routledge, C. (2006). Nostalgia: Content, triggers, functions. *Journal of Personality and Social Psychology, 91*(5), 975–993. https://doi.org/10.1037/0022-3514.91.5.975.
Wildschut, T., Sedikides, C., & Routledge, C. (2008, January 3). *Nostalgia—from cowbells to the meaning of life.* The British Psychological Society. https://www.bps.org.uk/psychologist/nostalgia-cowbells-meaning-life.
Wildschut, T., Sedikides, C., Routledge, C., Arndt, J., & Cordaro, F. (2010). Nostalgia as a repository of social connectedness: The role of attachment-related avoidance. *Journal of Personality and Social Psychology, 98*(4), 573–586. https://doi.org/10.1037/a0017597.
Williamson, S., & Boisvert, A. (Producer). (2021). *The Mighty Ducks: Game Changers* [Television series]. United States: Disney Platform Distribution.
Wilson, T. (1993). *Watching television: Hermeneutics, reception, and popular culture.* Polity.
Zheng, L. (2014) Narrative transportation in radio advertising: A study on the effects of dispositional traits on mental transportation. *Journal of Radio & Audio Media, 21*(1), 36–50. https://doi.org/10.1080/19376529.2014.891213.

Recognizing the Princess as a Plus

Tracing <Princess> as an Ideograph for Contemporary Representation and Progressive Revisions

Erika M. Thomas *and* Mindy Burnett

The release of the full-length animated film *Snow White and the Seven Dwarfs* (1937) was a seminal moment for the Walt Disney company. The introduction of the character Snow White provided audiences with a new heroine, a naïve, young princess whose kindness, domesticity, and beauty served as a model for young girls. While Mickey Mouse is recognized as the definitive icon of Disney, Snow White and the many princesses who followed remind us that Disney princesses are quintessential characters. Popularity continues to grow around classic princess characters, such as Cinderella and Aurora, and modern characters, like Moana and Raya. Clearly, Disney princesses remain highly recognizable to girls in many cultures.

Compared with other "mediated princess stories" or "fantasy figures" from the 1990s on, Nash (2015) notes that "Disney's were the most profitable and influential" (p. 3). Their dominance in the global media market can be attributed to the strategic inclusion of female protagonists and gendered narratives, especially those that react to cultural shifts in gender relations (Schiele, Louie & Chen, 2020). The empowered and liberated princess qualities reveal an ongoing paradox. On one hand, the mass-produced narratives and branding of Disney princesses potentially conforms young girls to certain roles and expectations (e.g., idealistic and normative beauty standards, passivity, and heteronormative romance culture). On the other hand, the same characters have progressed, promoting women's individuality (e.g., independence, fearlessness, perseverance, and embracing one's culture). Regardless of the various pros and cons of princess culture, there is no denying that "princesses are everywhere" (Forman-Brunell & Hains, p. xi) and that these representations, part of a multi-billion-dollar media industry, will not disappear anytime soon.

New Disney princess films are steadily released. Examples include the *Frozen* films (2013, 2019), *Moana* (2016), and *Raya and the Last Dragon* (2021). The ongoing and frequent references of established princess characters and narratives, made even more accessible by the company's streaming application Disney+, point to a need to understand and compare shifting meanings and changing identities of the term princess. As such, we approach this textual analysis through a feminist lens, conducting an ideographic analysis of the term <princess>.[1] We argue that <princess> operates as a shifting ideograph, a theoretical concept traced in public discourse that marks evolving denotations. In the context of Disney's use of the word <princess>, we argue that <princess> aligns with the understanding of contemporary womanhood, consistent with, at the very least, liberal, mainstream feminism and, at times, radical feminist thought. We show how the Disney+ streaming service is a cultural text in and of itself, because of its ability to frame and construct, contextualize, inform, shift, and expand the meanings in other texts in a particular way. This essay, then, traces the Disney <princess> as changing ideological force in our cultural understanding of feminine identity and further attributes the shift in meaning to Disney+.

We first provide a brief literature review of the Disney princess, tracking its cultural significance and meaning over the decades. Next, we present our method of ideographic analysis and use it to conduct a close textual and visual analysis of the <princess> ideographs in the Disney+ original programming, including *Disney Princess Remixed, One Day at Disney (Shorts)*, and *Disney Insider.*

The Origin of the Disney Princess and Their Early Cultural Significance

For decades Disney films and television shows have fed cultural imaginations and influenced audiences and popular culture in innumerable ways. Davis (2009) notes that Disney is recognized as a "modern-day storyteller" (p. 13), teaching values, expectations, and social roles. According to Bell, Hass, and Sells (1995), animated films are an important place to examine Disney as both a company and a series of persuasive media representations built from storybook characters and fictional figures who tend to originate in an animated film and are later re-released, replicated, or referenced throughout Disney content and properties.

Among the many Disney characters, the princess is a symbolic and treasured commodity due to its social association for girls (Hains, 2014; Forman-Brunell & Hains, 2015; Koontz, Norman, & Okorie, 2017; Coyne, et al., 2021). Yet, the Disney princess undoubtedly has baggage. The princess archetypes have long raised concern that their tales and images contain obvious dated detachments from women's contemporary advancement. As noted earlier, the classic princesses, Snow White, Cinderella, and Aurora, portray qualities like innocence, softness, and beauty. Princesses are also "awarded" for acts of domesticity, falling in love, and submissiveness, which ultimately lead to their "happy ending" or dreams coming true.

Starting with the most classic of the Disney princesses, gender representations of female characters were consistently critiqued for qualities that are static and regressive, which continued even as more "progressive" princesses were introduced at the end of the twentieth century (Bell, Haas, & Sells, 1995; Gilliam & Wooden, 2008; Davis, 2009; Giroux & Pollock, 2010). It is this reason that feminist critics caution enthusiasm around the more empowered character qualities, especially in the "Renaissance" princesses, like Ariel, Belle, Pocahontas, and Mulan. This period developed in the late 1980s and 1990s when the princess protagonists become less passive but remain committed to traditional values, including a willingness to return to wifely duties and dependence despite their original desires of independence and rebellion. Despite some liberating potential, the princesses maintained conventional feminine qualities and gender roles. The protagonists were made more complicated, but the overall message still resulted in showcasing limited gender expectations and the stereotype of becoming "the appendage, if not the property of a man" (Giroux & Pollock, 2010, p. 108).

The narratives and predictable plotlines of princesses during the Disney "Renaissance" period often showcased "passive prettiness" as an ideal, but, most detrimentally, represented romantic relationships as the solution to a problem or the key to saving a kingdom (Hains, 2014; Hains, 2015). Bell (1995) explains the leading woman character/classic princess heroine is physically beautiful with a specific body image, and good or kind "tropes" that become a predictor of the character's attainment of "happily ever after," therefore reinforcing attractive physicality, feminine behavior, and rewards of marriage and money to impressionable, young audiences (Bell, 1995). Rutherford and Baker (2021) label this the "princess bubble."

Finding a similar conclusion in their research, Garlin and Sandlin (2017) identify a form of cruel optimism fueled by Disney princess narratives that spark a desire in women to attain the compulsory, heterosexual love and patriarchal structures that limit social advancement and individual agency. For example, Ariel, in *The Little Mermaid* (1989), is introduced as less submissive since she is initially presented as a mobile, defiant, and resilient teenage girl. However, Sells (1995) concludes that

Ariel's willingness to give up her voice in exchange for Prince Eric's love teaches girls they are only granted access to a White man's world "if we remain silent, and if we sacrifice our connection to 'the feminine'" (p. 181). Similarly, Jasmine, in *Aladdin* (1992), feels trapped by a system that does not respect her autonomy, yet once she falls for Aladdin, and she is content marrying him and settling for a life in the palace. Thus, Nash (2015) cautions that while feminine goodness is expanded with their new qualities, the princesses post–1989 are still restricted to traditional elements of goodness with the desire to find a man or engage in actions that are often choices of others. In short, these messages reveal the problematic, restrictive sub-texts that remain in many Disney princess films.

Not surprisingly, the elevated position of a Disney princess was assisted by the explicit media franchise known as the Disney Princess line or collection. Created in 2000 under Disney executive Andy Mooney, it developed into a billion-dollar enterprise consisting of media, dolls, theme park attractions and appearances, live shows, and apparel (Davis, 2009; Nash, 2015; Condis, 2015). Additionally, while Disney has re-released classic animated films from its "vault" on VHS and DVD for decades, today that content is archived on Disney+. Princess narratives are widely popular texts. They are easily accessible to young girls through the application and serve as models for children's social learning. Natasia and Uppal (2015) conducted a study on how girls from different countries understood princesses in relation to their own identities. They conclude girls, "regardless of ethnicity and age, seemed to have appropriated Disney princesses as part of their identities," explaining that many suggested "they were like princesses" (p. 131). While some girls struggled with identification when they focused on their ethnic differences in comparison to the princesses, and Western biases toward attractiveness, all girls generally recognized their ability to be princesses contingent on feeling beautiful and viewing oneself as a "good" person. These examples reveal that Disney princesses are, indeed, recognized around the world for contributing to gender roles and qualities, even if relating to them operated differently for girls from various geographical regions.

Examinations of Shifting Princesses in Contemporary Representations

Currently, a plethora of publications focus on the "princess" as a form of transmedia through revised fairy tales, original stories, and the construction and marketing of corresponding princess culture (Do Rozario, 2004; Davis, 2006; Hains, 2014; Forman-Brunell & Hains, 2015; Nash, 2015; Higgs, 2016). As more contemporary Disney princesses were created in the twenty-first century, cultural critics began to view them as heroic and holding increasingly independent qualities. Today's princesses are continually disrupting expected performative gender roles by questioning and dismissing passivity and subordinate positions, engaging independently, or in actions of resistance against patriarchal structures (Do Rozario, 2004). In the instances of "Revival" princesses, a category of princesses developed after the "Renaissance" princesses, the characters are hard-working, butting up against (and making attempts to reform) a system of patriarchy (Higgs, 2016). One example includes Merida in *Brave* (2012), who successfully pushes back against rigid social restraints, resists her parents' decision to arrange her marriage, and rejects the tradition followed by male suitors. Like Merida, Tiana in *The Princess and the Frog* (2009) and Rapunzel in *Tangled* (2010) both have dreams and ambitions other than romance, their confident and independent nature leading them to save the men they love. Despite the progress in storylines, these characters are still limited by elements of normative culture, which is not entirely changed by the end of the film. Nonetheless, such princesses are among the most "highly assertive princesses" and storylines have changed from romantic happy endings to achieving their own freedoms (Nash, 2015, p. 13; Hains, 2014).

More recently, scholars have viewed TV series and films as altering the princess identity in more direct and deliberate ways. The most recent princesses continue to push boundaries by gender expectations. For example, Moana ventures across the ocean to find the god, Maui, confront the monster, Te Ka, entirely on her own, and, as a result, saves her people from peril. Likewise, Maben (2020) views Princess Sophia from the Disney animated series *Sophia the First* (2013–2018) as redefining the princess persona, noting that Sophia's acts of kindness and ethical behavior embody characteristics of a "true" princess that successfully challenge traditional gender roles. This reflects more agency than the mere luck or coincidence of a royal birth. Similarly, *Frozen* (2013) calls into question gender roles when Anna saves Kristoff from a fall, and with her sister, Elsa, rejects and interrogates toxic masculinity and patriarchal ruling tendencies (Hackett, 2020). Their stories also suggest, when they save each other, they are true to themselves.

Consistent with these findings, textual analyses have shown Disney's deliberate rebranding of princesses contain imagery and messaging consistent with mainstream, third wave feminist ideologies. Third wave feminism, a dispersed approach to women's liberation activism, developed after the 1960s and 70s. Continuing the advocacy for women's rights, third wave feminism specifically acknowledges multicultural and diverse women's needs, recognizes a wider range of acts that constitute everyday activism, and embraces qualities of girl culture and the media. In much the same way that films like *Frozen* or the live-action remake of *Beauty and the Beast* (2017) are credited for reflecting the ideologies endorsed by feminist social movements (Weidman-Winter, 2020), the 2016 campaign "Dream Big, Princess" (Disney's global video series and an initiative to work with Girls Up of United Nations Foundation) fuels feminist sensibilities in a younger generation by representing contemporary girls' goals and ambitions and by emphasizing the most independent and heroic qualities found in both girls and princess characters (Thomas, 2019; Bickham & Roberts, 2020). Although there is risk that such marketing campaigns will lead to commodifying activism, depoliticizing women's advancement, or communicating a superficial, watered-down understanding of feminism, the content is nonetheless empowering compared to previous imagery. By showing young girls achieving their dreams and goals in relation to the princesses' liberating moments, the commercials reframe the "princess" through messages of independence, severing the stereotypical associations of traditional expectations in girlhood.

Given this context, it is not surprising that Coyne et al. (2021) found the opposite of many early studies on princess culture, concluding it does not cause the child to adhere to traditional gender conceptions and stereotypes. On the contrary, feminist associations related to princess messaging (e.g., allowing princesses to serve as the heroes, rescuers, or leaders in their own stories) is actually moving away from patriarchal biases and the hegemonic masculinity seen in the past. Therefore, new princess narratives have altered past representations of traditional, "feminine" expectations and heterosexual romance. Princess figures are now viewed as representing empowerment, individuality, and personal choices. In the next section, we provide an overview of our method, an ideographic analysis. Going forward, we trace and reference <princess> as a shifting and developing ideograph that further informs these previous studies and explores its most recent denotative power.

Method: Ideographic Analysis

One way to understand the rhetorical power behind terms such as "princess" is to examine how such a rhetorical concept developed through the formation of ideological beliefs and material "myths" of society. Scholars analyze the development of a popular term or word, which has taken on greater ideological understanding in the social consciousness and within public discourse. This term was coined an "ideograph" by McGee (1980), who provided examples, like "liberty" or "religion," and explained how their meanings changed over time. Since McGee's initial study, numerous scholars have applied the methodological approach to understand what influences cultural and meaning changes in interpretations of words (Lucaites & Condit, 1990; Delgado, 1995; Cloud, 2004; Williams & Young, 2005; Hayden, 2009; Hamilton, 2018). Critics read for the ways a term changes diachronically, meaning the changes in usage in historical and empirical contexts, and synchronically, which shows how the term evolves or clashes over periods of time. The shifts in meanings in public discourse expose how ideologies construct or influence identities and results in new or developed constituted meanings (Lee, 2009). For example, ideographs have been recognized for regulating gender norms (e.g., the use of suffrage-era postcards to feminize men and represent women's behavior as inappropriate during a period of growing support for the attainment of voting rights) (Palczewski, 2005). The public's response in this instance, and others, reveals the influence and power of circulating ideographs found in language and images.

Our ideographic criticism then is similarly informed through the lens of feminist theory and analyzes how <princess>, in the form of the broad media reference and strategy, takes on the meaning of empowered girl or woman diachronically and synchronically. The diachronic analysis uses literature discussing recent film content and analyzes specific Disney <princess> campaigns to expose how <princess> has changed meaning over time. The synchronic ideographic examination reveals the meaning of <princess> according to two strategies examined in Disney+ original content. The first strategy highlights how definitions are explicitly changed within content. The second strategy explores the ongoing focus of character's traits, both the labeling and reframing, which takes focus away from characters' qualities and narratives that are contrary to society's new understanding of <princess>.

Analysis

The <Princess> Through Diachronic Shifts

Before turning to an analysis of content on Disney+ contributing to the ideograph of the <princess>, we examine the <princess> diachronically or vertically. Consistent with the previous literature review, critics have traced a progression or evolution in the Disney <princess> archetype as films, characters, and messaging around princesses break from traditionally ideological scripts and negotiate cultural meanings (Do Rozario, 2004; Davis, 2006; Forman-Brunell & Hains, 2015; Nash, 2015; Higgs, 2016; Thomas, 2019).

Davis contends that these negative distinguishing qualities belonging to early princesses reflect the times of a classic era (late 1930–1950s), as she describes that Snow White, Cinderella, and *Sleeping Beauty*'s Aurora as "least active and least dynamic" (p. 102) for their traditional roles in caretaking and passive roles that require princes to save them from entrapped states of being. This is compared to more contemporary princesses characterized by "independence, strength of will, determination to engineer their own fates, and insistence on being true to themselves" (p. 176). Davis credits the changing connotation of <princess> as one influenced by the normalizing, feminist ideals of Western culture. For example, Moffitt (2019) argues that Tiana in *The Princess and The Frog* (2009) represents the evolution of traits with "vocal and increased on-screen presence, demonstrated abilities, and established goals" that challenge previously regressive princess imagery (p. 472). Thus, Tiana has agency, working hard to acquire cooking skills, saving money for her own restaurant, and eventually showing the arrogant Prince Naveen that she is equally capable of taking care of herself and saving him.

In similar ways as character qualities and narratives shift in Disney animated films, the <princess> ideograph is also formed with the influence of diachronic shifts in the various Disney princess campaigns over the years. As Davis (2006) aptly notes, "The marketing of 'The Princess Collection' seems to be an attempt by Disney to reconstruct its image as a friend and supporter of women's solidarity" (p. 227). Thus, the transitions in the Disney Princess line since its introduction operate as a means for conforming to society's changing views of women.

Since the development of the Disney Princess line, there have been four official Disney Princess campaigns with corresponding songs (https://disney.fandom.com/wiki/Starting_Now). The song "If You Can Dream," released in 1996, focuses on princesses, but emphasizes their connection to princes and finding heterosexual romance. In the music video, the love interests of the princesses, including Aladdin, the Beast, the various "Prince Charmings," John Smith, and Captain Li Shang (*Mulan*), are included and displayed along with the princesses. As such, their presence becomes instrumental to the princess role. Messages in the song include dreaming to fulfill the heart's wishes and finding love, equating romance with heroism. Sadly, the lyrics of this princess song downplay any progression in feminist qualities adopted by the "Renaissance" princesses and emphasized in their storylines. Judy Kuhn, voicing Pocahontas, sings her signature ballad "The Colors of the Wind" from the 1995 animated film, but instead of continuing its original theme of understanding the spiritualism in every living creature and respecting nature, the song turns the lyric into a love theme about connecting the hearts of significant others. In other words, rather than the song representing the princess's significant passions and interests, it changes the symbolism to only represent their love interests and dream of romance.

Fifteen years later, the next Disney princess song, "The Glow" (2011), was released. The song does not contain any references to romance, but rather declares that when a person believes in one's self their identity as a <princess> will emerge. <Princess> is now a direct signifier and connotation for all girls, disconnecting it from entitlement. Therefore, finding one's self and unearthing the <princess>/self is open to all girls. Additionally, although the message is more empowering, it is also more ambiguous, lending itself to include a wider range of dreams and goals. The lack of specificity leads girls to equate the dreams of achieving personal goals with the desire of attaining romance. The music video predominantly includes images of heterosexual romance that contributes to this conflation. For example, numerous scenes from the various animated films show the romantic interactions, including kisses between Aurora and Prince Phillip, Aladdin and Jasmine, Tiana and Prince Naveen, Belle and the Beast, Ariel and Prince Eric, Rapunzel and Flynn, and Snow White and Cinderella with their respective Prince Charmings.

Throughout the song, clips of the princesses are shown, often surrounded by literal glowing color changes as they occurred in the animated films. Perhaps most problematic is that the literal glowing surrounding their bodies are affiliated with acts of self-sacrifice for love, such as when Ariel's father turns her fins into legs so she can give up living under the sea for a life with Prince Eric, or when Rapunzel cuts her powerful hair to save her love interest, Flynn (later known as Eugene), from otherwise certain death. Although this song's lyrics start to move the campaign away from defining the roles of princesses to solely heterosexual romance, it does not go far enough. The song fails to focus on the story of the princesses' individuality, and the video still emphasizes the role of princesses in symbolizing the attainment of heterosexual and "true" love.

"Live Your Story" (2018) moves further away from the previous themes of passivity and romance. It tells girls to find agency, through dreaming, seeing, or writing their own narrative. The song is sung by Auli'i Cravalho, the voice of Moana, a princess known for her courage and independence since there are no plot elements about romance in the 2016 film. Thus, this song, like "The Glow," contains no explicit references to romance. Unlike "The Glow," "Live Your Story" makes direct reference to individualized qualities and achieving goals. While some claims are vague enough to stand in for achievement of romantic relationships, the phrasing makes it less likely to be understood in the context of partnering and finding love. Lyrics, instead, reference power that is attainable or roads that can be paved. According to the song, girls defy, fulfill goals, and are described as creating and believing in themselves. Most significantly, in the official music video, the imagery of animated princesses only shows them alone or in their element, like Merida in *Brave* (2012) shooting arrows, or Belle from *Beauty and the Beast* (1991) searching books in the town book shop. Additionally, the animated princesses are also doing good works, showing skills, succeeding, and completing remarkable feats. Another version of the video (the official lyric video) combines many of the clips from the "Dream Big Princess" commercials/campaign, which consist of girls acting in athletic, scholastic, philanthropic, political, or career-oriented activities alongside with animated princesses doing similar acts. Romantic encounters have been nearly stripped entirely from the music video with only a character, like Aladdin, briefly present alongside Jasmine.

Most recently, the release of "Starting Now," the 2021 theme song of the "Ultimate Princess Celebration," reveals the most progressive of the songs, continuing with the imagery started in "Live Your Dream," but significantly expands <princess> to include an even broader, more diverse audience and undeniably independent and empowering actions. Our analysis in the next section will further explore how the song reflects these changes through synchronic patterns or clusters that inform one another.

<Princess> in Synchronic Patterns: Ways of (Explicitly) Redefining/Reframing <Princess>

First, Disney shifts the actual definition of <princess> by using their Disney+ programming to provide an explicit, altered meaning for the term <princess>. One program that is vital for targeting young girls and changing what it means to be a princess is called *Disney Princess Remixed* (*DPR*) (2021). This program initially aired on the Disney Channel but is accessible by searching for "princess" on the Disney+ streaming application. *DPR* is a collection of five 22-minute music videos starring a young tween named Harper (Txunamy Ortiz) who operates as the show's virtual "DJ," "mixer," or host. In this fictional setup, Harper returns home to an artificial intelligence voice welcoming her and the audience to the Ultimate Disney Celebration. Harper makes herself comfortable in what is likely her bedroom, where she awakens "Flora," the smart speaker that provides her virtual assistance. Flora's technology is not dissimilar from Amazon's Alexa, a Google Home device, or Apple's Siri; yet, this fictional artificial intelligence serves as a kind of virtual Fairy Godmother (the name also belongs to one of the fairies caring for Aurora in *Sleeping Beauty*). Like fairies, magical godmothers, or guiding parental figures in Disney princess films, Flora encourages Harper while she remixes, telling her she is "smart" and "courageous" and she "can do anything," inspiration that derives from twenty-first-century <princess characters>.

This fictional setting is also significant. First, within Harper's bedroom we see context clues that serve to modernize both representations of girls and the <princess>. For example, Harper's room is decorated with a lighted sign that reads GRL PWR. The light is emphasized when Harper directs Flora to set lights at "chill mode," which darkens the room and brightens the sign, drawing attention to it. As we and other critics have addressed in earlier essays, the Disney <princess> is now synonymous with values and principles of contemporary Western feminist ideology as "doers" capable of social, academic, sports, or career advancements. Harper's personality and confidence becomes a model of the traits associated with <princesses> or girl's and women's empowerment.

Second, Harper communicates a strong sense of selfhood to viewers. In this program, her character exhibits such traits as creativity, kindness (to Flora), and responsibility when she sets her own screen time limited to half-hour. Though she herself is never called, referenced, or implied to be a <princess>, it is obvious that she feels a strong association with them and learns from them.

Third, Harper is not just observing and watching these music videos, she is also putting the measures in place to *produce* and *control* what she sees. Harper is using her imagination, opinions, and creative choices to recreate the representation of the <princess> in the videos about to be played. Harper is not actually selecting animated or real-life princesses; instead, she is choosing other recognizable young actors who started their careers as tween or teenage actors on the Disney Channel or in Disney programs like *High School Musical: The Musical: The Series* (2019–) and *Under Wraps* (2021). In addition to selecting a princess-specific song and a performer to sing the role, Harper can select details such as the performer's dress, such as when she selects a song from *The Little Mermaid* and an outfit with pants for the singer. Flora warns Harper that mermaids cannot wear pants due to their tails. Harper responds, "not if I give her legs to dance." Thus, "remixing" has two meanings throughout the show. First, the performances are obvious remixes of an original princess song from an animated film redone in an entirely different genre. Second, Harper is capable of remixing her understanding or vision of a <princess>, in this case, by making and/or adjusting the characteristics belonging to the <princess> upon which the song is based. In doing so, she can alter or revise the <princess>, so <princess> is relevant to her contemporary understanding of capabilities and choice.

Every song operates through a shift in genre. For example, "Almost There" shifts from jazz to pop, and "Into the Unknown," a ballad, is now performed as a techno song. The best example of the remixing, or re-envisioning, comes from the Harper's remix of *Beauty and the Beast: The Broadway Musical*'s song "Home." The animated Belle is a controversial <princess> character, as her literal imprisonment leads to falling in love with her captor and securing a heterosexual relationship (Hains, 2016). Yet, Weidman-Winter (2020) argues that Belle, especially in the 2017 live action version, represents "freedom, independence, and relationships built on trust and respect" (p. 206). In *DPR*, "Home" is sung by Julia Lester, who performed a ballad version of the same song in *High School Musical: The Musical: The Series.* Harper, however, remixes it into a rock song, and selects Belle based on her quality of loyalty. Lester is also accompanied in the music video by an all-female rock band. The song utilizes Princess Belle's signature colors of yellow and red in costumes and scenery, but instead of adorning a gown, Lester and the band wear leather jackets and pants, and the color red also dominates through lasers, rose petals, and fog from the stage lights. The song's bridge takes on new meaning because without direct reference to a beast, the song becomes an anthem of resistance. Lester croons about there being no merit to losing one's freedom, which her back-up singers confirm. The remix operates in the spirit of the Riot Grrrl Rock movement of the early 1990s, a less mainstream punk movement that addressed issues of patriarchy and women's empowerment. While "Home" cannot escape the obvious references to the domestic sphere as a sacred space, the song also works to deconstruct the home as a limitation. Therefore, this song reflects Belle's spirit in *Beauty and the Beast* (1991, 2017), reflecting empowerment as she resists changing herself, her heart's desires, and her interpretation of "freedom" in this new "home," remaining uninhibited and "free" in her heart. The genre of a rock ballad represents symbols of Riot Grrrl, the underground feminist music subculture, and further secures a "liberating" interpretation of meaning for a <princess> identity.

Near the end of Harper's remixing session, Harper has a video call with various performers. In this segment, the performers thank Harper, but in doing so, they discuss what defines a <princess> and, in the dialogue, further clarify its meaning. One of the stars of *DPR*, Sophia Hammons, from *Under Wraps* (2021), the Disney Channel Original Movie, describes the purpose of the show as being about "finding *courage* and *kindness* within yourself," two qualities now commonly associated with contemporary Disney <princesses>. She also asserts that the show will aspire many individuals. Another actress, Dara Reneé of *High School Musical: The Musical: The Series* provides the most direct reframing, stating, "What it means to be a princess today, is be yourself, have courage behind your actions, continue to be kind, and do you." In short, a Disney

<princess> is not that different from the messaging of liberal feminism in Western culture today, especially the ideologies presented in media targeting young children and adolescents. The idea of all people living their truth and aspiring to achieve their dreams, while also steeped in American Dream mythology, has become more realistic since civil rights and women's rights ideologies became widely accepted and understood.

Furthering the meaning of <princess> is the final song that Harper creates. It is a music video, the *official* music video, for the song "Starting Now," sung by Brandy. "Starting Now" is the theme song for the 2021 "Ultimate Princess Celebration," which is another iteration of the Disney princess campaign. The video stars Brandy Norwood, who also played Cinderella in 1997's musical telefilm *Rogers and Hammerstein's Cinderella*. The song incorporates references to at least eight other princess-themed songs, which span from Cinderella to Moana. In other words, phrases and song titles of previous <princess> songs are built into the lyrics so the association with princesses is obvious. "Starting Now" also endorses re-envisioning oneself as a <princess>. The chorus endorses a new vision for the audience, allowing the <princess> a makeover or remix of who we want her to be moving forward. Thus, the song references letting go of the past, the familiarity of the princess, synonymous with a neighbor girl, but also the ability to move beyond limitations. Thus, the act of saving the day or breaking curses, two actions that were historically enacted with the support of a prince or a man, are now attributed as capabilities of <princesses> everywhere.

While *DPR* contributes to a *new* meaning of <princess>, it also works to embrace the shifting and evolving meanings to come. The theme is symbolized in the music video, through Brandy's changes. When she looks at her reflection, she sees herself in her very first music video, "I Wanna Be Down" (1994), but then sees her present-day self, working within a recording studio. The growth of <princesses> are also apparent in the images of real children actors growing into "their" future identities as a skilled skateboarder, an aspiring fashion designer, and a future marine biologist.

As part of this transition in meaning, "Starting Now" is also unique for expanding the definition of <princess> to boys and others outside traditionally dominant demographics. While the song still references feminine gender pronouns, the video highlights a young, Black male child, watching *Cinderella*, designing his own clothing with aspirations to become a fashion designer. Thus, for the first time, a <princess> is expanded beyond a girl's gender identity. This is furthered by Harper's earlier remix of "Into the Unknown," that includes actor Frankie Rodriguez who teams up with Dara Reneé. Rodriguez describes Anna and Elsa as "optimistic" and "caring," explaining he relates to them because he embraces the future and is always attempting to better himself. Likewise, throughout Disney+ content, the Disney <princess> is no longer described as a static figure. Rather, through the act of remixing, the <princess> is constructed as dynamic, and the view is reiterated through corresponding discourse like in the *One Day at Disney Shorts* (2019–2020). In Episode 18, highlighting Patti Murin who plays Anna in *Frozen: The Broadway Musical,* Murin describes aspects of Anna's character as having "so much energy and so much hope." In her interview, Murin also emphasizes the developing and changing of Anna, explaining, "to be able to inhabit her and go through her literal journey, physically, emotionally, I feel like I still—I'm still finding new things every single—every single time I do it." In Murin's discussion of Anna and *DPR*, transition in identity is emphasized and embraced consistently in discourse around the <princess>. In other words, the meaning of <princess> has changed, and will continue to do so.

Finally, it is important to note that while the diachronic changes of <princess> have been traced in terms of Disney+ content, the archive of previous Disney princess campaign videos does not exist on the streaming service. While archival content is available online on other platforms, like YouTube, the lack of access to these campaigns on Disney+ is arguably a positive for the corporation since some previous representations can be read as a minus because of their traditional feminine portrayals. Disney+ controls the narrative and the contemporary ideograph of <princess> by providing only *DPR* to its audiences and viewers. Thus, it can keep and make accessible all the original animated Disney princess films, while the framing from *DPR* provides a buffer to the criticisms of traditional princess messaging. As a further dismissal of the "minuses," e.g., the problematic plotlines and traditional gender role characteristics, Disney's additional framing of princess traits is key to the creation of the contemporary <princess> ideograph.

Character Traits Over Plotlines

The second way Disney+ is shifting the <princess> ideograph is with their focus on <princess> character traits over <princess> narratives. Consider, for example, how Tiana is utilized differently from her story in the animated film *The Princess and the Frog* despite Tiana's role in a story about romance. In the film, significant portions of the plot focus on Prince Naveen, who wishes to avoid marriage and responsibility. It is only after meeting Tiana, his eventual love interest, that they develop an inevitable romance. Given the criticism of heterosexual romance plots in <princess> films, it is not a surprise that Disney would want to downplay this aspect of the story, that is, her love for a prince, that makes Tiana a

<princess>. Consistent with the shift to focus on character traits, Tiana is widely recognized and continually labeled in <princess>-focused scenes as hard-working, persevering, and determined despite life's challenges as a waitress working multiple jobs to save money for her restaurant. This part of Tiana's story is also emphasized in *DPR* in Harper's video calls with the performers who sang "Almost There," two Disney Channel actors, Izabela Rose (*Upside-Down Magic*, 2020) and Ruth Righi (*Sydney to the Max*, 2019–2021). Rose states, "I am hard-working like Tiana for sure," and Righi explains that she relates to Tiana's "resilience" and carries it with her.

Additional Disney+ programming further supports the trait-focused approaches and even reveals the intention behind this strategy. In *Disney Insider* (2020) Episode 9, the segment "Princess Provisions" includes Kristin Rodack, Director of Commercial Integration and Franchise Management at Walt Disney World Resort in Florida. She discusses the park's method for bringing princesses to life in order to honor them, creating products that represent "the characteristics and the qualities that those princesses possess." In this instance, the pastry chefs receive inspiration from the princesses and their creative pastries are the result. The segment shows how Tiana's physical appearance is captured on a cake, with green floral leaves of lily pads that represent her signature dress and pay homage to her transition into a frog. Lauren West, Pastry Chef Assistant at Amorette's Patisserie in Disney Springs, explains in her interview, "What I like about Tiana is that she's very hard-working, she's courageous. I think those are really important princess qualities, but they're also qualities that I try to have in my life as well." She also equates her dream to be a pastry chef to Tiana's dream of opening a restaurant, which Tiana eventually achieves in the film. West relates to Tiana since she now has a dream career, a pastry chef in a premier bakery in a Disney park, a goal that she has been working towards her entire life.

The sentiment is similar for Desirey Gibson, a Pastry Chef Assistant at Disney's Polynesian Village Resort. She discusses the Moana cupcake, where the icing is made to look like the ocean and shoreline and garnished with Moana's signature flower and boat. In this case, the cupcake represents the journey taken by Moana in the film. Moana and the film's plotline are particularly applicable to the shifting ideograph of the <princess>, since the character and narrative is consistent with the new image of a <princess> that Disney wants to legitimize. Even so, Gibson stresses Moana's traits and their similarity to her identity, stating, "I connect with Moana, with her courage and her strength, the love that she has in everything she does, the passion and the drive."

In *DPR*, traits of all <princesses> are emphasized throughout the series of videos and recognized by Harper. As she makes selective choices in her remixes, she picks from <princesses> alongside their dominant character attribute. In her first selection Pocahontas is "giving," Ariel is "fierce," Cinderella is a "dreamer," and Merida is "brave." In the next remix, Belle is "loyal," Rapunzel is "adventurous," Snow White is "sweet," and Mulan is "courageous." Finally, in the last creation which results in Brandy's music video of "Starting Now," Harper produces it by combining all the <princesses>'s characteristics, listing "fierce, hopeful, courage, kindness, and spirit."

This type of character trait framing is consistently used in synopses accompanying the Disney princess films on Disney+. We can note that while some plot elements are discussed, the role of the <princess> is emphasized along with their individual qualities. For example, Merida from *Brave* is a "skilled archer and headstrong." *Beauty and the Beast*'s Belle is "brave" and "independent." In *Aladdin*'s description, his qualities are minimized only to include the information that he is "paired up with a *clever, confident* Princess Jasmine" (emphasis added). Even before mentioning her beauty, Snow White is qualified as "kind." Throughout *DPR* and in nearly all the original programming that contributes to a larger discourse about a Disney <princess> or <princesses> in general, characteristics and traits are continually emphasized. As Kristin Rodack, the Disney World Director overseeing commercialization, franchising, and marketing, again emphasizes giving inspiration to others is what makes the <princesses> beloved. While this may be true, such inspiration would not be possible if Disney had not contributed to the meaning of an ideograph, making the revised <princess> thrive in contemporary culture.

Conclusion

Using an ideographic analysis, we have argued that not only are contemporary <princesses> disrupting the stereotypical and overly feminine, "damsel-in-distress," archetype, the Disney+ streaming service is also reinforcing revisionary and revolutionary messages about <princesses> through additional media and materials, including original programming and textual content. Thus, the discursive moves in framing and programming on Disney+, including princess-themed content and summaries accompanying the films' descriptions, craft <princess> representations through subtle rhetorical strategies that reappropriate, re-envision, and, arguably, resist previous patriarchal norms and assumptions, such as heterosexual romance narratives. We have shown that programs have altered <princess> in ways that include multiple identities/genders and as infinitely expanding or revisionary. Additionally, the new iterations of <princess> avoid messages about plotlines, unless stories are in line with freedom or significant gender advancement for the character. Thus, character traits and/or empowering qualities are consistently emphasized in order to envision the <princess> according to twenty-first-century standards.

We conclude that the changes occurring to Disney <princesses> provides a roadmap for future archetypes that seek to upend tradition and challenge patriarchal messages. Altering <princesses> introduces children to feminist values that will likely influence them to have confidence in their personal abilities and aspire for independence and leadership roles. As Maldonado (2017) notes, and we agree, despite the initial damage from Disney's construction of <princess> culture, "Disney's apparent newfound dedication to the empowerment of children, especially young women, is both necessary and welcome" (para. 12).

Tracing this ideographic change, and its apparent success, reinforces the value of cultural criticism and its importance in reconstructing traditional ideas so they reflect progressive societal changes. Thus, this textual analysis reveals how women's liberation rhetoric is transferred in shifting and alternative representations, meanings, and qualities of <princess> discourse and images. The strategy has the effect of representing change and, in turn, constituting this reality for society.

While we can generally endorse the rhetorical moves of Disney <princesses> on Disney+ as positive mediated representations directed toward girls, we also urge caution against embracing it uncritically. Due to contemporary exigencies, including the #MeToo Movement and the overturning of *Roe v. Wade* in 2022, our cultural moment signals the precarious state of women's rights. While ideologies of feminism and women's liberation rhetoric have seemingly permeated society, the commercialization of Disney <princesses>, even with their empowering messages, will do little to alter current conditions that restrict women and other marginalized groups. Without addressing the ongoing reality of structural inequities for women, such <princess> representations seem problematic. They contain shallow messages of feminism, risk conflating past gender roles with contemporary representations that are more illustrative of advancement and empowerment, minimize the persistent patriarchal structure, and misrepresent "girl power" as personal ownership instead of political activism. Disney and Disney+ risk fueling gender myths by pretending that self-confidence, ambitions, and acceptance of <princess> character traits are all that is necessary to overcome glass ceilings (barriers to perceptions of equal qualifications), glass walls (exclusions of certain roles) and glass elevators (the lack of fast-tracking of marginalized individuals to positions of leadership) and other structural limits in today's society. Yet, it is at this same crossroads we can find some hope. If enough current and younger generations can internalize these messages, which are obviously progressive, these individuals may become politically active and endorse material and policy changes. Ultimately, it depends on whether we truly adopt the ideologies reflected in our favorite, "most beloved" Disney characters and stories and whether we extend such ideals to the material experiences of girls and women everywhere.

Note

1. The brackets surrounding <princess> denote the indexing of the specific ideograph. In this essay we include the word without angle brackets when we reference the term in previous articles and usages. The angle brackets draw attention to the deliberate ways the wording reflects its ideological meaning that we explore in this textual analysis. Following Cloud (2004), we use the symbols to follow "standard notation style for ideographs" (p. 288).

References

Bell, E. (1995). Somatexts at the Disney shop: Constructing the pentimentos of women's animated bodies. In E. Bell, L. Haas, & L. Sells (Eds.), *From mouse to mermaid: The politics of film, gender, and culture* (pp. 107–124). Indiana University Press.

Bell, E., Haas, L., & Sells, L. (1995). *From mouse to mermaid: The politics of film, gender, and culture.* Indiana University Press.

Bickham, S.B., & Roberts, S. (2020). Diversity sells: The dollars and cents of "woke" rebranding. In S. Roberts (Ed.), *Recasting the Disney princess in an era of new media and social movements* (pp. 21–42). Lexington.

Cloud, D.L. (2004). "To veil the threat of terror": Afghan women and the <Clash of Civilizations> in the imagery of the U.S. War on Terrorism. *Quarterly Journal of Speech, 90*, 285–306. DOI: 10.1080/0033563042000270726.

Condis, M. (2015). Applying for the position of princess: Race, labor, and the privileging of whiteness in the Disney Princess Line. In M. Forman-Brunell & R.C. Hains (Eds.), *Princess cultures: Mediating girls' imaginations and identities* (pp. 25–44). Peter Lang.

Coyne, S.M., Linder, J.R., Booth, M., Keenan-Kroff, S., Shawcroft, J.E., & Yang, C. (2021, November/December). Princess power: Longitudinal associations between engagement with princess culture in preschool and gender stereotypical behavior, body esteem, and hegemonic masculinity in early adolescence. *Child Development, 92*(6), 2413–2430.

Davis, A.M. (2009). *Good girls and wicked witches: Women in Disney's feature animation.* John Libbey.

Delgado, F.P. (1995). Chicano movement: Rhetoric: An ideographic interpretation. *Communication Quarterly, 43*(4), 446–455.

Do Rozario, R.C. (2004). The Princess and the magic kingdom: Beyond nostalgia, the function of the Disney Princess. *Women's Studies in Communication, 27*(1), 34–59.

Forman-Brunell, M., & Hains, R C. (2015). *Princess cultures: Mediating girls' imaginations and identities.* Peter Lang.

Garlin, J.C., & Sandlin, J.A. (2017). Happily (n)ever after: The cruel optimism of Disney's romantic ideal. *Feminist Media Studies, 17*(6), 955–971.

Gilliam, K., & Wooden, S.R. (2008). Post-princesses models of gender: The new man in Disney/Pixar. *Journal of Popular Film and Television, 36*(1), 2–8.

Giroux, H.A., & Pollock, G. (2010). *The mouse that roared: Disney and the end of innocence.* Rowman & Littlefield.

Hackett, S.R. (2020). "Let It Go" as radical mantra: Subverting the princess narrative in *Frozen*. In S. Roberts (Ed.), *Recasting the Disney princess in an era of new media and social movements* (pp. 211–225). Lexington.

Hains, R.C. (2014). *The princess problem: Guiding our girls through the princess-obsessed years*. Sourcebooks.
Hains, R.C. (2015). If I were Belle: Performer's negotiations of feminism, gender, and race in princess culture. In M. Forman-Brunell & R.C. Hains (Eds.), *Princess cultures: Mediating girls' imaginations and identities* (pp. 209–231). Peter Lang.
Hamilton, H. (2018). Can you be patriotic and oppose the war? Arguments to co-opt and refute the ideograph of patriotism. *Controversia, 8*(1), 13–35.
Hayden, S. (2009). Revitalizing the debate between <life> and <choice>: The 2004 March for Women's Lives. *Communication and Critical/Cultural Studies, 6*(2), 111–131.
Higgs, S. (2016). Damsels in development: Representation, transition, and the Disney Princess. *Screen Education, 83*, 62–69.
Koontz, A., Norman, L., & Okorie, S. (2019). Realistic love: Contemporary college women's negotiations of princess culture and the "reality" of romantic relationships. *Journal of Social and Personal Relationships, 36*(2), 535–555.
Krueger, B. (2010). Making sense of the no on Proposition 8 campaign: The failure of non-ideological argumentation. In D. Gouran (Ed.), *The Functions of Argument and Social Context: Proceedings of the 16th NCA/AFA Summer Conference on Argumentation* (pp. 266–273). National Communication Association.
Lee, R. (2009). Ideographic criticism. In J.A. Kuypers (Ed.), *Rhetorical Criticism: Perspectives in action* (pp. 285–319). Lexington.
Lucaites, J.L., & Condit, C.M. (1990). Reconstructing <equality> culturetypal and counter-cultural rhetorics in martyred black vision. *Communication Monographs, 57*, 5–24.
Maben, S. (2020). *Sophia the First*: A princess life fit for a preschool audience. In S. Roberts (Ed.), *Recasting the Disney princess in an era of new media and social movements* (pp. 43–58). Lexington.
Maldonado, A. (2017, September 20). *Can Disney fix its broken "princess culture"?* Salon. https://www.salon.com/2017/08/20/disney-princesses-dream-big-girl-up/.
McGee, M.C. (1980). The ideograph: A link between rhetoric and ideology. *Quarterly Journal of Speech, 66*, 1–16.
Moffitt, K.R. (2019). Scripting the way for the 21st-century Disney Princess in *The Princess and the Frog*. *Women's Studies in Communication, 42*(4), 471–489. https://doi.org/10.1080/07491409.2019.1669757.
Natasia, D., & Uppal, C. (2015). Mono- or multi-culturalism: Girls around the world interpret non–Western Disney Princesses. In M. Forman-Brunell & R.C. Hains (Eds.), *Princess cultures: Mediating girls' imaginations and identities* (pp. 115–138). Peter Lang.
Palczewski, C.H. (2005). The male Madonna and the feminine Uncle Sam: Visual arguments, icons, and ideographs in 1909 anti-woman suffrage postcards. *Quarterly Journal of Speech, 91*, 365–394.
Rutherford, A., & Baker, S. (2021). The Disney "Princess Bubble" as a cultural influencer. *M/C Journal, 24*(1). https://doi.org/10.5204/mjc.2742.
Schiele, K., Louie, L., & Chen, S. (2020). Marketing feminism in youth media: A study of Disney and Pixar animation. *Business Horizons, 63*, 659–669. https://doi.org/10.1016/j.bushor.2020.05.001.
Sells, L. (1995). Where do mermaids stand? Voice and body in *The Little Mermaid*. In E. Bell, L. Haas, & L. Sells (Eds.), *From mouse to mermaid: The politics of film, gender, and culture* (pp. 175–192). Indiana University Press.
Thomas, E.M. (2019). Empowerment through Disney? Third wave feminist discourse in the "Dream Big, Princess" campaign. In K.A. Foss (Ed.), *Beyond Princess Culture: Gender and children's marketing*. Peter Lang.
Weidman-Winter, R. (2020). Belle: Beyond the classic story for the modern audience. In S. Roberts (Ed.), *Recasting the Disney princess in an era of new media and social movements* (pp. 199–210). Lexington.
Williams, D.C., & Young, M.J. (2005). In P. Riley (Ed.), *Engaging argument: Proceedings of the 14th NCA/AFA Summer Conference on Argumentation* (pp. 97–103). National Communication Association.

Doogie Kameāloha, M.D.

Gen Z to AAPI Direct Marketing and Its Effects on Native Hawaiians

Samantha Tecson

> "She's like a real-life Doogie Howser. That's why we call her Doogie!"—*Doogie Kameāloha, M.D.*

Remakes, reboots, and reimaginings are not unusual territories for Disney. The company's connection to these concepts is generally attached to their much-lauded animated film remakes, but to think Disney's scope only encompasses these properties undermines their corporate visions. With Disney+ the company has modernized its past television properties for newer audiences. Tactically, this allows Disney to exploit viewer familiarity while molding a show for a different audience demographic. An example of this is the Disney+ exclusive series *Doogie Kameāloha, M.D.* (2021) which serves as a reworking of ABC's *Doogie Howser, M.D.* (1989–1993).

Created by Kourtney Kang, *Doogie Kameāloha, M.D.* (*DKMD*) centers on the half White, half Native Hawaiian teen doctor Lahela (Peyton Elizabeth Lee) as she navigates the medical and young adult worlds. By injecting her own biracial White and Asian heritage into the piece, Kang challenges *DKMD*'s White male point of view. Much like her predecessor, Lahela is labeled an adolescent prodigy—a "Doogie Howser," as the show states—and struggles with being a normal young adult. Kang's willingness to interact with race and gender allowed Disney to market the series to modernly progressive teens. Those teenagers, largely part of Generation Z (those born after 1996), are "the most racially and ethnically diverse generation in U.S. history" and seek content reflective of that representational mélange (Bakhtiari, 2022, para. 2; Igielnik, R., & Parker, K., 2020). Advertisements and interviews placed special emphasis on the diversity within the casting and production staff. Yet the most attention was given to *DKMD*'s AAPI (Asian American Pacific Islander) connections.

Akin to other people of color (POC), the AAPI community has low television representation in most acting and production positions. These minute numbers work against the medium's overrepresentation of White non–Hispanic people (Umoh, 2020). The onset of digital platforms was purported to increase diversity, yet they did not. According to the University of California, Los Angeles' *2021 Hollywood Diversity Report Part 2: Television*, digitally scripted shows had only 2.8 percent of Asian people as leads, 24 percent writers of color, and 21.7 percent of digital series episodes directed by non–White groups (Hunt & Ramón, 2021). This meant that most shows on streaming platforms lacked diversity and rarely had Asian actors in the main roles. Additionally, the Geena Davis Institute on Gender in Media in 2021 found that within Hollywood productions API (Asian Pacific Islander) people were often experiencing racism, and API characters were treated as jokes or sexualized. They reported that "80.9% of [their] respondents have experienced microaggressions, blatant racism (55.6%), and tokenization (72.5%) in the workplace. Seventeen percent of female API characters are verbally objectified, and 13.0% are visually objectified in the top 10 grossing domestic films from 2010 to 2019. Audiences are asked to laugh at almost half of the API characters (43.4%)." These intersecting AAPI trends provided Disney with an opportunity to market a series toward an underutilized and misunderstood demographic. As showrunner for *DKMD*, Kourtney Kang constructed an AAPI-guided staff and cast. Because of these AAPI voices, Kang permitted Disney access to the AAPI community. Through their association with Kang and her team, Disney was seen as supporting authentic AAPI stories. However, not all AAPI people were satisfied.

Doogie Kameāloha, M.D. centralizes Hawaiian culture and is publicized as credibly portraying it. This legitimacy is attributed partially to Kourtney Kang who identifies as a Hawaiian Native due to having familial ties on the island (S. Mark, 2021). However, the show's credibility faded in the eyes of some Indigenous Hawaiians. On social media Native Hawaiians took issue with half–Chinese actress Peyton Elizabeth Lee playing Lahela. The character is part Indigenous Hawaiian, a group rarely seen in media. For this essay, I will use the terms Native Hawaiian and Hawaiian Native to describe two different sets of populaces in Hawai'i. Native Hawaiians are the indigenous people of Hawai'i, also referred to as the Kānaka Maoli. Hawaiian Natives are the prescribed Westcentric view of anyone who was born on or lives in Hawai'i regardless of connections to the Kānaka Maoli people. The latter grouping includes other Pacific Islanders such as Samoans and Asian communities (Desmond, 1999). These definitions give the framework as to why Native Hawaiians took issue with the show's casting and highlight problematic aspects *DKMD* presents in its goal of depicting a realistic Hawai'i.

Textually, the show's portrayal of the islands illustrates landmark tourism with its typical iconography of Hawaiian surf, beaches, and tropical greenery. Its images become an advertisement for Hawai'i yet skips over the land's torrid history with the colonization of the Kānaka Maoli people. Not surprisingly, it also serves as a not so subtle commercial for Disney's tourism ventures which includes Hawaiian vacations. When *DKMD* does spotlight Native Hawaiians, they are often in the background or buffoonish characters. These depictions of Native Hawaiians and their land perpetuates existing dominant images of the Kānaka Maoli.

In this essay the complexities surrounding *Doogie Kameāloha, M.D.* will be discussed. First, its positive appeal to Gen Z using a relatable young cast and Disney's valuable working relationship with the AAPI community will be analyzed. Then, *DKMD*'s negative depictions of the Native Hawaiian people are examined through the lens of social media criticisms regarding casting choices, the production's struggle of defining who is Hawaiian, and the series' touristic affiliations. *DKMD* is a series built on Disney's good intentions of inclusivity, but through representational missteps the series falls short of this premise.

Aloha, Gen Z's Dr. Doogie!

Angharad N. Valdivia writes that during the late '90s to early 2000s, the Disney Channel, "One of the bastions of whiteness … [began] to expand its offerings to include a broader range of representations" (Valdivia, 2008, p. 271). Valdivia connects these youth culture as being a "blend of this age/gender/race strategy and a serious dose of postfeminist politics that foregrounds style and consumption over political and social gender politics" (p. 275). For Valdivia, Disney's want for greater audience interactions during that era meant appealing to and including the needs of the tween to teen (ages 10 to 18) demographic. Years later, the adolescents of the mid–2000s to 2010s would be the new target audiences of the Disney Channel. That younger audience, as scholar Jenifer Gillan argues, wanted Disney shows and marketing materials that provided "reassuring counter-narratives about current ideological flashpoints" (Gillan, 2015, p. 150). What both Gillan and Valdivia assert is that young adult audiences have repetitively sought creative works divergent from their social norms. These would be pieces reflexively working against a largely White hegemonic world. For the Disney Channel era teens, Disney shows needed to be modern, female, and diverse. Disney Branded TV, formerly Disney Channel Worldwide (2005–2020), carries on this tradition of diverse youth-centered content on Disney+. Launching in 2019, the streaming service's new youth demographic is Generation Z which consists of people born after 1996 (Igielnik & Parker, 2020). Generation Z is vocal about needing diversity in media; it is no longer a suggestion but a requirement for them (Miller, 2021). *Doogie Kameāloha, M.D.* responds to these desires by branding their young stars as the diversified faces of Generation Z.

In *DKMD*'s media kit on the Disney Media & Entertainment Distribution site, Disney spotlights prior progressive content actress Peyton Elizabeth Lee, who portrays Lahela, worked on under their company:

> Peyton is most well known for playing the title character on Disney Channel's "Andi Mack." "Andi Mack" has been the number one rated show on Disney Channel and the highest rated cable television show across all youth demographics. It has been well received for breaking new ground in young adult television by touching upon previously taboo subject matter for the genre [Disney Media & Entertainment Distribution, n.d.].

From this description, Disney builds Lee to be a credible actress, able to act in socially groundbreaking shows and attract a wider youth audience. They double-down on this position by mentioning her work in the Disney+ exclusive movie *Secret Society of Second-Born Royals* (2020) which they state "was developed by Disney with her direct input as a franchise vehicle for her. For her performance, she was nominated for a Critics Choice Award for Best Lead Actress in a Superhero Film" (Disney Media & Entertainment Distribution, n.d.). During an *Entertainment Tonight Canada*'s interview with Lee, she applauds *Secret Society of Second-Born Royals* and makes reference to social movements—like Black Lives Matter—as facilitating increased representational diversity within the entertainment industry (ET Canada, 2020). From Disney's description of Lee's involvement in the *Secret Society of Second-Born Royals* to her keying in on larger progressive campaigns, Disney is positioning Lee as a socially cautious lead actress. Linking Lee's past projects back to *DKMD* shows that she can reliably fulfill Gen Z's need for diversity.

Gillan would consider this interlinking promotional work part of Disney's "brand-casting." Gillan defines this as the company's practice of hiring third-party digital marketing companies, such as 7ate9, to craft short, video, and content-promotional hybrids to promote a Disney Channel TV series (Gillan, 2015, pp. 165–167). These hybrids referenced social themes approved by Disney corporate as a way to enlist parents' support for their programming. In this case, it is Disney's in-house marketing teams reminding potential viewers of Lee's credentials via her actress biography on the *DKMD* webpage and media tour interviews. In turn, this gives the audience reasons to watch her current work on *DKMD* since she built up familiarity with Gen Z and their desire for diverse content current. This is best seen in a series of interviews with teen-focused magazine *J-14*. In these Zoom interviews, the young cast member's diverse faces are on display as they speak about their experiences filming *DKMD*. They are asked about how the series reflects their own teen life, the importance of a strong female teen lead, and about an *Andi Mack* reboot (J-14 Magazine, 2021a). Now instead of just Lee, the young cast is hitting Gen Z's markers of diversity and inclusion while brandcasting Lee's credentials from *Andi Mack*. Gillan notes that part of Disney's brandcasting is relatability to their target demographic and that in itself is not a bad objective (Gillan, 2015). A company needs to be able to relate to, and have knowledge of, its target audience. Disney selected a diverse Gen Z cast; three of the four young actors are non–White and two of the four are female (Studio System, n.d.). Disney promoted an understanding of *DKMD*'s Gen Z audience by having their young stars speak about the series' inclusive production practices and connecting to modern teen's nostalgia surrounding Lee's prior shows.

Diagnosis, an Asian Dr. Doogie

During the initial promotions for *Doogie Kameāloha, M.D.*, Disney prioritized speaking about the show's diversity. In a radio interview with Kiss 104.1 FM, Jeffrey Bowyer-Chapman reflected on his work playing Doogie's coworker Dr. Charles Zeller:

> In the sense that the stories that were so often ... told—[where] the protagonists and the heroes that are often ... clothed in white skin—that isn't necessarily the case in the show. We get to show the strength and power and genius and brilliance and perseverance of everyone else. Everyone who's existed in the margins for so long. The cast is built of majority people of color, majority Hawaiian natives, tons of AAPI representation. I mean, myself, as a Black biracial queer person, as a series regular on the show, it's something that is not often seen, especially in Disney entities [Williams, 2021].

By speaking about the deficits in Disney's prior attempts with diverse content, Bowyer-Chapman articulates that *DKMD*'s inclusive casting demonstrates Disney's growth as a company, and for the show, with its specific ties to the AAPI community. Bowyer-Chapman's estimation of a majority AAPI cast is factually correct as six of the nine regular actors are from that community. Peyton Elizabeth Lee, Matthew Sato, Wes Tian, Mapuana Makia, Jason Scott Lee, and Ronny Chieng are all Asian or Pacific Islanders (Studio System, n.d.). Additionally, Kourtney Kang serves as showrunner while Melvin Mar is an executive producer; both are Asian and worked on ABC's popular Asian American show *Fresh Off the Boat* (2015–2020) (Ramos, 2021a). Just like Peyton Elizabeth Lee's involvement in diverse Disney projects, Mar's and Kang's work on *Fresh Off the Boat*, and their Asian Heritage, gives AAPI authenticity to the *DKMD* brand. They are not only knowledgeable about the Gen Z demographic, but also willing to feature AAPI voices through community-driven stories recognized by AAPI organizations. The Americans Advancing Justice Southern California awarded Mar for his AAPI media productions: "Congratulations to #DoogieKamealohaMD executive producer Melvin Mar on receiving the Public Image Award from @AAAJ_LA for his positive impact on Asian American Native Hawaiian Pacific Islander communities" (Disney Branded TV PR [@DisneyBrandTVPR], 2021c). In a series of tweets, Disney Branded TV mentioned prominent AAPI figures guest starring on *Doogie Kameāloha, M.D.*, such as actors Margaret Cho, Randall Park, and Al Harrington, along with musician Jake Shimabukuro and master Hawaiian dance teacher Vicky Holt Takamine (Disney Branded TV PR [@DisneyBrandTVPR], 2021a, 2021b, 2021d). Additionally, beyond his multi-episode guest appearance, Park had also directed Episode 5 of *Doogie Kameāloha, M.D.* titled "Dunk Cost" (Studio System, n.d.). What these social media posts illuminate are strong celebrity AAPI authenticators for the show. For example, both Cho and Park are well-known Asian American actors who appear regularly on Asian American media, and actively speak out against Hollywood's lack of support towards AAPI people. The show's AAPI forward casting, creative team, and auxiliary stars firmly place *DKMD* in the AAPI bubble, but were not its sole entries into this community.

Asian American media scholars have long spoken of the community-driven institutions that attempt to preserve and push for AAPI stories. In *Asian American Studies Today: Making Asian American Film and Video: History, Institutions, Movements* (2015) author Jun Okuda notes organizations such as the Center for Asian American Media (CAAM) and VC (Visual Communications) bring together Asian American workers across the media landscape allowing their voices to be heard. These AAPI institutions give aid either financially, through their industry connections, or by holding events featuring AAPI visual arts projects. In 2021 the Disney corporation advertised *Doogie Kameāloha, M.D.* at AAPI events. Before the show's Disney+ debut, CAPE (Coalition of Asian Pacifics in Entertainment) tweeted a promotion for the series and how cast member Mapuana Makai provided a table read during one of CAPE's New Writers Fellowship (CAPE—Coalition of Asian Pacifics in Entertainment [@CAPEUSA], 2021a, 2021b). After the show's debut, Disney had special programming slots for *DKMD* at VC's 2021 Los Angeles Asian Film Festival and Mixed Asian Media's first annual Mixed Asian Media Fest

(Sirikul, 2021; Visual Communications, 2021). Both festivals played the first episode for the audience and had interviews with the AAPI actors and creative team including Kang, Mar, Lee, and Scott Lee. They spoke about the integration of their own AAPI experiences into the show, the diverse crew, and the care put into accurately representing Hawai'i and the AAPI people. Kang has mentioned on several occasions that she wanted to make a show in which she and her children could see a mixed-race Asian family much like their own (101.9 The Mix, 2021). Kang's vision, along with her mainly AAPI cast and crew, reflect the desire of AAPI media and organizations for more visibility and believable community stories.

By attaching themselves to these AAPI organizations and events, Disney had its proverbial mouse ears on the ground. Their global outreach credibility to AAPI causes Kent A. Ono and Vincent N. Pham to argue in *Asian Americans and the Media* (2009) that the AAPI organizations and institutions

> "may gain or otherwise acquire the power to apply constant pressure for change and can become involved in the dominant media in order to create change from within with varying degrees of success" since some of them "hold more clout and power than individuals, as they are able to pool resources, argue for space through a collective voice based on numerical representation, and attend to both institutional and individual levels" [Ono & Pham, 2009, p. 254].

They further state that due to these abilities, "these organizations are pressuring mainstream media outlets to move beyond ridicule and stereotypes to produce representations that are respectful and intelligent" (p. 254). Disney's presence in the mainstream media then amplifies organizations like VC and CAPE by widening their visibility to the public and connecting them to fellow communications conglomerates. In response, Disney's symbiotic relationship to AAPI organizers allows the company to swiftly respond to the community's aspirations of restructuring conventional AAPI images. Ono and Pham believe that Asian American media independence requires not only smaller actions from individuals, but larger ones asserted by organizations and institutions. Through Disney's vast networking and economic support systems, AAPI businesses can use these negotiated benefits to progress Asian American independence and storytelling away from the dominant cultural hegemony in the media landscape. However, this does not mean that *Doogie Kameāloha, M.D.* was always accurate with its AAPI representation.

A Cast Full of "Hawaiian" Spirit?

Disney's announcement of *DKMD* did not come without complications. On social media sites like Twitter and TikTok people were quick to point out that the show did not cast a Kānaka Maoli actor to play Lahela. Instead, Disney chose White-Asian actress Peyton Elizabeth Lee. For example, one tweet stated, "@disneyplus you're telling me you can search all of the Pacific Islands to find a girl to play Moana but you couldn't do the same for this show? Make it make sense. #DoogieKamealohaMD," and another said, "I basically just repeated myself at dis [*sic*] point w [*sic*] #DoogieKamealohaMD but I'm just so tired n [*sic*] hurt by the sidelining of Native Hawaiian artists in favor of Asians playing US!??! [*sic*] & the favor of lighter skinned natives over brown natives. It [*sic*] just shows how Hollywood is still racist" (pualalea [@pualaleapanaewa], 2021c; Sipping Koko [@sipping_koko], 2021). These viewers believe that Disney allowed for what Pine Mei Lin Mark would call "Hawaiian Fac[ing]" where non–Native Hawaiian actors will play Kānaka Maoli characters (D.M.L. Mark, 1991). Unfortunately, there is a precedent of this in media where even part Kānaka Maoli actors are not put into lead roles (Oh, 2022). These constant dismissive casting practices deplete the chances to have accurate Native Hawaiian portrayals and mark the community as replaceable.

In an interview with *Mixed Asian Media*, Peyton Elizabeth Lee admits:

> [She] personally don't have any Hawaiian in [her]. But, because of that, it was very important for me to learn as much as [she] possibly could and talk to as many local people as possible to bring the story to life in the most truthful way. Being in Hawaii, immersing [her]self in the culture, researching, and talking to the local cast and crew that [they] had, [she] learned a lot and tried to bring their story to life as much as possible [Chester & Tanabe, 2021].

Her argument for being able to play a Hawaiian alludes to being Hawaiian as performative. She can play Hawaiian if she studies their culture. According to Native Hawaiian scholar Lisa Kahaleole Hall, "'Hawaiians at heart' assume that knowing and appreciating Hawaiian culture is enough to transform them into being Hawaiian" (Hall, 2005, p. 410). This is not dissimilar to statements made by showrunner Kourtney Kang who considers herself to be a Hawaiian:

> I was born in Hawaii. My dad is Korean, fourth-generation—his family was on like the first boat from Korea that came to Hawaii. And my mom is an Irish Catholic girl from Wilkes-Barre, Pennsylvania. They fell in love and had us three kids, and then my mom missed everybody, so we basically grew up in Pennsylvania. But we would go back to Hawaii, so I have family there [Hullender, 2021].

Having family living in Hawaiʻi and being born there does make someone a Native Hawaiian. Kang's statements reflect Hall's "Hawaiian at heart" definition which she furthers by hypothesizing that non–Hawaiians "who pretend they are Hawaiian are reaching for an identity that others will recognize and legitimate, since it has been so thoroughly advertised and commodified" (Hall, 2005, p. 410). Kang exemplifies this "Hawaiian at heart" further by mentioning how *DKMD* would embody the "spirit of aloha" (Chew, 2021). To the Kānaka Maoli people, aloha "signifies a deep, abiding kinship within Hawaiian culture based on practices of reciprocal care and the work it takes to be in community, but [they] also know that aloha has been turned into a concept for tourism, emptied of its cultural context when displayed in advertisements or postcards" (Teves, 2018, p. 28). Aloha is then transformed from something of cultural importance into a snappy catchphrase that attaches itself to an "accurate" Hawai'i. Through society's loose definition of Hawaiian, and the concept of "Hawaiian at heart," Lee was a mixed Kānaka Maoli character studying the Hawaiian culture while Kang could serve as an "authentic Hawaiian voice" due to her connections to the islands.

Ironically, *DKMD* does have actors and crew members who are not "Hawaiian at heart" but true Native Hawaiians. Kourtney Kang said in an interview that she wanted to respect and honor Native Hawaiians. She mentions, "Jason is Native Hawaiian, Matt Sato, who plays the older brother Kai is Hawaiian, Mapuana is Hawaiian. Several of our key crew and department heads are Native Hawaiian" (Chester & Tanabe, 2021, para. 31). What Kang fails to mention is how they settled on Lee when they were able to cast other Native Hawaiian actors and use Kānaka Maoli people in non-key cast and crew positions (Chester & Tanabe, 2021; Nakamura, 2021) and mainly served as extras. For example, some are fellow students in Episode 1, "Aloha—The Hello One," fellow surfers in Episode 7, "Mom-mentum," and farmers market venders in Episode 8, "Talk-Story" (Kasdan, 2021; Kavanagh, 2021; Rodriguez, 2021). Not surprisingly, there are few comments from extras about their role as background characters. However, there was one tweet from an extra in Episode 4, "Lahela & Stitch," who was asked to cover their indigenous tattoo. This request was confirmed by another extra who explained that to the Kānaka Maoli tattoos are culturally significant and that hiding them is disrespectful (Kawelu, 2021). Like the tattoo, having the Native Hawaiians as extras rather than central characters undercuts the respect Kang claims *Doogie Kameāloha, M.D.* has for the Kānaka Maoli. This problem is exacerbated when considering the three actual Native Hawaiian regulars on the show serve as comic side characters to Lahela's strait-laced doctor persona.

The three main Native Hawaiian cast members are what Colby Miyose would describe as "buffoonish" Kānaka Maoli stereotypes due to their comedic roles (Miyose, 2021). Matt Sato's Kai Kamealoha is the laid-back bothersome older brother; Mapuana Makai's Noelani Nakayama is the gossipy, somewhat misguided older medical assistant; and Jason Scott Lee's Benny Kamealoha is the heartwarming father who does not take life too seriously and serves as the viewer's guide to Hawaiian culture. Benny, at many points in the series, performs silly or eccentric actions rooted in Hawaiian cultural stereotypes. In Episode 1, "Aloha—The Hello One," he mentions that he is going to throw an octopus in the washing machine to tenderize it (Kasdan, 2021). This is punctuated by his youngest son, Brian Patrick Kamealoha (Wes Tian), telling him that other kids think that it is weird to have another washing machine just for octopuses. Kang and Scott Lee discuss the octopus scene with *The Wrap*, mentioning how it is authentic to some octopus preparation they heard about as Hawaiians (Nakamura, 2021). The educational side to the sequence is lost when considering it is played for laughs at Benny's and somewhat all Native Hawaiians' expenses. That damaging side of the humor is echoed in the running gag of the strangeness with Benny's food truck. Benny's truck sells both leis and Hawaiian shaved iced because he has a passion for both (Kasdan, 2021). Financially this truck would be unstable, and the combination of flowers and shaved ice is not practical. Benny's truck then represents comical naivete wrapped in tourist machinations by having stereotypical vacationist images attached to Hawai'i. Miyose, through Sharpe and Haynes, ties the use of humor into acts of everyday reinforcement of cultural stereotyping (Miyose, 2021, p. 90; Sharpe & Hynes, 2016, p. 89). Using humor through Benny, and thus Native Hawaiians, normalizes othering of the Kānaka Maoli and paints their culture as unusual. They are a people that have already suffered years of colonization and commodification of their culture. What *Doogie Kameāloha, M.D.* does for the Kānaka Maoli is harmfully erase them from Hawaii's narrative by uplifting the ideas of "Hawaiian at heart" and misrepresenting their culture with humor at their expense and having Native Hawaiian extras fade into Hawaii's backdrop.

Cruising for Tourism

Although they promised to respect Native Hawaiians and the land of Hawai'i, *Doogie Kameāloha, M.D.* is still attached to the problematic effects of tourism. The show uses idyllic tourist-associated images of Hawai'i and has been used to promote Disney's Hawaiian vacation resorts. As a result, the series ignores the effects of colonization Hawai'i has suffered that has displaced the Kānaka Maoli people and commodified their culture.

In February of 2021, *DKMD* was granted access by the State of Hawai'i Department of Business, Economic Development & Tourism (DBEDT) to film the show in Hawai'i (Department of Business, Economic

Development & Tourism, 2021). The DBEDT Director, Mike McCartney, welcomed the show to Hawai'i, expressing that it "will deliver a new perspective for viewers that embraces our island home" (DBEDT, 2021, p. 2). Analyzing how the cast speaks of Hawai'i and how Hawai'i is depicted in the series, the hopes of McCartney's may be dashed. When speaking about filming in Hawai'i, the cast of *DKMD* called it an "island paradise" with wondrously breathtaking beaches, mountains, and ocean (J-14 Magazine, 2021b; Shine On Media, 2021). Mirroring the cast's idyllic memories of Hawai'i, the show uses picturesque shots of the island including its beaches and mountain ranges. An example of these scenic displays is in the opening sequence of Episode 1. Lahela and her father Benny surf in the crystal-blue water and then walk along the sun-speckled beach until the scene cuts to her driving on the roads surrounded by lush green hills (Kasdan, 2021). From the cast gushing about Hawaii's beauty, to the show's painting-like snapshots of the islands, the reaffirmation of tourist imagery is present. The show was even filmed at iconic tourist destinations such as 'Iolani Palace, Waikiki, and the Duke Kahanamoku Statue (Desborough, 2021). Vacationers in Hawai'i often go for the aforementioned "island paradise" seeking a tropical escape only the islands can provide. These images of tropical enchantment further entice people to vacation in Hawai'i. Tourism itself is a double-edged sword for Hawaiians because it provides the state money, but has contributed to locals losing land to tourist industries (C. Miyose, personal communication, August 1, 2022). The Kānaka Maoli do not gain much from these intrusions as they are shifted out of their space. In *Hollywood's Hawaii: Race, Nation, and War* (2017) Delia Malia Caparoso Konzett examines the interconnection between land, race, and poverty within Hawai'i influenced by the expansion of mass tourism. Konzett explains:

> The profit shares from all these projects stayed mostly within the hands of the white elites, cutting in here or there some emerging elites among Japanese and Chinese Hawaiians. However, for most of Hawaii's local population these changes produced little economic improvement and instead were often accompanied with forceful dislocation from areas to be developed, a problem that continues today and underlies, along with the high costs of rent and real estate, Hawaii's acute crisis of homelessness, the highest in the nation [Konzett, 2017, pp. 197–198].

From Konzett, the active tourism industry decimates the indigenous Hawaiian population leaving them little land and little money. The irony of *DKMD* is that the show does not address these issues, nor mentions them.

The Kamealoha family lives in a beach house mere feet away from the shores of Waimānalo. Beachside housing is expensive and is not usually given to Native Hawaiians due to poverty and land rights claims (C. Miyose, personal communication, August 1, 2022; Stevenson, 2020). The family is Kānaka Maoli through the father's side, but the White mother Dr. Clara Hannon (Kathleen Rose Perkins) seems to be the breadwinner due to her status as a head doctor at the hospital. Their home then represents a part of what Konzett mentioned, the benefits non-Hawaiians gain from the land. Reclamation of Native land could have been shown if the father was the one to own the house and the financial disparities between the parents were lessened. However, by having the White mother as the head of the family, the ownership of the Indigenous land is claimed more by her. The idea of reclaimed land could have also been discussed in Episode 6 where Kai Kamealoha decides to become a farmer. With the shifting of Kānaka Maoli–owned lands, few farming locations were left for them especially as some are owned by corporate industries (Stevenson, 2020). The farm in which Kai works is in an undisclosed mountainous location with unknown owners. The focus of the episode is on Kai having a passion for farming, but it could have challenged who benefits from farming on native lands. Instead, like with the Kamealoha house, the relations between Native Hawaiians and land ownership are ignored.

As a large conglomerate, Disney has an entire business sector dedicated to resorts and vacations, some of which are stationed in Hawai'i (Hallman, 2018). On the island of Oahu, Disney has the Aulani Resort which they say is "inspired by the natural wonders and rich traditions of Hawai'i, Aulani Resort is the ultimate family getaway—celebrating the beauty, history and welcoming spirit of the island" (Disney Aulani, n.d.). Using *Doogie Kameāloha, M.D.*, Disney created advertisements with Peyton Elizabeth Lee to promote Aulani. In the ads she plugs the series and her favorite things to do at the "ultimate Hawaiian vacation destination," Aulani Resort, such as snorkeling, floating in the lazy river, and eating shaved ice (Disney Parks, 2021). Instead of the obvious appeals to tourism inherent within the series, these advertisements explicitly relate *DKMD* to it. Like other tourist corporations, Disney is not returning or respecting Kānaka Maoli's land. John Willis in *Disney Culture* (2017) argues that the many Disney vacation ventures are to profit off those familiar with their product and Disneyfy those who are not. What he means by Disneyfy is Disney's tendency to saturate its brand in every generation, various mass entertainment formats, and the hospitality industry. For example, within the MickeyBlog article for Aulani, Lee poses with Disney animated characters Stitch, Moana, and the Hawaiian shirt–wearing Mickey and Minnie (Roden, 2021). This makes Disney seem authentically Hawaiian while enticing Disney resort guests to meet those characters and see the land that inspired their projects. As a result, the commodification of Native

Hawaiian culture and the loss of Native lands continues as Disney expands their tourist footprint using *DKMD* as an additional promotional tool.

Conclusion

Doogie Kameāloha, M.D. represents a complicated media artifact that is an amalgamation of good intentions, misguided attempts, and corporate desires. The series truthfully provides diversity in its cast and crew with many of them being from the AAPI community. Yet the show fails to fully embrace its Native Hawaiian perspective. Instead, it erases and commodifies the Kānaka Maoli people. Writer Dino-Ray Ramos best summarizes the show's conflicting aspects when he discusses his own experiences with the show's content and criticisms:

> As a series, *Doogie Kamealoha M.D.* hits all the sweet spots and beats to make it a great watch. However, upon voicing this opinion, it will be met with scrutiny because of the representation of Pacific Islanders ... or as some locals and Pacific Islanders might say, "misrepresentation." The main source of criticism of the show is the fact that Lee is not from Hawaii. In an age of authentic representation, this is a problem for many. As an advocate and someone in the industry who helps bolster diversity, I admit this was [a] blindspot for me. When the first two episodes were sent to me to screen, I had a smile on my face the entire time and the series just shined. However, when people started to point out to me the flaws in its casting of the lead it burst my bubble [Ramos, 2021b].

Ramos is reckoning with enjoying the series' progressive nature and the reality that it still failed an underrepresented group. His opinion is not unique as scholars and cultural critics have had mixed reactions to the show.

On social media there is continued criticism of the *DKMD*'s portrayal of Native Hawaiians. In a tweet from a Native Hawaiian, she expresses her deep regret that Hollywood undermines her people by putting Asian actors in Kānaka Maoli roles (pualalea [@pualaleapanaewa], 2021a, 2021b). Similarly, TikTok user dreamfromvenus created a skit surrounding the casting of *DKMD* satirizing the conflation of Hawaii's large Asian population as "Native Hawaiian" representation (Dreama, 2021). As Native Hawaiians, both users are denouncing the series because it misrepresents their underrepresented culture. On the other hand, others acknowledge the show's misstep in casting Peyton Elizabeth Lee to play a Kānaka Maoli character, but overall view the show as an accurate snapshot of Hawai'i. The YouTube channel *Hello from Hawaii*, hosted by a Hawaiian local named Chris (his last name is not shared), highlights portions of the island where *DKMD* was filmed. Chris argues the series referenced niche local knowledge, reflected the diverse populace of the island, and did not play into Hawai'i as a tourist spot (*Hello from Hawaii,* 2021). He does note that he understands Lahela should have been played by someone from Hawai'i or that was Native Hawaiian. TikTok personality marmaryeesa2022 begins her video on *DKMD* addressing the issues with Lahela's casting, but then states the show provides a realistic take on living in Hawai'i (marmaryeesa2022, 2021). From their Hawaiian Native perspective, these positive views acknowledge *DKMD*'s shortcomings are balanced by its effort to depict a Hawaiian's Hawai'i.

Kourtney Kang is not unaware of the show's criticisms. She had spoken about her depiction of Hawai'i and how she wishes to do better. On the topic of Native Hawaiian representation, she says:

> That said, I still think we can do a better job of it. And season two, I would love to dig more into the Hawaii of it all, you know? Get more into their stories that only this show can tell, because it's set in Hawaii. We're only at the tip of the iceberg. I'm proud of the show we did, and I think there's always things that we could do better moving forward [Chester & Tanabe, 2021].

Certainly, some of these issues could have been fixed in the show's development, such as the casting of non–Hawaiian Peyton Elizabeth Lee and implementing plotlines that created dialogue around the Kānaka Maoli. However, her sincere interest to do better in terms of storytelling should not be overlooked, and not all blame for *DKMD*'s representational issues should be pinned on her.

Doogie Kameāloha, M.D. shows it is important to give underrepresented groups voices and to evaluate criticisms. Its discussions in the press and social media tell us to celebrate the achievements of AAPI people, but to be cautious of erasing the Pacific Islander portion of the acronym. Ignoring the Native Hawaiians' presence dangerously elongates their struggles with colonization. Soon before this volume went to the publisher, Disney+ released a second season of *DKMD*. It will be interesting to see if Disney tries to rectify the issues Kang, critics, and viewers noticed about the series. The best way for *DKMD* to do this is to give agency back to the Kānaka Maoli people who were misused and misrepresented, using the show as a platform to denounce the Native Hawaiian loss of land, culture, and finances. If Kang and Disney always respected the Native Hawaiians through *Doogie Kameāloha, M.D.*, they could work harder to fully realize that promise.

References

Bakhtiari, K. (2022, June 5). Gen-Z demand racial justice, not just diversity, equity and inclusion from brands. *Forbes.* https://www.forbes.com/sites/kianbakhtiari/

2022/06/05/gen-z-demand-racial-justice-not-just-diversity-equity-and-inclusion-from-brands/.
CAPE—Coalition of Asian Pacifics in Entertainment [@CAPEUSA]. (2021a, August 27). Catch the trailer to #DoogieKamealohaMD! Arriving on @disneyplus on 9/8! @ leecommapeyton @alexaiono @jasonscottlee @ronnychieng @mapuanamakia @mattksato @chineseguy88 @kourtneykang [Tweet]. Twitter. https://twitter.com/CAPEUSA/status/1431330258398023684.
CAPE—Coalition of Asian Pacifics in Entertainment [@CAPEUSA]. (2021b, August 27). Special shoutout to #MapuanaMakia in the cast. She graciously provided her talents for @brysonchun's table read during our CAPE New [Tweet]. Twitter. https://twitter.com/CAPEUSA/status/1431395887666774017.
Chester, A., & Tanabe, S. (2021). *Mixed Asian media—Disney+ breaks barriers with Doogie Kamealoha*. Mixed Asian Media. https://mixedasianmedia.com/disney-breaks-barriers-with-doogie-kamealoha-interviews-with-peyton-elizabeth-lee-kourtney-kang.
Chew, E. (2021, September 7). *How the spirit of "aloha" is channeled through Disney's "Doogie Kamealoha M.D."* AsAmNews. https://asamnews.com/2021/09/07/how-the-spirit-of-aloha-is-channeled-through-disneys-doogie-kamealoha-m-d/.
Department of Business, Economic Development & Tourism. (2021, February 2). DBEDT news release: The state welcomes Doogie Kamealoha, M.D. https://governor.hawaii.gov/newsroom/dbedt-news-release-the-state-welcomes-doogie-kamealoha-m-d/.
Desborough, J. (2021, September 8). Filming locations revealed for Doogie Kamealoha M.D. *Newsweek*. https://www.newsweek.com/doogie-kamealoha-filming-locations-hawaii-1627069.
Desmond, J. (1999). *Staging tourism: Bodies on display from Waikiki to Sea World*. University of Chicago Press.
Disney Aulani. (n.d.). *Aulani Hawaii Resort*. Aulani Hawaii Resort. Retrieved September 27, 2022. https://www.disneyaulani.com/about-aulani/story/.
Disney Branded TV PR [@DisneyBrandTVPR]. (2021a, October 6). #DoogieDeets: #RandallPark returns as a guest star and directs this week's episode of #DoogieKamealohaMD. Additionally, the late Al Harrington guest [Tweet]. Twitter. https://twitter.com/DisneyBrandTVPR/status/1445830775593582594.
Disney Branded TV PR [@DisneyBrandTVPR]. (2021b, October 13). #DoogieDeets: @margaretcho #JaeSuhPark and #GabbyDuran's #KylieCantrall guest star in this week's episode of #DoogieKamealohaMD, now streaming on @DisneyPlus. [Tweet]. Twitter. https://twitter.com/DisneyBrandTVPR/status/1448371324045254661.
Disney Branded TV PR [@DisneyBrandTVPR]. (2021c, October 21). Congratulations to #DoogieKamealohaMD executive producer Melvin Mar on receiving the Public Image Award from @AAAJ_LA for his positive impact on [Tweet]. Twitter. https://twitter.com/DisneyBrandTVPR/status/1451285895953354752.
Disney Branded TV PR [@DisneyBrandTVPR]. (2021d, November 10). #DoogieDeets: In the season finale of #DoogieKamealohaMD @JakeShimabukuro guest stars as himself & performs a new original song. Plus, the late [Tweet]. Twitter. https://twitter.com/DisneyBrandTVPR/status/1458571753660243972.
Disney Media & Entertainment Distribution. (n.d.). *Doogie Kamealoha, M.D.* Media Kit. Retrieved September 29, 2022. https://dmedmedia.disney.com/disney-plus/doogie-kamealoha-md.
Disney Parks (Director). (2021, September 8). *Peyton Elizabeth Lee shares her favorite things from Aulani, a Disney Resort & Spa*. YouTube. https://www.youtube.com/watch?v=1m6m2dg5jIk.
Dreama. (2021, September 8). Dreama on TikTok. TikTok. https://www.tiktok.com/@dreamafromvenus/video/7005490324348964102?_t=8VscrgF3DwJ&_r=1.
ET Canada (Director). (2020, September 14). *Peyton Elizabeth Lee talks diversity in "Secret Society of Second-Born Royals" | EXTENDED*. YouTube. https://www.youtube.com/watch?v=s6IIZ4h8j4g
Geena Davis Institute on Gender in Media. (2021). I am not a fetish or model minority:

Redefining what it means to be API in the entertainment industry. *Geena Davis Institute on Gender in Media.* https://seejane.org/research-informs-empowers/api-study-i-am-not-a-fetish-or-model-minority/.

Gillan, J. (2015). *Television brandcasting: The return of the content-promotion hybrid.* Routledge, Taylor & Francis Group.

Hall, L.K. (2005). "Hawaiian at Heart" and other fictions. *The Contemporary Pacific, 17*(2), 404–413. https://doi.org/10.1353/cp.2005.0051.

Hallman, C. (2018, June 25). *Every company Disney owns: A map of Disney's worldwide assets.* TitleMax. https://www.titlemax.com/discovery-center/money-finance/companies-disney-owns-worldwide/.

Hello from Hawaii (Director). (2021, September 15). *Does Disney's Doogie Kamealoha M.D. represent the real Hawaii?* YouTube. https://www.youtube.com/watch?v=s898BMImHk4.

Hullender, T. (2021, September 7). *Kourtney Kang interview: Doogie Kamealoha, M.D.* ScreenRant. https://screenrant.com/kourtney-kang-interview-doogie-kamealoha-md/.

Hunt, D., & Ramón, A.-C. (2021). 2021 Hollywood Diversity Report part 2: Television (No. 8; Hollywood Diversity Report, 1–78). University of California, Los Angeles. https://socialsciences.ucla.edu/wp-content/uploads/2021/10/UCLA-Hollywood-Diversity-Report-2021-Television-10-26-2021.pdf.

Igielnik, R., & Parker, K. (2020, May 14). On the cusp of adulthood and facing an uncertain future: What we know about Gen Z so far. Pew Research Center's Social & Demographic Trends Project. https://www.pewresearch.org/social-trends/2020/05/14/on-the-cusp-of-adulthood-and-facing-an-uncertain-future-what-we-know-about-gen-z-so-far-2/.

J-14 Magazine (Director). (2021a, September 7). *Peyton Elizabeth Lee talks "Andi Mack" reboot.* YouTube. https://www.youtube.com/watch?v=68YpVdkbZV4.

J-14 Magazine (Director). (2021b, September 9). *The cast of "Doogie Kamealoha, M.D." share favorite parts about filming in Hawaii.* YouTube. https://www.youtube.com/watch?v=OnZfoWoyWsc.

Kasdan, J. (Director). (2021, September 8). *Aloha—The Hello One* (Season 1, Episode 1). Doogie Kameāloha, M.D.

Kavanagh, S. (Director). (2021, October 20). *Mom-Mentum* (Season 1, Episode 7). Doogie Kameāloha, M.D.

Kawelu, K. (2021, August 28). Kamahaʻo kawelu on TikTok. TikTok. https://www.tiktok.com/@kuakamahao/video/7001626178402438406?_t=8VscjPL3MhG&_r=1.

Konzett, D.C. (2017). *Hollywood's Hawaii: Race, nation, and war.* Rutgers University Press.

Mark, D.M.L. (1991). The reel Hawaii. In R. Leong (Ed.), *Moving the image: Independent Asian Pacific American media arts* (pp. 109–117). UCLA Asian American Studies Center and Visual Communications, Southern California Asian American Studies Central.

Mark, S. (2021, September 5). Life mimics art in Kourtney Kang's reboot, "Doogie Kamealoha, M.D." *Honolulu Star-Advertiser.* https://www.staradvertiser.com/2021/09/05/features/life-mimics-art-in-kourtney-kangs-reboot-doogie-kamealoha-m-d/.

marmaryeesa2022. (2021, September 11). Mar Mar :) on TikTok. TikTok. https://www.tiktok.com/@marmaryeesa2022/video/7006731898881871110?_t=8VscdmQvOoN&_r=1.

Miller, J. (2021, February 18). For younger job seekers, diversity and inclusion in the workplace aren't a preference. They're a requirement. *Washington Post.* https://www.washingtonpost.com/business/2021/02/18/millennial-genz-workplace-diversity-equity-inclusion/.

Miyose, C. (2022, August 1). Interview with Colby Miyose on Native Hawaiian Representation (S. Tecson, Interviewer) [Personal communication].

Miyose, C.Y. (2021). *Aloha Media: Negotiating Kānaka Maoli representation and identity in television, film, and music.* University of Massachusetts Amherst. https://doi.org/10.7275/22278875.0.

Nakamura, R. (2021, September 8). "Doogie Kamealoha, MD" showrunner explains the origin of the octopus washing machine. *Yahoo!* https://www.yahoo.com/entertainment/doogie-kamealoha-md-showrunner-explains-224506589.html.

Oh, D.C. (2022). *Whitewashing the movies: Asian erasure and white subjectivity in U.S. film culture.* Rutgers University Press.
Okada, J. (2015). *Making Asian American film and video: Histories, institutions, movements.* Rutgers University Press.
101.9 The Mix. (2021, September 8). Kourtney Kang reveals how her three daughters helped inspire the "Doogie Howser" reboot. *101.9fm The MIX—WTMX Chicago.* https://wtmx.com/kourtney-kang-reveals-how-her-three-daughters-helped-inspire-the-doogie-howser-reboot/.
Ono, K.A., & Pham, V.N. (2009). *Asian Americans and the media.* Polity.
pualalea [@pualaleapanaewa]. (2021a, August 28). @CAPEUSA really hurts when you're an organization that's for asians AND pacific islanders yet not commenting on how this show [Tweet]. Twitter. https://twitter.com/pualaleapanaewa/status/1431540702249304070.
pualalea [@pualaleapanaewa]. (2021b, August 28). @CAPEUSA times in Hollywood in the past. We are highly underrepresented and misrepresented in media which is sick and no [Tweet]. Twitter. https://twitter.com/pualaleapanaewa/status/1431541019594485761.
pualalea [@pualaleapanaewa]. (2021c, August 28). I basically just repeated myself at dis point w #DoogieKamealohaMD but I'm just so tired n hurt by the sidelining [Tweet]. Twitter. https://twitter.com/pualaleapanaewa/status/1431542335368663043.
Ramos, D.-R. (2021a, August 26). *"Doogie Kamealoha, M.D." Cast and EPs talk Hawaiian authenticity in remake, possible NPH cameo and …"White Lotus."* DIASPORA. http://thediasporatimes.com/2021/08/26/doogie-kamealoha-m-d-cast-and-eps-talk-hawaiian-authenticity-in-remake-possible-nph-cameo-and-white-lotus/.
Ramos, D.-R. (2021b, September 8). *"Doogie Kamealoha, M.D." is charming to some, but problematic to others because of its Pacific Islander representation Shortcomings.* DIASPORA. https://thediasporatimes.com/2021/09/08/doogie-kamealoha-m-d-is-charming-to-some-but-problematic-to-others-because-of-its-pacific-islander-representation-shortcomings/.
Roden, M. (2021, April 25). Peyton Elizabeth Lee from upcoming "Doogie Kamealoha M.D.," visits Aulani resort. *Mickeyblog.com.* https://mickeyblog.com/2021/04/24/peyton-elizabeth-lee-from-upcoming-doogie-kamealoha-m-d-visits-aulani-resort/.
Rodriguez, G. (Director). (2021, October 27). *Talk-Story* (Season 1, Episode 8). Doogie Kameāloha, M.D.
Sharpe, S., & Hynes, M. (2016). Black-faced, red faces: The potentials of humour for anti-racist action. *Ethnic and Racial Studies, 39*(1), 87–104. https://doi.org/10.1080/01419870.2016.1096405.
Shine on Media (Director). (2021, September 9). *DOOGIE KAMEALOHA cast talk season 1 & filming in Hawaii (Exclusive interview).* YouTube. https://www.youtube.com/watch?v=y1teG8AlYuM.
Sipping Koko [@sipping_koko]. (2021, August 31). @disneyplus you're telling me you can search all of the Pacific Islands to find a girl to play Moana but [Tweet]. Twitter. https://mobile.twitter.com/sipping_koko/status/1432572708685062146.
Sirikul, L. (2021, September 7). *Mixed Asian media presents first annual mixed Asian media fest!* The Nerds of Color. https://thenerdsofcolor.org/2021/09/07/mixed-asian-media-presents-first-annual-mixed-asian-media-fest/.
Stevenson, J. (2020, March 27). Kānāwai: Using ancient Hawaiian law to prepare for the future. *UCLA Law Review.* https://www.uclalawreview.org/kanawai-using-ancient-hawaiian-law-to-prepare-for-the-future/.
Studio System. (n.d.). Doogie Kameāloha, M.D. (2021). *The Studio System.* Retrieved September 27, 2022. https://app.studiosystem.com/p/doogie-kamealoha-m-d/overview.
Teves, S.N. (2018). *Defiant indigeneity: The politics of Hawaiian performance.* University of North Carolina Press.
Umoh, R. (2020, December 3). Streaming platforms are driving diverse representation in television. *Forbes.* https://www.forbes.com/sites/ruthumoh/2020/12/03/streaming-platforms-drive-diverse-representation-in-television/.
Valdivia, A.N. (2008). Mixed race on the Disney Channel: From Johnny Tsunami through

Lizzie McGuire and ending with the Cheetah Girls. In M.C. Beltrán & C. Fojas (Eds.), *Mixed race Hollywood* (pp. 269–289). New York University Press.
Visual Communications. (2021). *C3: DOOGIE KAMEALOHA, M.D.—A New Legacy—2021.* Los Angeles Asian Pacific Film Festival. https://festival.vcmedia.org/2021/special_events/c3-doogie/.
Williams, C. (2021, October 8). Jeffrey Bowyer-Chapman calls "Doogie Kameāloha, M.D." "revolutionary" in spotlighting stories of the marginalized. *KISS 104.1 FM.* https://www.kiss104fm.com/news/jeffrey-bowyer/OVZONXCSMHQ7REBW3VWEMBDJDA/.
Wills, J. (2017). *Disney Culture.* Rutgers University Press.

"Stick to the Status Quo" or the "Start of Something New"?

Exploring the Highs and Lows of Disney+'s High School Musical: The Musical: The Series

LORI BINDIG YOUSMAN

Introduction

While the sequels, prequels, reboots, and spin-offs built on existing media properties expand beloved characters and stories, they also expand the reach and profitability of a franchise. This means modern media franchises are inherently commercial endeavors that allow companies to maximize earnings on already lucrative properties (Benson, 2022). The most successful franchises transcend a property's original medium—increasing revenue across a range of media (television series, books, video games, etc.). Likewise, ancillary products (like toys and clothing) work to extend the franchise while simultaneously generating more profit. However, to maintain the power of an expanding franchise, media companies must engage in "franchise refurbishment," which ensures franchises speak to contemporary audiences and are culturally relevant. In other words, franchise refurbishment is the process by which a "franchise can be resurrected, reshaped, and ultimately managed" (Benson, 2022, p. 440).

As one of the leading media conglomerates in the world, it comes as no surprise that the Disney corporation has been wildly successful in developing and maintaining lasting franchises. The creation of its own Disney+ streaming service has provided new possibilities for franchise expansion and refurbishment as exemplified by *High School Musical: The Musical: The Series* (*HSMTMTS*). This essay explores the Disney+ series, which builds upon the original *High School Musical* (*HSM*) franchise. Through franchise refurbishment, the new series appears to push the boundaries of traditional Disney storytelling. However, as this essay will show, *HSMTMTS* adheres to, and continues to perpetuate, many of the tropes from the previous films.

Building the *HSM* Franchise

On January 20, 2006, the Disney Channel debuted its 63rd original movie, *High School Musical* (*HSM*), in hopes of appealing to growing tween (nine- to 12-year-old) audiences. The film featured then-unknown actors Vanessa Hudgens and Zac Efron as Gabriella, a top student, and Troy, a basketball star, who disrupt the status quo of their high school by breaking free from their cliques and performing in the annual musical. The initial broadcast drew 7.7 million viewers making *HSM* the most watched premiere in Disney Channel history at the time (Graff, 2007). In 2006 alone, *HSM* reached over 100 million unduplicated viewers globally (Wagmeister 2016), and by 2011 the made-for-TV movie had been watched by over 295 million people world-wide (Potter, 2011).

The film was so well-received that it spawned a second Disney Channel Original Movie, *High School Musical 2* (*HSM2*), in 2007. The sequel, which follows the students as they work at a country club during summer vacation, also broke records with 18 million U.S. viewers tuning in to watch its premiere—making it the highest rated telecast at the time (Potter, 2011). In 2008, Disney followed this success with *High School Musical 3: Senior Year* (*HSM3*), a major motion picture released in theaters that chronicled the students' final year of high school. Like its predecessors, the third film drew audiences; taking in $42 million—the largest opening weekend box office for a movie musical at the time (Potter, 2011). Taken together, it has been estimated that the first two *HSM* films earned Disney $1 billion in 2006 and 2007 and that the global box office gross for *HSM3* was $252 million in 2008 (Huddleston, 2016).

Beyond the films, the *HSM* franchise includes a host of ancillary media and merchandise that was readily consumed by fans. For instance, the original soundtrack (including beloved songs like "Start of Something New," "Stick to the Status Quo" and "Breaking Free") was the best-selling CD in the United States in 2006; the DVD of the original film sold 7.8 million copies worldwide, making it the fastest selling television movie at the time; and the *High School Musical* book series has sold 4.5 million copies (Potter, 2011). Other *HSM*-branded products and experiences (such as video games, toys, clothing, a concert series, and even an ice show) contributed to the financial success of the franchise. Overall, the *HSM* commercial juggernaut generated $4 billion in retail sales during its first five years (Rubin, 2021).

Expanding the Franchise: HSMTMTS

Although Disney was rumored to be working on a fourth *HSM* project in 2009 and then again in 2016 (Wagmeister, 2016), it was not until 2019 when the next installment appeared. *High School Musical: The Musical: The Series* (*HSMTMTS*) was introduced as part of the initial lineup for the Disney+ streaming service, which launched on November 12, 2019. As Radulovic (2019) notes, "the franchise has enough of an era-defining legacy that Disney placed it alongside *The Mandalorian* as a priority to sell the service to a skeptical audience. *High School Musical: The Musical: The Series* has pride of place as the only other original nonreality TV title on the site at its launch" (para. 1). In fact, *HSMTMTS* was considered the ideal vehicle to "appeal to both the older original 'High School Musical' fans alongside a new generation" (Bundel, 2021, para. 7), which would help Disney+ draw the "all important tween/18–35 demographic" (Tapp, 2022, para. 20).

The new series—which is inspired by, but deviates from, its predecessors—is currently comprised of 30 episodes that range from 30 to 40 minutes in length and take a mockumentary approach. The first season of 10 episodes follows a group of students from East High (where the original *HSM* movie was filmed) as they stage their own production of *High School Musical*. In the second season (with the first of 12 episodes released on May 14, 2021), the East High students perform *Beauty and the Beast* as part of a theater competition where they face off against rival, North High. A third season of 8 episodes chronicling the students' adventures as they mount a production of *Frozen* at summer camp was released July 27, 2022. Prior to the release of the third season, Disney renewed the series for a fourth season (Petski, 2022). In addition, there was also a *HSMTHTS* holiday special that was released on Disney+ between the first and second seasons on December 11, 2020. Continuing the lucrative legacy of the original films, "the series has garnered record numbers for its soundtracks across the first two seasons and holiday special, with two billion combined streams to date" (Petski, 2022, para. 4).

Refurbishing or Reiterating: Comparing Representations

Historically, children's media—Disney in particular—has been criticized for stereotypical representations of gender, race, and sexuality. However, in recent years Disney has been considered a leader in providing more progressive representations in their films and on the Disney Channel (Hentges & Case, 2013; Hine et al., 2018; Schiele, 2020). Artz (2021) attributes this representational shift to the fact that

> Disney themes, characters, and animation style have been thoroughly institutionalized in practice and procedure—from the scriptwriters, animators, and technical producers who create the actual films to the market researchers and integrated marketing directors who conduct product research and focus groups to spot trends and advise editors on socially sensitive issues—all are geared to maximizing corporate profits [p. 418].

Nevertheless, critical media scholars suggest that this perception of progress is merely an illusion and that in actuality, Disney continues to reproduce hegemonic ideologies (Rutherford & Baker, 2021; Turner, 2012). At first glance, the original franchise appears to be a testament to diversity and inclusivity—exemplified by the *HSM* anthem "We're All in this Together." Therefore, it comes as no surprise that *HSMTMTS* would also adopt this same approach. However, a closer examination of the franchise exposes the superficiality of these representations. Furthermore, a comparative analysis of the original films and the Disney+ series reveals that rather than using franchise refurbishment as an opportunity to rectify problematic tropes in regard to gender, race and sexuality, *HSMTMTS* simply reifies them.

Through the Eyes of Guys

Historically, male characters have been featured more prominently in youth media than young women (Hine et al., 2018). Yet, scholars and popular media (Henges & Case, 2013; Pulver, 2016) have noted a shift in contemporary gender representations—with female characters appearing in a less stereotypical fashion and in more central roles. Given the intended audience[1] for the *HSM* franchise, it would be reasonable to expect that young women would take centerstage. However, both the original films and new series privilege their respective male leads: Troy (Zac Efron) and Ricky (Joshua Bassett).

Although *HSM* is comprised of an ensemble cast with subplots for multiple characters, Troy is established as the most central through his prominently featured storylines. As Sørenssen (2018) notes, "In all three movies Troy goes through different 'crises' forcing him to reflect on who he is" (p. 216). For instance, in the first film, Troy must negotiate his sense of self; he feels torn between the expectations of his father and the possibility of exploring new interests like the musical. Likewise, in the second film, Troy is pressured to follow in his father's footsteps and earn a college basketball scholarship, which complicate his relationships and self-image. Finally, in the third film, Troy must decide what path to take in college—ultimately choosing UC Berkeley where he can play basketball, pursue theater, and be close to Gabriella (Vanessa Hudgens). At the end of each *HSM* film, Troy has not only persevered through any personal hardship but also established himself as a basketball star, dazzling performer, loving boyfriend, and loyal friend. Of all the characters, Troy is the most fully developed and multi-dimensional; he is also the character that gets to "have it all." Beyond his story arcs, the films also demonstrate that Troy is the central character in other ways. For instance, in opening moments of *HSM*, it is Troy who steps up to the microphone and takes the first verse of a karaoke duet with Gabriella—making her comfortable enough to join in. Likewise, in *HSM2* it is only because of Troy that his friends are hired to work at the country club for the summer. *HSM3* removes any doubt about Troy's primacy, opening with a closeup of his face, inviting the audience to see the world through his eyes as he looks at the scoreboard, and hearing his voice call out "Let's go!"—simultaneously calling his teammates to action and setting the story in motion. Troy's graduation speech at the conclusion of *HSM3* acts as a bookend—literally giving him the last word of the film as well as the trilogy.

In *HSMTMTS* Ricky functions similarly to Troy. While the series opens with Miss Jenn (Kate Reinders), the drama teacher, watching the finale of the original *HSM* film on her phone, Ricky literally moves the action forward as he rides by her on his skateboard and enters East High with his best friend. In those first moments, the premise of the series is established by Ricky as he lays out his plan to rekindle his relationship with Nini (Olivia Rodrigo). Although Nini proclaims that she is no longer interested in Ricky, the first season of *HSMTMTS* revolves around Ricky winning Nini back by starring as Troy in their production of *High School Musical*. Likewise, the second season also follows Ricky and Nini's relationship and the third season focuses on Ricky's growing feelings for Gina (Sofia Wylie). In addition to Ricky's love life, like the original franchise, *HSMTMTS* explores Ricky's internal struggles. While Troy was torn about basketball, the first and second seasons of *HSMTMTS* follow Ricky as he comes to terms with his parents' divorce, their moves to different homes, and their relationships with new partners. Despite any personal turmoil (and lack of musical theater knowledge), Ricky successfully performs as the male lead in all three of the musical productions featured in *HSMTMTS* and is clearly the romantic male lead both onstage and off.

She Shines Because He Validates

Beyond serving as the protagonists, the *HSM* franchise repeatedly depicts young men as a source of validation for other characters particularly women. In both the films and the new series, Troy and Ricky champion others—giving them the confidence, insight, or approval that they need to achieve their goals. Although Troy and Ricky could be perceived as being supportive—a trait that is often associated with female characters—they are presented as authorities, which conforms to stereotypical notions of masculinity where men know best (Gauntlett, 2008). However, the underlying patriarchal nature of this trope is often overlooked because the emphasis is on the outcome rather than the reason for it.

In both the original film and the first episode of *HSMTMTS*, Troy and Ricky help their respective love interests overcome stage fright and (in some cases, quite literally) find their voice. For example, in *HSM* when Gabriella is unable to sing at her callback, she says, "I can't do it Troy—not with all those people staring at me." Troy encourages her by telling her to look at him and reminding her of the first time they sang together. Like the start of the film, Troy once again steps in and begins their duet—giving Gabriella both the time she needs to collect herself and the courage she needs to perform "Breaking Free." Tellingly, the lyrics of the song reflect what has occurred moments before—with Troy's faith in Gabriella giving her the strength to soar. Similarly, in the very first episode of *HSMTMTS*, Ricky supports Nini at her audition. Although Nini claims that she is "not thrown" by Ricky showing up or the sudden loss of electricity, she begins her song tentatively. Seeing this (and knowing she can do better), Ricky quickly stands and shines his cellphone flashlight onto her. As Nini turns towards him and is bathed in his light, her confidence blossoms. Ricky's face and phone then become an imaginary spotlight, physically transforming Nini as she magically appears in a red dress reminiscent of what Gabriella wears in the *HSM* finale. Thanks to Ricky, Nini performs with newfound confidence. While the franchise makes clear that both Gabriella and Nini are gifted singers, it is only because Troy and Ricky draw out their abilities that their talent is recognized, and they are cast as leads.

In addition to performing, both Troy and Ricky are shown actively supporting their love interests' talents and goals. For instance, in *HSM3*, Troy encourages Gabriella to enroll in Stanford's prestigious summer program even though it will mean leaving East High before the end of the school year. Although Gabriella is introduced as the "freaky genius girl" in the first film, it is Troy who figures out a way for Gabriella to attend Stanford and return to East High to participate in the musical and graduation. In other words, when Gabriella's academic prowess becomes an obstacle, Troy finds a solution, all while affirming Gabriella. Likewise, in the second season of *HSMTMTS*, Ricky supports Nini when she decides to leave East High to attend an acting conservatory in Colorado. He makes plans to talk to her regularly, gives her a snow globe to help when she misses him, and even travels to Denver to surprise her for Valentine's Day. When Nini chooses to leave the conservatory and returns to East High, Ricky advocates for her to join the musical despite the show already being cast. Due to Ricky's insistence, Nini is given the opportunity to write an original song, "The Rose Song," which serves as the catalyst for a new social media account that launches her music career. Therefore, while Troy and Ricky encourage their love interests to follow their dreams and cultivate their talents, the young women only do so with their stamp of approval—suggesting that their decisions are not valid without their support and suggesting that young men are integral to their success.

Beyond instilling confidence in Nini, Ricky also plays a pivotal role in Miss Jenn's professional and romantic life. When Miss Jenn's job is in jeopardy because she lied on her resumé, Ricky devises a plan to defend his drama teacher and successfully convinces the school board to reinstate her in Episode 106. Later in Episode 212, when Miss Jenn becomes obsessed with winning a theater competition and inappropriately tells him to "jump off something high," Ricky benevolently forgives her, helps assuage her guilt and affirms that she is a good teacher. Ricky also plays a significant role in Miss Jenn's personal life—initially encouraging his recently divorced father Mike (Alex Quijano) to pursue Miss Jenn in Episode 108. Bolstered by his son, Mike asks Miss Jenn out and the pair date until Episode 206, when it becomes clear that Ricky is uncomfortable with their romance. However, in 212 Ricky tells Miss Jenn, "You have my blessing if you want to date him again" and reminds her that she deserves to be happy thus allowing Mike and Miss Jenn to resume their romance. Through these storylines, not only is a high school boy depicted as more sensible than an adult woman, but he ensures positive outcomes for her that she cannot manifest on her own.

Ambition in Women = Villain

In popular culture, young women who are nice, reserved, and modest are framed as "good" girls while those who are assertive and ambitious are framed as "bad" (Bindig Yousman, 2021). Disney has often perpetuated stereotypical feminine ideals, punishing those who fail to conform and rewarding those who do (Hine et al., 2018). While the *HSM* franchise has no issue with young men working towards basketball championships, college scholarships, or leading roles in musicals, when young women actively strive for the spotlight, they are portrayed negatively. Furthermore, while the franchise shows young men achieving their goals and finding love, success and love elude ambitious young women unless a young man curbs their behavior.

The antagonist in the original *HSM* films is Sharpay Evans (Ashley Tisdale)—an ambitious diva who will stop at nothing to become a star.

In the first film, Sharpay attempts to secure the lead role in the musical by changing the time of callbacks so it overlaps with Gabriella's academic competition and Troy's championship basketball game. Similarly, in the second film, Sharpay engineers a well-paid position for Troy at her country club as part of a plan to have him help her win the annual talent show award. In the third film, Sharpay tries to eliminate her competition for the musical by revealing to Troy that Gabriella was accepted to the Stanford Honors program, which conflicts with the musical. Despite her talent and ambition, Sharpay's schemes never come to fruition; she always loses out to the always sweet and ever-humble Gabriella. In fact, it is not until Sharpay is introduced to a young man named Peyton (Austin Butler) that she exhibits modesty and humility and is rewarded with love and success in *Sharpay's Fabulous Adventure* (a 2011 direct-to-video companion to the *HSM* trilogy).

Like *HSM*, *HSMTMTS* also paints ambitious women as "bad." While there is no diva like Sharpay in the series, Gina, a new student, is established as the villain of the first season due to her ambition. In Episode 101, Gina's competitive nature is revealed when she responds snidely to Nini, who was simply trying to be welcoming to the newcomer. Once Nini is cast as the lead, Gina devises a plan to cause Nini so much distress that she drops out of the musical. Although Gina attempts to upset Nini by manipulating her ex-boyfriends, her plans, like Sharpay's, backfire. In Episode 105, Ricky makes clear that Gina's behavior is unacceptable when he harshly admonishes, "Maybe you are what everyone says—too ambitious for your own good." In response to Ricky, Gina exhibits previously unseen vulnerability, opening up about her family issues and insecurities. Once Ricky reveals that Gina's ambition is alienating her from others, she stops striving to be the star and starts developing friendships with the other cast members—making her significantly happier in the process. Gina's transformation does not go unnoticed by the other characters; in fact, it is explicitly acknowledged by Ashlyn (Julia Lester) in Episode 201 when she states, "Six months ago I thought Gina was borderline the *Bad Seed* but now she's borderline my number one confidant."

Like Sharpay, Gina's ambition reemerges temporarily in the second season of *HSMTMTS*. In Episode 202, Gina initially chooses a chance at stardom over her friends when she rejects Ashlyn's invitation to audition "as a girl group" and dismisses Carlos's (Frankie A. Rodriguez) offer to be co-choreographer. Gina makes clear that ambition is driving her decision-making when she looks directly to camera and says, "Okay, I don't mean to sound ungrateful. I don't, but why does everyone suddenly want to do 'co' stuff with me? I'm trying to make my mark, not co-make-my-co-mark." While Gina does ultimately end up joining the trio for auditions and serving as co-choreographer, it is only after Carlos confronts Gina in Episode 204 that she once again softens and becomes less ambitious. This new version of Gina (or "Gina 2.0" as Ashlyn refers to her in later episodes) is rewarded with EJ (Matt Cornett) as her love interest for the remainder of the second season.

With Nini's absence[2] in the third season, Gina emerges as the female lead and the primary love interest in *HSMTMTS*. To take on this new role, the series requires Gina's ambition to be acknowledged and controlled. In Episode 302, Gina tells her camp bunkmates, "I'm just letting it be known that I am going for gold at auditions today. I'm finally ready to play the lead. No apologies, no prisoners." Upon hearing Gina's statement, Ashlyn frowns and says, "Sounds like you brought Gina 1.0 to camp." Gina defends herself and says she just wants to stand on her own to which Ashlyn responds, "okay, 1.0." Ashlyn's comments serve not only as a critique of female ambition but as a reminder of how Gina had moved on from that ambitious self-centered version of herself. Following their conversation, Gina sings the song "Balance," which allows her to explain how she is negotiating her ambitious tendencies with being more down-to-earth. Thus, it is only because she says she is willing to step out of the spotlight after dancing the solo that she can assume the role of romantic leading lady, both in the camp's production of *Frozen* and in the series. While Gina's performance of "Balance" demonstrates her character's personal growth, the song perfectly encapsulates the double-bind of young femininity in contemporary society—that trying to balance idealized femininity with ambition is akin to walking on a tightrope. While feminist scholars have long problematized this double-bind, *HSMTMTS* frames it as achievable for Gina so long as she navigates the metaphorical tightrope slowly on tiptoes—making it clear that if she is not careful, she will return to being cast as the villain.

Faux Feminism

Emerging out of post-feminist discourse in the 1990s, girl power assumes "that girls are powerful and that gender equality exists, or even that girls are dominant" (Taft, 2004, p. 72). Thus, girl power adopts a "more positive version of girlhood, one that is assertive, dynamic, and unbound from the constraints of passive femininity" (Gonick, 2006, p. 2). At the same time post-feminist girl power still embraces stereotypical beauty ideals in the pursuit of heterosexual romance. In the three original *HSM* films, the primary female characters reflect the post-feminist "girl power" ideology prevalent in popular culture at the time. As Jin (2012) notes, Gabriella, Taylor (Monique Coleman), and Sharpay are empowered by their intelligence and drive while maintaining their femininity. They are the embodiment of

Harris's (2004) notion of "can-do" girls—young women who are "individualized, resilient, self-driven and self-made" (p. 16). Although the original franchise never explicitly addresses gender politics, the young women are presented as capable of achieving their goals as demonstrated by the academically gifted Gabriella and Taylor attending elite universities and the talented and driven Sharpay (eventually) performing on Broadway while still conforming to traditional femininity and earning the affection of young men. Not surprisingly, *HSMTMTS* picks up where the original franchise left off—adopting the same plucky girl power approach for Nini, Kourtney (Dara Reneé), Gina, and Ashlyn. Like their predecessors, the young women in *HSMTMTS* are "can-do" girls who can overcome adversity—whether overcoming stage fright, taking the stage last minute, composing an original ballad, or climbing a rock wall—while still being feminine and finding love.

Interestingly, the new series does seemingly differ from the films by incorporating explicitly feminist rhetoric; however, *HSMTMTS* continues to only make superficial nods to gender equality and ultimately reproduces *HSM*'s post-feminist approach. From the start, *HSMTMTS* appears to adopt a feminist stance. In the first episode, Kourtney tells Big Red (Larry Saperstein), "I'm dismantling the patriarchy this year and I'm not afraid to start with you." Later in the same episode, Kourtney reiterates her feminist identity when she tells Nini, "looking this good while fighting for intersectional feminism is my summer job." Nini also adopts also feminist language in Episode 105 when she claims she is not angry, but "empowered," as she flushes her homecoming dress down the toilet in response to her breakup with EJ. Likewise, when Ashlyn writes the tercet "1-2-3" in Episode 202 so she, Kourtney, and Gina can audition as a girl group, the song is described as having "girl power vibes." Regardless of the use of terms like "patriarchy," "intersectional feminism," "empowered," and "girl power," *HSMTMTS* fails to engage with feminism in any meaningful way. Instead of showing young women addressing systemic injustice through collective action, *HSMTMTS* simply adopts feminist language as a shortcut to communicate the characters' personality. Hence, the young women in *HSMTMTS* reflect a highly individualized version of post-feminism, which Gill notes (2016) is not about a political movement, but instead is a temporary identity that speaks more to personal confidence, self-love, and self-esteem than social injustice.

In addition to employing feminist rhetoric, *HSMTMTS* appears to embrace feminism through situations when the young women seemingly challenge traditional notions of romantic relationships. For example, in Episode 102 Ashlyn reminds EJ that dating Nini "doesn't mean you own her." Later, in Episode 208, Nini tells Ricky that her choice to leave boarding school and open new social media accounts for her music are not about him. The young women also do this when talking to each other—as exemplified in Episode 105 when Kourtney informs Nini, "Ever since you discovered boys, you've spent way too much time trying to see yourself through their eyes" and in Episode 212, when Nini tells Gina, "I'd say any guy would be lucky to have you but that's not the point." By attempting to decenter romance and young men, these declarations of female independence appear to reinforce the notion that these are strong and assertive young women. However, when looking at the *HSMTMTS* more broadly, these are only isolated moments. Rather, the majority of the young women's storylines focus on boys and romance. Throughout the three seasons that have been released, Nini, Kourtney, Gina, and Ashlyn have all been involved romantically with young men and have numerous conversations about the state of their relationships. Furthermore, each season culminates with a romantic resolution: Nini and Ricky rekindle their relationship in the first season finale, Gina asks EJ to be her first kiss at the end of the second season, and Gina and Ricky end the third season with a kiss. Consequently, although there are times when the series celebrates female friendship and camaraderie, there is no doubt that heteronormative romance still reigns supreme in *HSMTMTS*. Taken together, the faux feminism established in the first three *HSM* films and expanded in the new series, offers "a solution for producing socially responsible, feminist media that constantly questions gender norms in a way that will mitigate the alienation of mainstream consumers" (Schiele et al., 2020, p. 668).

Erasing Race

At first glance, the *HSM* franchise appears to be the embodiment of multiculturalism. In the original *HSM* films, the racial makeup of the six main characters is equally distributed among those that can be identified as black, indigenous, and people of color (BIPOC)—Gabriella, Chad (Corbin Bleu), and Taylor—and White—Troy, Sharpay, and Ryan (Lucas Grabeel). Although the Disney+ series expands the size of the cast, it maintains a similar balance between BIPOC characters—Nini, Kourtney, Carlos, and Gina—and White characters—Ricky, EJ, Big Red, Ashlyn, and Seb (Joe Serafini). Because the racial balance avoids the complete absence or blatant tokenism of people of color, the franchise appears responsible in terms of inclusive representation.

The franchise then builds on this perception of multiculturalism by presenting interracial friendships and romances as commonplace. While Troy and Gabriella are the only interracial romance in the films, they both have best friends of differing racial backgrounds. *HSMTMTS* expands upon this practice by increasing the number of interracial pairings (both romantic and platonic). While Ricky and Nini's romance mirrors Ricky and Gabriella's relationship, Nini has a far more diverse friend group. Like Gabriella, Nini's best friend, Kourtney, is Black, but she also establishes close friendships with two other young women from different racial backgrounds: Ashlyn (who is White) and Gina (who appears racially ambiguous in the series but is played by mixed-race actress Sofia Wylie). While Carlos, who is Mexican, is the only non–White male character, he is fully integrated into the friend group and is in a romantic relationship with Seb. Other interracial romances include EJ and Nini, EJ and Gina, and Ricky and Gina. Thus, rather than self-segregating by race, which is the reality at many U.S. high schools (Daniel Tatum, 1997), East High appears to be a bastion of integration and racial harmony.

Despite the inclusion of diverse characters and interracial relationships, the *HSM* franchise overwhelmingly ignores issues of race and ethnicity by taking a color-blind approach. In other words, while the audience may be able to infer the race and ethnicity of the characters based on their appearance (i.e., skin tone) or their names (Gabriella Montez or Carlos Rodriguez), neither the films nor the series acknowledge the racial and ethnic identities of the characters in any substantive way. This approach is beneficial to companies like Disney because it allows them to appeal to wider audiences without alienating White audiences. However, Turner (2012) acknowledges the problematic nature of colorblindness by explaining, "Not seeing race effectively erases race and suggests that 'we are all the same,' and yet this seemingly liberal viewpoint works to deny the existence of social, cultural, economic, and/or political disenfranchisement that is the result of institutionalized racism" (p. 127). By failing to engage with issues of race and ethnicity, characters essentially become "raceless," which frees the franchise from grappling with systemic biases and inequalities that impact the daily lives of people of color. As a result, "colorblindness serves to legitimize racism and certain racial (read White) privileges. Thus, audiences can see and celebrate multicultural assimilation while disregarding existing racial hierarchies" (Turner, 2012, p. 127). By continuing to employ the colorblind approach that was established in the *HSM* films, *HSMTMTS* is complicit in perpetuating a neoliberal post-racial ideology that suggests that racism no longer exists while profiting off the work of people of color.

Convenient Culture

While there is an overall erasure of race and ethnicity in the *HSM* franchise, it must be acknowledged that there are three isolated instances where cultural heritage is explicitly highlighted: once in *HSM3* and once in the first and second seasons of *HSMTMTS*. Rather than genuinely exploring issues of cultural identity, these three examples show that the *HSM* franchise only reference a character's ethnic background when it is convenient. As a result, instead honoring cultural difference, the films and series dismiss it.

The only explicit acknowledgment of race and ethnicity in the original films appears halfway through *HSM3* when Gabriella's mother, Lisa (Socorro Herrera), tells her daughter that she loves her in Spanish. The scene is puzzling, as the rest of the conversation takes place in English, as do all other conversations between the pair in *HSM3* and the first film.[3] To be clear, Gabriella does not respond to her mother in Spanish, nor does she ever speak Spanish in any of the *HSM* films. By having Lisa speak Spanish, the audience is reminded of Gabriella's cultural heritage; however, Gabriella's response in English is confirmation that she is no different from the other characters. In other words, Lisa's use of Spanish lends credibility and "authenticity" to Gabriella's Latinx identity without Disney having to delve into any actual issues related to race or racism.

Like the original franchise, there are also two clear instances when *HSMTMTS* acknowledges race and ethnicity, but they ultimately work to uphold the status quo. In Episode 107, Nini asks her grandmother, Malou (Jeanne Sakata), to tell the story of her immigration to the United States. Malou explains to her granddaughter that she had once believed the America was "paved with gold" but discovered that was not the case once she arrived. To be clear, Malou's story does not explore family history or the hardships immigrants face. In fact, the country Malou immigrated from is never even named. Instead, Malou uses the story to stress the importance of "always seeking new shores." Thus, rather than encouraging Nini to reflect on her cultural heritage, Malou's story urges Nini to look to the future. Within the overarching narrative of the series, Malou's story has nothing do with race, ethnicity, or cultural heritage, but rather functions as a form of foreshadowing and as an implicit endorsement of Nini's decision to leave East High to nurture her talent at an acting conservatory in Denver.

Cultural heritage also appears to be present in Episode 205, when Gina and Seb organize a "quinceañero" for Carlos. While a quinceañera is a rite of passage for Latinx young women when they turn fifteen, Seb explains, "It's a birthday party but seriously zhuzhed up." There are no other discussions about the cultural importance of quinceañeras except when Gina notes that a quinceañero was something Carlos "always wanted and never got." Planned by his non–Mexican friends, Carlos's quinceañero features Mexican-inspired décor, a banner that reads, "Feliz Quinceañero," and a special Latin dance performed Gina (dressed as a toreador). However, none of Carlos's family members are present at the party even though family plays a central role at traditional quinceañeras. Although the actor who plays Carlos, Frankie Rodriguez, says, "it was so special to see my culture represented" in the episode (Matarese, 2021, para. 3), he is the only Mexican character present, and his Mexican roots are never mentioned. Therefore, unlike Lisa and Malou, whose presence provides clear links to Gabriella and Nini's cultural heritage, Carlos lacks any generational connections to his Mexican identity. As a result, *HSMTMTS* erases any true cultural significance from the event, and so it becomes just another themed party—no different than Homecoming in Episode 105 or the 1970s prom that takes place in Episode 307.

Don't Say Gay

In the original *HSM* films there are no characters that explicitly identify as part of the LGBTQ+ community. However, Sharpay's brother, Ryan, was assumed to be gay although his sexuality was not explored or even mentioned in the films. In an interview, *HSM* director Kenny Ortega acknowledges the portrayal (or lack thereof) of Ryan's sexuality when he says, "We decided he [was] probably going to come out in college. It was less about coming out and just more about letting his true colors come forward" (Delgado, 2020, para. 3). Later in the interview, Ortega takes responsibility for this creative decision, explaining:

> Disney is the most progressive group of people I've ever worked with [but] I was concerned because it was family and kids, that Disney might not be ready to cross that line and move into that territory yet.... So, I just took it upon myself to make choices that I felt that those who were watching would grab. They would see it, they would feel it, they would know it and they would identify with it. And that is what happened [Delgado, 2020, para. 4].

Using Ryan as a point of comparison, *HSMTMTS* appears to have made significant strides with the inclusion of several queer characters over the first three seasons. The first two seasons feature Carlos and Seb and follows their burgeoning romance and subsequent relationship. The third season introduces Maddox (Saylor Bell) and Madison (JoJo Siwa)—two young women who had been in relationship the previous summer. The third season also concludes with Ashlyn and Big Red—who were presented as a heterosexual couple in the first two seasons—realizing they are bisexual. Although *HSMTMTS* has been celebrated for including LGBTQ+ characters and queer romances, the series depicts displays of affection among heterosexual couples more often than queer couples.[4] In addition, *HSMTMTS*'s queer characters conform to traditional stereotypes with Carlos and Seb being framed as feminine[5] while Maddox and Madison adopt more masculine[6] characteristics. Most notably, the series echoes the original films by relying on implied meanings rather than directly addressing queer issues. In fact, *HSMTMTS* only uses explicit language about sexual orientation twice throughout the series. The word "gay" is not used until the second season when Carlos retorts, "I'm Mexican and gay" in Episode 201 and the word "bisexual" is only uttered once when Big Red says, "I'm Ashlyn's boyfriend and I'm bisexual" in the final minutes of Episode 308. The words "lesbian" or "queer" have not been uttered in the series to date.

In lieu of adopting clear language about the character's identities, *HSMTMTS* chooses to rely on vague allusions and visual cues. For instance, instead of using the word "gay," Carlos uses the phrase "there's not like a ton of me at this school" in Episode 204 to describe himself. Later in Episode 210, Seb is the source of implied language when he says, "there's not a lot of other choices for a boy like Carlos at here East" and when Big Red reports that Seb is worried Carlos is with him by default because "he's the only other boy at school who watches *Drag Race Canada*." Similarly, when Ashlyn comes to the realization that she is bisexual she does not use that word in the show. Instead, in Episode 307, she says, "So, I learned something new about myself last night, and it goes a little deeper than a rising sign. It is possible that I have a crush on Valerie, the choreographer, and all that that implies." Later in the same episode when talking to Carlos, Ashlyn uses implied language when she tells him, "I'm still me. Just more." Carlos responds in kind, presenting Ashlyn with a rainbow flag pin—a recognizable symbol of the LGBTQ+ movement—but only saying "Welcome to the community," which alludes to, but does not explicitly address her queer identity.

Despite the presence of queer characters, *HSMTMTS* ultimately downplays queer visibility by favoring implied language and visual cues. Through the reliance on vague allusions and references, the series places the onus of recognizing queer characters and issues on the audience. The lack of explicit dialog about queer identity, removes an essential marker of difference—subsequently making the LGBTQ+ characters largely indistinguishable from the straight characters. As a result, this assimilationist approach ultimately reinforces heteronormativity and offers a very narrow view of the queer experience (Hilton-Morrow & Battles, 2015). Furthermore, because queer characters are the ones opting to use implied language, they appear to be implicitly endorsing this approach. As a result, *HSMTMTS* obfuscates how the series undermines, rather than promotes, progressive queer representations.

Conclusion

On the surface, the Disney+ series *HSMTMTS* appears to be the "start of something new" in terms of representations of gender, race, and sexuality. However, as this essay demonstrates, in actuality, *HSMTMTS* decides to "stick to the status quo" by "presenting diversity in such a way as to reify the position and privilege" of those in power and reinforce hegemonic ideologies (Turner, 2012, p. 127). Rather than breaking new ground, the series simply offers superficial updates to the original films as part of franchise refurbishment. This approach can be understood as part of a savvy commercial strategy designed to appeal to viewers who had once been ignored by Disney as well as those that demand a modicum of social progress to be reflected in the company's content. However, as Valdivia (2008) notes, "Disney does not pursue new representational strategies unless it is certain that profits will increase without alienating the bulk of its audience" (p. 286). Therefore, it is not just unlikely, but frankly unrealistic, to expect that *HSMTMTS* would deviate significantly from the *HSM* films. To be clear, *HSMTMTS* is just one example of the co-optation of progressive representations that work against real social change—both on Disney+ and across contemporary media. Despite the plethora of media platforms that exist today, authentic representations are still rare. While streaming has been said to offer a wider array of voices and content (Andrews, 2022), as Disney+'s *HSMTMTS* demonstrates, even updated, refurbished, and rebooted properties can be limited or regressive.

Furthermore, as Benson (2022) reminds us, "in addition to these textual and cultural functions, refurbishment is also inherently a practical process guided by industrial and legal realities" (p. 443). In other words, by refurbishing the *HSM* franchise, Disney extends its intellectual property and copyright, thereby increasing the company's ability to generate profit and police its image. As a result, *HSMTMTS* provides a unique opportunity for the Disney corporation to promote and capitalize on existing holdings while at the same time generating a variety of new products associated with the reboot. Rather than "breaking free" from the past, *HSMTMTS* allows Disney+ to tap into the nostalgia of *High School Musical* while drawing new audiences through seemingly fresh stories and characters, which not only helps to solidify the financial viability of the new streaming service, but also ultimately increases Disney's revenue overall. Yet, as the marketplace becomes increasingly saturated and subscription prices rise, audiences are becoming more discerning about their streaming services (Andrews, 2022; Fitzgerald, 2023). To ensure audiences don't "walk away,"[7] Disney+ must "work this out" by offering characters and stories that truly reflect the diversity of "right here, right now."

Notes

1. Tween and teen girls were the key audience for the original *HSM* films. The new series expands the target demographic to also include 20-somethings (Radulovic, 2019).

2. Actress Olivia Rodrigo's status has changed from regular to reoccurring cast member in the third season of *HSMTMTS* and only appears in three episodes.

3. Lisa is mentioned but does not appear in *HSM2*.

4. For example, Carlos and Seb only kiss on the lips once in Episode 205 while multiple heterosexual couples kiss throughout the series: Nini and Ricky (Episodes 110 and 204), Ashlyn and Big Red (Episodes 110 and 201), EJ and Gina (Episode 301), and Ricky and Gina (Episode 308).

5. In the first season, Seb is literally cast as Sharpay in East High's production of HSM while Carlos has Sharpay's pink locker, sings Sharpay's song "Fabulous" in the third season, and makes reference to dressing like female characters from musicals.

6. Maddox's camp name is Gadget reflecting her technical stage crew knowledge and both she and Madison refrain from wearing stereotypical feminine clothing.

7. "Walk Away," "Work This Out" and "Right Here, Right Now" are songs from *HSM 3*.

References

Artz, L. (2021). Disney: 21st century leader in animating global inequality. In B. Yousman, L. Bindig Yousman, G. Dines, and J.M. Humez (Eds.), *Gender, race and class in media: A critical reader*, 6th edition (pp. 413–420). Sage.

Andrews, T.M. (2022, September 7). Streaming TV is having an existential crisis, and viewers can tell. *Washington Post*. Retrieved September 14, 2023. https://www.washingtonpost.com/arts-entertainment/2022/09/07/streaming-tv-changes-crisis/.

Bindig Yousman, L. (2021). Good girls go bad. In B. Yousman, L. Bindig Yousman, G. Dines, and J.M. Humez (Eds.), *Gender, race and class in media: A critical reader*, 6th edition (pp. 209–216). Sage.

Benson, N. (2022). "For your future enjoyment": Managing intellectual property through franchise refurbishment. *Media Culture & Society, 44*(3), 428–444.

Bundel, A. (2021, May 12). Disney+'s "High School Musical" spinoff doesn't realize only adults view high school with irony. NBCnews.com. Retrieved September 14, 2022. https://www.nbcnews.com/think/opinion/disney-s-high-school-musical-spinoff-doesn-t-realize-only-ncna1267104.

Daniel Tatum, B. (1997). *Why are all the Black kids sitting together in the cafeteria? And other conversations about race*. Perseus.

Delgado, S. (2020, July 1). "High School Musical" director explains why Ryan Evans wasn't openly gay. *Teen Vogue*. Retrieved September 14, 2022. https://www.teenvogue.com/story/high-school-musical-director-explains-why-ryan-evans-wasnt-openly-gay.

Fitzgerald, T. (2023, August 9). Disney+ sheds record 11.7 million subscribers, announcing price increase and password crackdown coming. *Forbes*. Retrieved September 14, 2003. https://www.forbes.com/sites/tonifitzgerald/2023/08/09/new-record-for-disney-sheds-117-million-subscribers-password-crackdown-coming/?sh=4568ca651d7b.

Gauntlett, D. (2008). *Media, gender, and identity*. Routledge.

Gill, R. (2016). Post-postfeminism? New Feminist Visibilities in Postfeminist Times. *Feminist Media Studies, 16*(4), 610–630.

Gonick, M. (2006). Between 'Girl Power' and 'Reviving Ophelia': Constituting the neoliberal girl subject. *NWSA Journal, 18*(2), 1–23.

Graff, G. (2007, August 21). "High School Musical" kids soaking up success. *Billboard*. Retrieved September 14, 2022. https://www.billboard.com/music/music-news/high-school-musical-kids-soaking-up-success-1049761/.

Harris, A. (2004). *All about the girl: Culture, power, and identity*. Routledge.

Hentges, B., & Case, K. (2013). Gender representations on Disney Channel, Cartoon Network, and Nickelodeon broadcasts in the United States. *Journal of Children & Media, 7*: 319–33.

Hilton-Morrow, W., & Battles, K. (2015). *Sexual identities and the media*. Routledge.

Hine, B., England, D., Lepreore, K., Skora Horgan, E., & Hartwell, L. (2018). The rise of the androgynous princess: Examining representations of gender in prince and princess characters of Disney movies released 2009–2016. *Social Sciences, 7*: 245–268.

Huddleston, T., Jr. (2016, February 24). Disney's "High School Musical" franchise by the numbers. *Fortune*. Retrieved September 14, 2022. https://fortune.com/2016/03/02/disney-high-school-musical-4/.

Jin, S. (2012). *Screening girls in High School Musical: Identity, femininity, and empowerment*. Retrieved September 14, 2022. https://repositories.lib.utexas.edu/bitstream/handle/2152/ETD-UT-2012-05-5519/JIN-THESIS.pdf?sequence=1&isAllowed=y.

Matarese, J. (2021, June 11). Rodriguez, Serafini talk powerful quinceañero episode on "High School Musical" Disney+ series. Retrieved September 14, 2022. https://abc7.com/high-school-musical-the-series-joe-serafini-carlos-rodriguez-disney/10775332/.

Petski, D. (2022, May 20). *High School Musical: The Musical: The Series renewed for season 4*. Deadline. Retrieved September 14, 2022. https://deadline.com/2022/05/high-school-musical-the-musical-the-s...es-renewed-season-4-season-3-premiere-date-disney-plus-1235029013/.

Potter, A. (2011). It's a small world after all: New media constellations and Disney's rising star—the global success of High School Musical. *International Journal of Cultural Studies, 15*(2), 117–130.

Radulovic, P. (2019, November 14). Yes, High School Musical: The Musical: The Series is for adults. *Polygon*. Retrieved September 14, 2022. https://www.polygon.com/disneyplus/2019/11/14/20964676/high-school-musical-the-musical-the-series-review-disney-plus.

Rubin, R. (2021). "High School Musical" turns 15: A look back at the humble origins of Disney Channel's billion dollar franchise. *Variety*. Retrieved September 14, 2022. https://variety.com/2021/film/features/high-school-musical-anniversary-zac-efron-vanessa-hudgens-1234886967/.

Rutherford, A., & Baker, S. (2021). The Disney 'princess bubble' as a cultural influencer. *M/C Journal, 24*(1). https://doi.org/10.5204/mcj.2742.

Schiele, K., Louie, L., & Chen, S. (2020). Marketing feminism in youth media: A study of Disney and Pixar animation. *Business Horizons, 63*: 659–669.

Sørenssen, I. K. (2018). Disney's High School Musical and the construction of the tween audience. *Global Studies of Childhood, 8*(3), 213–224.

Taft, J.K. (2004). Girl power politics: Pop-culture barriers and organizational resistance. In A. Harris (Ed.), *All about the girl: Culture, power, and identity* (pp. 69–78). Routledge.

Tapp, T. (2022, February 9). Disney Plus: Everything you need to know about Disney's subscription streaming service. NextTV.com. Retrieved September 14, 2022. https://www.nexttv.com/news/disney-plus.

Turner, S.E. (2012). Disney does race: Black BFFs in the new racial moment. *Networking Knowledge, 5*(1), 125–140.

Valdivia, A.N. (2008). Mixed race on the Disney Channel: From Johnnie Tsunami through Lizzie McGuire and ending with The Cheetah Girls. In M. Beltrán and C. Fojas (Eds.), *Mixed race Hollywood* (pp. 269–289). New York University Press.

Wagmeister, E. (2016). Disney Channel begins casting on "High School Musical 4." *Variety*. Retrieved September 14, 2022. https://variety.com/2016/tv/news/high-school-musical-4-disney-channel-casting-1201719833/.

When the World Finally Sees Us

The Coming Out of the High School Musical *Franchise*

JENNESSA HESTER

I Want It All

High School Musical (2006) (*HSM*) remains the most successful programming event ever hosted on children's cable television network the Disney Channel. Part of the network's illustrious line of made-for-TV features known as Disney Channel Original Movies, or DCOMs, advertisements at the time pitched the movie as a "crescendo" to a week of new and repeat programming centered around song and dance numbers (Miller, 2019). The premiere on January 20, 2006, certainly lived up to this promise, pulling in an estimated 7.7 million viewers to become the channel's second-highest rated movie up to that point. The unassuming teen romance quickly proved to be a hit with young viewers, and Hollywood's ancillary market soon generated Wildcat fever. A second screening of the movie on July 22, 2007, garnered an additional 5.7 million viewers, a number which equals and exceeds the premiere numbers for many other DCOMs, and subsequent airings on the network averaged around 4.6 million each (Keveney, 2007). Disney sold nearly eight million DVDs of *HSM* within their first year, and that number does not include digital purchases made via the iTunes store, where *HSM* became the very first feature-length film offered for purchase (Cypress, 2006). A concert adaptation of the musical entitled *High School Musical: The Concert* (Buena Vista Concerts, 2006), featuring the original cast members, save lead actor Zac Efron (who was replaced by his singing double from the original film Drew Seeley), garnered an additional $25 million for Disney. Indeed, by the time the movie's sequel, *High School Musical 2* (*HSM 2*), hit Disney Channel a year and a half later on August 17, 2007, it was well positioned to become the highest rated premiere in the network's history, an honor it still holds.

A threequel, *High School Musical 3: Senior Year* (*HSM 3*), quickly entered development, and parent company Walt Disney Pictures chose to capitalize on it via a wide theatrical release on October 24, 2008. This decision resulted in a $250 million worldwide gross on its scant $11 million production budget for a profit margin of over 2100 percent (Box Office Mojo, 2008).

Given the franchise's remarkable success during the 2000s, and since its initial viewer base now possesses disposable income and is a prime target for nostalgic marketing tactics, it is no surprise that Disney positioned *HSM* as a flagship brand to help launch their on-demand video streaming service Disney+. Though largely ignored in the press due to the overwhelming popularity of Lucasfilm's *The Mandalorian* (2019–present) and the live-action adaptation of *Lady and the Tramp* (2019), the Wildcats of East High were one of the premiere attractions for the fledgling service (Disney+, 2019). This new serialized addition to the franchise, a weekly program entitled *High School Musical: The Musical: The Series* (2019–present) (*HSMTMTS*), has proven an undisputed success for the company. While it does not rack up the Nielsen ratings of *Star Wars* or Marvel releases on Disney+, *HSMTMTS* has attained consistent enough viewership to be renewed for a second, third, and (as of now final) fourth season. Moreover, the performance and vocal talents of lead actress Olivia Rodrigo led to a record contract with Interscope Records, where her first single, "driver's license" (2021), and debut album, *SOUR* (2021), hit number one on the charts (Caulfield, 2021). Even as the majority of Disney+ subscribers' attention remains doggedly fixed on far off galaxies and multiverses, the Wildcats have silently resumed their position as significant cultural arbiters, subtly shaping Walt Disney's content as well as the broader landscape of American media.

Among the most impactful of these changes is that *HSMTMTS* has become a trailblazer for its inclusion and representation of LGBTQ characters and themes. The extent of this inclusivity is so pronounced that the Gay & Lesbian Alliance Against Defamation recognized the show at their annual media awards ceremony in 2020, celebrating it as a milestone in kids and family programming. In accepting the accolade, cast members from the series expressed their excitement about the honor, noting that "growing up [we] wished we could have seen more people like us on screen. It means so much to us to be able to tell these stories and to be a small part of the representation we wish to see in the world" (GLAAD, 2020). For a franchise whose original incarnation featured no major openly gay characters, and whose parent company has been notoriously reluctant to include LGBTQ persons in family fare, this shift toward an unambiguous and assertive endorsement of queerness marks a fundamental departure from both *HSM* and Walt Disney's previous approaches to queer representation. This essay charts the process by which such an incredible change of heart came to be. In doing so, it argues that *HSMTMTS* has helped the series come out of the closet, making visible an underlying tenor of queerness that has been present since the first film. Moreover, that coming out has gone far beyond the superficiality of mere representation, with the show altering the central *phenomenological structures*—or the systems in a text that produce certain feelings while experiencing them—by which LGBTQ viewers interact with the franchise as well as Disney-related content as a whole.

Stick to the Status Quo

At first glance, *HSM* appears to wear its heterosexual heart on its sleeve. The original film's story follows the romantic escapades of Troy Bolton (Zac Efron), a superstar on the East High School Wildcats basketball team, and Gabriella Montez (Vanessa Hudgens), a nerdy introvert who excels on the school's academic decathlon squad. However, the two possess a shared love of theater, and as they break out of their cliques and comfort zones to become leads in the school musical, they also manage to dance into each other's arms. It is a classic boy meets girl, boy falls for girl, boy impresses girl through his ability to learn complex choreography and hit the high notes type of tale—could the writers make it any more obvious? And, to be sure, a majority of the movie's initial viewers interpreted the film in this way, as indicated by its frequent comparisons to other heterosexual romances like *Romeo & Juliet* (1597) and *Grease* (1971), and by widespread support of Troy and Gabriella's pairing amongst young fans. Audiences knew from the first few minutes of the film that *HSM* would be a straight tale about a straight couple falling in unambiguously straight love. The sequels doubled down on this interpretation, with *HSM 2* following the couple through relationship strife and eventual triumph, and *HSM 3* detailing their struggles to remain together as college looms. Throughout an entire arc of ups and downs, the structures of heterosexuality nevertheless seemed to remain intact.

However, the open secret of the *HSM* franchise is that for as straight as it seems on the surface, it is, in actuality, one of the most subcutaneously queer pieces of media that Walt Disney has ever released. In a recent interview with *Variety*, director of the original trilogy and openly gay filmmaker Kenny Ortega posited that a "queer aesthetic runs through all [his] movies," and "whether it's screaming at you, or whether it's just sort of quietly there, it's there" (Setoodeh, 2020, para. 27). He specifically noted *HSM* supporting character Ryan Evans (Lucas Grabeel), who he wrote as a closeted teenager who would come out later in life. This hesitancy to present Ryan as he truly was came from the cultural climate of the time, with Ortega stating:

> I have to be honest with you. I didn't think at the time [that Ryan could be openly gay]—and Disney is the most progressive group of people I've ever worked with.... I was concerned because it was family and kids, that Disney might not be ready to cross that line and move into that territory yet. So, I just took it upon myself to make choices that I felt that those who were watching would grab. They would see it, they would feel it, they would know it and they would identify with it. And that is what happened [Setoodeh, 2020, para. 31–32].

The aesthetic practice the director references here, known as *queer coding*, is by no means unique to *HSM*. The notion that musicals are in some way essentially and by their very essence gay products runs through the history of Hollywood, to the point where "the term musical has long been used as a coded reference to homosexuality; to describe someone as 'musical' or 'into musicals' is to describe them as homosexual" by association (Farmer, 2000, p. 74). To this end, instances of the genre which play up the stereotypically flamboyant or campy traits frequently associated with homosexuality, especially those which "disrupt notions of appropriate gender behaviour" for men by substituting masculinity with femininity, end up "[acting] as a heavily gendered method of signifying gay male identity" (McKinnon, 2013, p. 105–107).

Once one knows what to look for, queer coding starts to appear throughout the *HSM* film trilogy, from Troy's frequent use of effeminate hand gestures and wispy dance moves to express emotion, to antagonist Sharpay Evans' (Ashley Tisdale) mannerisms and shady commentary recalling the diva—and thereby, for queer viewers especially, the drag queen—social archetype. Unsurprisingly, however, the signs of homosexuality are most apparent in the character of Ryan and his interactions with rival-turned-friend Chad Danforth (Corbin Bleu). As a particularly potent illustration, look to the musical number "I Don't Dance" from *HSM 2*. The sequence takes place on a baseball diamond, a location choice which immediately (albeit subconsciously) calls to mind erotic metaphors like "getting to third base" and, especially relevant when discussing homosexuality, "batting for the other team." As the music starts, Ryan and Chad take their places at the pitcher's mound and batter's box respectively. The film then cuts to a medium shot of Gabriella and female friend Taylor McKessie (Monique Coleman) making their way to the spectator benches, seats filled primarily by other girls and only a handful of boys. As Gabriella and Taylor look off screen at the sporting duo, surrounded by signifiers of femininity, the default ocular system of the male gaze becomes inverted.

The movie asks its young viewers to look upon Chad and Ryan through the framework of a female gaze, through the eyes of desiring and, given the objects of their glance, heterosexual women. This subtle shift in aesthetic communication opens up space for female and male viewers alike to conceive of Chad and Ryan as focalizing points for desire. For any boys in the audience, the natural byproduct of this decision is that they come phenomenologically close to homosexuality via the adoption of a gaze which, for them, is directly adjacent to what one might refer to as a gay-ze.

The content of the scene builds upon this erotic framework through sexual signifiers. Most obvious are the balls and bats of baseball proper. As the players swing around their phallic tools, eyes fixed firmly on those all-important balls with the hopes of scoring big, the idea that there is something gay about this whole event becomes easy to see, particularly for queer viewers. Small additional signifiers further this perception: dance moves which emphasize the players' crotches, as with one background dancer who does a headstand before fully opening and extending his legs; a sound mix which foregrounds effects like the *smack* of a hand or the *whip-fast whoosh* of a bat or the *dull thud* of balls hitting mitts, aggressive sounds which highlight the human body; a segment of the sequence which brings Chad and Ryan face to face in a mock tug-of-war game, the literal back and forth of their performances indicating (sexual) tension. And all this does not even account for the central lyrical premise of the song, which is on its surface about repression. Chad views himself solely as an athlete, declaring loudly and proudly that he does not dance. Meanwhile, the intentionally queer-coded Ryan responds with taunts, declaring Chad a closeted dancer who needs to take a tap dance on the wild side. Just as in everyday life, dancing here becomes a substitute for both courtship and intercourse, in this case between two men. That Chad protests this choreographed arrangement, but all the while actively participating in that arrangement, functions as a commentary on the queer codes in play—*I want to show you what's really going on between these two "bat boys,"* Kenny Ortega seems to say, *but we have to keep them closeted to appease straight people.*

As noted, this subversive aesthetic practice is common to musicals as an artistic genre, not just this franchise. Indeed, viewers who have witnessed the "carefully tailored pants" of Gene Kelly in *Singin' in the Rain* (1952) or the "homosocial rhetoric" between Jane Russell and Marilyn Monroe in *Gentlemen Prefer Blondes* (1953) will already have at least a passing familiarity with these concealed structures and how they operate (Doty, 1993, pp. 10–12). However, Ortega's explanation behind the inclusion of queer codes highlights an aspect which is rarely invoked: embodiment. Returning to his earlier comment Ortega notes, "I took it upon myself to make choices that I felt that those who were watching would grab. They would see it, **they would feel it,** they would know it and they would identify with it" (Setoodeh, 2020, para. 32, emphasis added). Most LGBTQ activists press the importance of representation in cinema, meaning the ability to *see* literalized representations of queerness. As some of the *HSMTMTS* cast members put it, we "wished we could have **seen** more people like us on screen" (GLAAD, 2020, emphasis added). However, Ortega's choice of words encourages us to consider that the forms of representation hidden within *HSM* are not merely the traces of particular types of gay persons, but various essences of queerness which one must feel instead of see. The franchise contains feelings transmitted from gay to gay, and the successful representation of those emotional faculties is just as important as including the ocular signifiers.

With this perspective in mind, Ryan takes on a much more complicated role as a closeted queer character. On the one hand, his flamboyant personality and actions mark him as gay, but only to observant audience members. This means he can at best partially, but not fully, fulfill a viewer's desire for LGBTQ representation, and that this encounter must happen in a way mediated by the closeted aesthetic standards of the time. He codes gay, so he can be *seen* as gay, but only in part, creating what one might think of as a half self. On the other hand, due to the thorough displacement of queer affect amongst all the characters in the trilogy, including those like Chad who are affirmed as straight within the explicit text of the narrative, only a handful of viewers will be able to *feel* Ryan as gay. Due to the feigned ignorance of homosexuality by the series—to borrow language from critic Ayden Ferdeline, *HSM* at best "tolerate[s] the flamboyant Ryan Evans," but does not do so openly (2011, p. 6)—a space of silence opens up wherein gay eroticism exists but is not present, does not present itself of its own accord. As a result, "that silence is rendered as pointed and performative as speech, in relations around the closet," its potency acting upon the narrative as an affective phenomena but without functioning as a clear marker of visual or emotional representation (Sedgwick, 2002, p. 4). Thus, since LGBTQ viewers do not have an unambiguously queer character with which to tie this floating queer affect and, by extension, their own marginalized body searching for a point of identification, said affect will instead float to a different character for each viewer. In lieu of actual representation, the sexual silence ends up performing itself within Troy, or Gabriella, or Chad, or Taylor, or Sharpay, making them *feel* gay despite being depicted as straight.

The result of this is at once positive and negative. In one way, the indeterminate homosexuality yields a more diverse range of characters upon which the LGBTQ viewer might drape their own sense of self. For a non-effeminate gay youth, Troy or Chad might make a more appropriate narrative surrogate than Ryan; for an effeminate but non-flamboyant gay youth, Gabriella or Taylor might be the perfect fit. The ability to transport between bodies (and therefore focalization points), to adopt the screen form most similar to, or indicative of, one's lived experience, is as beneficial here as in any media product. And yet, the lack of any clear *queer* focalization point means this floating method of identification can only ever yield a half self, not a whole self. Even as one relates intimately to Sharpay in demeanor, her straightness marks a point of difference that is not made up for by the imaginative construction of a world where queerness is permitted sans code. While watching the original *HSM* trilogy, an LGBTQ fan can only ever possess a truthful body (via transportable focalization) or a truthful sexuality (via coded on-screen focalization), the result in both cases being a half fulfillment of self. One can etch themselves into the specific signifiers of eroticism, or they can etch themselves into a broader character archetype, but the closet prohibits the two from fully integrating and intermingling. In this way, the franchise utilizes a "reception space that stands simultaneously beside and within that created by heterosexual and straight positions" (Doty, 1993, p. 15), a mode of spectatorship which is better than nothing, but still places queer persons on a permanent precipice between marginalization and disintegrative assimilation. For the franchise to at some point truly come out, then, it must find a way to merge these two halves of the viewer into a genuine whole, to bring queerness entirely into the boundaries outlined by straight reception standards. As the trilogy's drama teacher, Ms. Darbus (Alyson Reed), puts it near the start of *HSM 3*, "playing a role is easy, but being yourself, now that's a challenge." The contra-normative viewer cannot just prop their identity up in a half self and hope to find fulfillment, but must in fact find a way to perform their whole self within the designated aesthetic space.

The Start of Something New

In the decade following the conclusion of the original film trilogy, America changed dramatically with regard to its treatment of queer people. Most obviously, the Supreme Court's decision in *Obergefell v. Hodges* in 2015 extended the right of marriage to same sex partners, a massive shift which marks the point at which many culturally enforced closets of the past began to finally crumble away. At the time of this essay's writing, a majority of United States citizens have expressed happiness with the increased "acceptance of gays and lesbians in the nation," and those numbers have risen proportionally for other categories of queer people (Jones,

2022). Though still a hotly contested aspect of society—a fact aptly demonstrated by the Walt Disney Company's conflict with Florida governor Ron DeSantis, who signed into law the Parental Rights in Education Act, better known as the "Don't Say Gay" bill, which prohibits the discussion of sexual orientation or gender identity in certain public school settings (Diaz, 2022)—the status of queer liberation in America is leaps and bounds ahead of where it was when Kenny Ortega first started rolling on *HSM* way back in 2005. The director himself has even commented on this change, sharing a story about a queer encounter that would not have been possible during his youth:

> I would have never have [*sic*] dreamed that I would see the day [where homosexuality was accepted]. I was at McConnell's ice cream parlor with a friend ... [a]nd in walks these teenage boys, like six teenage boys, and they're laughing and holding hands. And it is clear to me that they are gay young men and that they're comfortable in their skin and in their shoes.... I pulled them aside, and I said, "It's just so exciting to be able to see you guys walk in with this kind of comfort and confidence, that you're not even having to think twice about who you are or that anybody would have a problem with it." And I said, "Just remember that it wasn't always that way" [Setoodeh, 2020, para. 24–26].

Meanwhile, this same period saw a sharp rise of LGBTQ influence within American media. Perhaps best evidenced by *TIME*'s declaration of a "transgender tipping point" in 2014—with said point marked visually on the magazine's cover via trans actress Laverne Cox, who gained prominence through a featured performance in the hit Netflix streaming show *Orange is the New Black* (2013–2019)—this new wave of rainbow-laced storytelling "helped expose the broader culture to trans people," gay and lesbian folks, and other facets of the United States' queer communities (Steinmetz, 2014, para. 19).

This rush of content came with its own aesthetic and generic codes, from the increased prevalence of blue and purple "bisexual" lighting styles to the incorporation of drag and Harlem ballroom fashion into typical Hollywood fare (see, for instance, *Dumplin'* from 2018). When talking about musicals, however, no property was quite so influential as Fox's jukebox dramedy *Glee* (2009–2015). Created by gay auteur Ryan Murphy and premiering but a single year after *HSM 3*, the show follows a frenetic high school glee club and its various teenage members. Throughout the series, the characters' own personal struggles and interpersonal relationships weave together with song and dance numbers, the narrative's choral framework providing ample opportunity to have the cast sing covers of classic and contemporary pop songs as expressions of their emotions. Though by no means identical, *Glee* bears striking resemblances to the *HSM* movies which immediately preceded it, and the show certainly positioned itself as a more mature and less saccharine take on that same basic formula. Part of that maturity involved the open incorporation of more marginal identities into the story, and especially issues related to LGBTQ persons. Sexual repression and coming out, (trans)gender identity and gender transition, and more all factored into the text (not subtext) of the series, and queer characters like Kurt Hummel (Chris Colfer) remain important touchpoints of queer media, having functioned as the first major source of fictional on-screen queer representation for many target viewers. Such spectators found this representation refreshing and incredibly empowering, with the perceived authenticity of the show and its subject matter generating praise even as *Glee* itself waned in popularity. As one fan noted in a survey conducted by Michaela Meyer and Megan Wood (2013), what made the series special is "that you have this kind of introduction to these topics, maybe before you can deal with them yourself so you can build your own thoughts on them, and prepare to deal with them in real life, whether it be bullying, or you know, being gay and coming out" (p. 441).

While deserving of such commendations, it is essential to note that part of the purported genius of *Glee*'s approach to sexuality stems from the fact that it builds upon musical signifiers of the past, just as *HSM* did. As Meyer and Wood note, that the participants in their survey frequently described *Glee*'s "narrative as 'singing and prancing around' subtly codes [their] meaning," which is that the show is gay both through form and content (2013, p. 443). The truthfulness of *Glee*, and where it diverges from the *HSM* trilogy, stems from the fact that the show allows those two halves to mingle and merge: actualized bodies, meaning the diverse range of character archetypes which musicals have utilized for generations; and actualized identities, meaning the diverse range of real world sexualities and genders present in the show. The coming out offered by *Glee* goes beyond surface level representation, offering instead a way for audience members to at once float between different characters until they find their perfect model for identification, while at the same time still tying the show's queer affects to actual queer points of origin. When watching *Glee*, a viewer can both inhabit their real, gay body and inhabit their chosen, fictional body at the same time, creating a whole self out of two halves.

You Are the Music in Me

It is within this new era of queer programming that Disney launched Disney+, accompanied from day one by flagship show *High School Musical: The Musical: The Series*. Pulling heavily from the aesthetics pioneered by *Glee*, this serialized project debuting November 8, 2019, does not see a return of Troy, Gabriella, or any of the other characters from the original movie trilogy. Instead, *HSMTMTS* takes viewers to a stylized version of Salt Lake High School East in Salt Lake City, Utah, the real-world shooting location for the classic films. In this narratively self-aware, or *meta*, space, a fictional group of characters sign up to perform in the school's yearly play, which will for the first time be a stage adaptation of *HSM*. As in *Glee*, the program focuses on the personal and interpersonal drama experienced by the characters, seamlessly weaving song and dance into the narrative by way of its choral framework; this time, however, the songs come from Disney's extensive movie library (alongside a selection of original tunes written for the series) instead of pop music. Though not nearly as assertive as its primetime predecessor *Glee*, *HSMTMTS* features a handful of queer characters, the most prominent of which is gay couple Carlos Rodriguez (Frankie Rodriguez) and Seb Matthew-Smith (Joe Serafini). The show foregrounds their romance in a way unprecedented both for the *HSM* franchise itself and Disney more broadly, centering them during school dances, parties, and other major events in a way unthinkable back in the hetero homecoming heydays of the first *HSM*. Thanks to the content featured on-screen as well as the formal conventions pulled from shows like *Glee*—indeed, the show was widely considered to be "a delightful Disneyfied *Glee*" (Lopez, 2019, article headline) due to the clear aesthetic overlap—*HSMTMTS* represented a full and unambiguous coming out of the *HSM* franchise. Heterosexual and homosexual spectatorship have, once again, mingled and merged, this time within the sanctified boundaries of the castle-shaped proscenium arch.

The reflexive approach Disney utilized for *HSMTMTS* has further consequences for queer spectatorship, and especially spectatorship of media produced by the House of Mouse itself. By foregoing now standard modes of serialization utilized by television and film studios to revive old franchises—including Disney's own "(multi-)linear" and "transmedial serialization" methods pioneered by the Marvel Cinematic Universe (Brinker, 2021, pp. 208–209)—in favor of a more meta take, Disney has enhanced the receptive practices of the original movies by enabling LGBTQ viewers to alter and incorporate the texts into their own identities as opposed to merely accepting them as originally constructed. Just as the half self which was produced by *HSM* transformed into a more specific and fulfilling variant produced by *Glee*, making it so homosexual positions were treated as equal to their heterosexual counterparts, *Glee*'s variant has now transformed into a self-aware style of identification in *HSMTMTS*. This mode of reception permits meta viewing practices whereby gay audience members may use their own identity to alter the straight text by segmenting it from its original context, thereby privileging their lived reality over the existing heterosexual fabulation.

To understand how this new mode of meta reception works, look to how it impacted one of the major musical numbers from the original film, "Breaking Free." Performed by Troy and Gabriella, the song marks a moment in the story when they have accepted their own love as well as their shared connection to musical theater. During callbacks, the duo walk on stage in stereotypical "jock" and "nerd" outfits which signify the status quo they have long been forced to accept. As Gabriella shakes off her nerves, the song opens with a three-measure piano melody that straddles the line between love and sorrow. Troy proceeds to sing about the duo flying so high that they can touch the heavens. The hopeful lyrics contrast with the anxious instrumental, intimating that conflict exists in the couple. Conflict in themselves? Between themselves? Troy continues singing, declaring that the outside world does not see the duo as they actually are. As it turns out, the conflict is that same repressive silence of the closet to which the queerness of the film already finds itself bound. Suddenly, for the LGBTQ viewer, the idea that this song is a treatise against concealing one's sexuality becomes clear, a notion reinforced when the duo split on stage to emphasize that the limitations placed on embodied expression quite literally tear a whole person in two (the half self versus the whole self). The two then rejoin together in a duet to declare that their partner empowers them, suggesting being able to connect with one's significant Other, the half of the self constantly negated by society, leads to full embodied actualization. Troy and Gabriella then repeat the opening lyrics with more confidence, and soon the entire auditorium starts clapping along. Gabriella quickly strips off her repressive wardrobe, and as the song continues, suddenly all is right with the world ... or so it seems.

For LGBTQ viewers, the problems with this number are likely already clear: despite being a song about busting down the closet door, the film itself has chosen not to do that and is, in this very moment, reinforcing the dominance of heterosexual courtship. However, the issues run deeper than this already troublesome surface, and they stem largely from Troy's performance. While Gabriella gets to escape the restrictive manacles of her outfit, Troy does not get to strip off his. There is no dramatic quick change into a flashy Broadway costume, no tearing away of his sporty pants to reveal sequins. Despite the musical genre already granting space to transgress social gender norms, Troy's body remains fixed to a single conception of masculinity. The fact that Zac Efron does not even provide the singing voice for Troy in this first film only highlights this inflexibility, with the hidden work of Drew Seeley symbolizing the heteronormatizing processes at play. Even as Troy reveals his truth to the world, letting loose the song in his heart he for so long repressed, the incongruence between that interior self and his prescribed body produces only a half measure of actualization as opposed to a whole measure.

Fast forward to *HSMTMTS*, and things have changed significantly. Now that the franchise has embraced homosexuality, has found a way to combine one's truthful desires with one's truthful body, the show contains the space necessary to accommodate a more genuine message of anti-repression. In the program's staged production of *HSM* during Season 1, the fictional cast's version of "Breaking Free" starts as one would expect. Troy, played by male character E.J. Caswell (Matt Cornett), approaches Gabriella, played by female protagonist Nini Salazar-Roberts (Olivia Rodrigo). E.J. sings his part as expected, but Nini cannot join in, a slight variation on Gabriella's nervousness from the original movie that does not fundamentally alter the song yet subtly indicates that things are different this time around. But then, the major shift happens. Nini's love interest, Ricky Bowen (Joshua Bassett), enters the performance auditorium and the two lock eyes. E.J. leaves the stage and, in the midst of audience confusion, Nini begins to sing Troy's part from the original number. In this moment, the character has partitioned the song from its original context, creating a new product by re-embodying an existing one. While the tune and lyrics of the song remain the same, the identity of the singer has shifted, allowing for a reincorporation of the text as initially composed but in a new mode of authenticity. Thus, "Breaking Free" has now been altered in a non-representational way, altered by a body it once viewed as incompatible. It took ten years, but Nini has finally exemplified *HSM 3*'s declaration that "playing a role is easy, but being yourself, now that's a challenge," overcoming the struggle for truth by legitimately *breaking free* from the constraints of heteronormative, or perhaps heteronarrative, storytelling.

Best of all, Nini is not the only one who gets to achieve this level of actualization. Another character on the show, Seb from the gay couple discussed earlier, mirrors the character of Sharpay from the classic trilogy by performing all of her parts as written, but *without* changing his normal gender presentation while on stage. Though the fullness of the diva's classic characterization remains intact, *HSMTMTS* does not force Seb to don drag or assume the role of a woman in order to take up her on-stage positionality. Instead, the show allows him to sublimate Sharpay and her affiliated lines, actions, and songs into his own lived experience, maintaining the authenticity of his identity as a gay male youth. This is easiest to see in his hair, makeup, and wardrobe choices during the fictional cast's production of "Stick to the Status Quo," also in Season 1. During this number in the original *HSM*, Sharpay dons a bright white top with sparkly trim, a pink blazer patterned with flowers and cinched at the waist via a thin belt, and semi-formal cream-colored pants. She has painted her face in a fairly traditional femme style (blush, contour, eyeliner, and a distinct but not overly dramatic lip color), and has accented her ensemble with a star necklace and long, dangly earrings. In contrast, while Seb carries over one signifier from the film's wardrobe by way of a similarly pink flower blazer, he chooses not to tie it at the waist and lets it hang open instead. This helps highlight the other changes to his wardrobe, namely reflective theater pants and a graphic top that would not look unusual on a Lady Gaga merchandise table. Moreover, while he has chosen to utilize makeup and accents to complete his ensemble, they take on a very different form than *HSM*'s variant of Sharpay; specifically, Seb dons a strong lip color and a bold streak of makeup across the left side of his head in place of more conservatively effeminate face paint, and he brushed glitter through his hair in lieu of wearing jewelry. Yet despite all these changes, *HSMTMTS* still allows Seb to deliver Sharpay's lines and vocals as written, his personal identity and gender expression not prohibiting access to them. Indeed, by sublimating the text through his body, the type of homosexuality which was previously rendered invisible (or at best half-visible) by *HSM* now becomes acceptable both visually and non-representationally.

Moreover, *HSMTMTS* intimates that one can apply these same logics to *all* properties within the Disney consumer umbrella, given that the second and third seasons take the same approach as the first but replace *HSM* with *Beauty and the Beast* (1991) and *Frozen* (2013), respectively. While these subsequent fictionalized productions do not feature the same immediately recognizable gender shakeups as Nini and Seb, the streaming series nonetheless offers routes for exploring the possibility of meta queer reception practices in relation to Disney's animated fairy tale fare. Perhaps most notable among these comes by way of the character Ashlyn Caswell (Julia Lester), who plays the lead and presumed heterosexual role of Belle from *Beauty and the Beast* in Season 2 prior to realizing she is queer in Season 3, a subplot which is expanded significantly in Season 4 as she accepts and acts upon her desire for women. In a more restrictive receptive framework, viewers rewatching or recalling previous episodes following this revelation might view the details as incongruous, leading to a conflict of identity which must be confronted and resolved. However, because the system of spectatorship outlined above places emphasis on one's lived truth over textual authority, Ashlyn can exist and identify in whatever way she needs to regardless of what character she plays (or has previously played) on stage. Her authentic reality trumps the original heteronormative tale, and she can simply adapt the source material to make it suit her.

We're All in This Together

Though the above examples all pull from what *HSMTMTS* depicts on screen, the true stakes of this argument do not lie in these narrative representations themselves. Instead, the potential benefits of attending to such meta reception practices all relate to how queer viewers model them in their actual lives—how a gay boy who sees himself in Troy or a trans girl who sees herself in Gabriella can at last sing a song like "Breaking Free" with confidence and total honesty, secure in the knowledge that in spite of the text itself, the world can finally see them as they are. Or better yet, can see *you* as you are. In keeping with the embodied framework of this essay I conclude now with a moment of direct address that asks you, the reader, to make these theories "dance a little" (Latham, 2002, p. 2000). As non-representational theorist Alan Latham describes, "we should work through how we can imbue traditional research methodologies with a sense of the creative, the practical, and being with practice-ness," as there are certain aspects of reality which only become legible when one expands beyond classical analysis and close reading (2002, p. 2000). With this in mind, take a moment to pull up "Breaking Free" on a streaming service and sing along with the number yourself, making sure to perform both the "male" portion of the track and the "female" portion. As you perform, think about how the song feels in your body, how it forces you to adjust your chest and your throat and your mouth.

As you sang, you no doubt felt various parts of your body straining, even if just by a little bit, to attain the right pitch and timber, to keep pace with the tune as written, to pronounce each word clearly but with passion. However, your identity did not change during this process. In spite of at least one portion of the song being textually coded in such a way as to be incompatible with most individuals' understanding of themselves as either entirely male, entirely female, or neither, performing it did not suddenly turn you into a man or woman if you were not one already—and if you were, it did not turn you into the particular kind of boy Troy is supposed to represent or the particular type of girl Gabriella signifies. No, in singing "Breaking Free," you have in turn altered the text through your body, have asserted the presentation of yourself as an actualized being who takes precedence over the will of the original song. You have broken free from the constraints of textual repression and made good on the liberatory promises that, due to its heterohegemonic structure, the original film could never fully live up to.

So what will you sing next?

References

Brinker, F. (2021). Transmedia storytelling in the "Marvel Cinematic Universe" and the logics of convergence-era popular seriality. In Matt Yockey (Ed.), *Make ours Marvel:*

Media convergence and a comics universe (pp. 207–233). University of Texas Press. http://dx.doi.org/10.7560/312490-009.
Box Office Mojo. (2008). Rollout: High School Musical 3: Senior Year. *Box Office Mojo.* http://boxofficemojo.com/releasegroup/gr1860260357/?ref_=bo_ydw_table_23.
Buena Vista Concerts. (2006–2007). *High School Musical: The Concert.*
Caulfield, K. (2021, December 2). The year in charts 2021: Olivia Rodrigo is the top new artist. *Billboard.* http://billboard.com/music/chart-beat/olivia-rodrigo-top-new-artist-2021-year-in-charts-1235004948/.
Cypress, A. (2006, March 15). iTunes offers first feature-length movie. *Washington Post.* http://washingtonpost.com/wp-dyn/content/article/2006/03/15/AR2006031501843.html.
Diaz, J. (2022, March 28). *Florida's governor signs controversial law opponents dubbed "Don't Say Gay."* NPR. http://npr.org/2022/03/28/1089221657/dont-say-gay-florida-desantis.
Disney+. (2019, November 12). *Disney+ launches today—and a new era of Disney entertainment begins.* The Walt Disney Company. http://thewaltdisneycompany.com/disney-launches-today-and-a-new-era-of-disney-entertainment-begins/.
Doty, A. (1993). *Making things perfectly queer.* University of Minnesota Press.
Farmer, B. (2000). *Spectacular passions: Cinema, fantasy, gay male spectatorships.* Duke University Press.
Federle, T. (Creator). (2019–present). *High School Musical: The Musical: The Series* [Television series]. Disney+.
Ferdeline, A. F. (2011). How TV helped me to come out. *The Gay & Lesbian Review Worldwide, 18*(4), 6.
GLAAD [@glaad]. (2020, July 30). The #GLAADawards for Outstanding Kids & Family Programming goes to… [Tweet] Twitter. http://twitter.com/glaad/status/1288838323046359047.
Jones, J.M. (2022, February 2). *Americans offer gloomy state of the nation report.* Gallup. http://news.gallup.com/poll/389309/americans-offer-gloomy-state-nation-report.aspx.
Keveney, B. (2007, August 9). Can "High School Musical" do it again? *USA Today.* http://usatoday30.usatoday.com/life/television/news/2007-08-09-high-school-musical2_N.htm.
Latham, A. (2003). Research, performance, and doing human geography: Some reflections on the diary-photograph, diary-interview method. *Environment and Planning, 35*(11), 1993–2017. http://dx.doi.org/10.1068/a3587.
Lopez, K. (2019, November 11). *High School Musical: The Musical: The Series is a delightful Disneyfied Glee.* Fansided. https://fansided.com/2019/11/11/high-school-musical-the-musical-the-series-review/.
McKinnon, S. (2013). Musicals are gay: A brief history of gay men, Hollywood divas and movie musicals. In G. Willett and Y. Smaal (Eds.), *Intimacy, violence and activism: Gay and lesbian perspectives on Australasian history and society* (pp. 105–118). Monash University Press.
Meyer, M.D., & Wood, M.M. (2013). Sexuality and teen television: Emerging adults respond to representations of queer identity on *Glee. Sexuality & Culture, 17*(3), 434–448.
Miller, C.J. (2019, March 22). *Disney Channel Gotta Sing Gotta Dance Week Promo 2006.* YouTube. http://youtube.com/watch?v=oYfE7AzITOg.
Murphy, R. (Creator). (2009–2015). *Glee* [Television series]. Fox.
Ortega, K. (Director). (2006). *High School Musical* [Film]. Buena Vista Television.
Ortega, K. (Director). (2007). *High School Musical 2* [Film]. Disney-ABC Domestic Television.
Ortega, K. (Director). (2008). *High School Musical 3* [Film]. Walt Disney Pictures.
Sedgwick, E.K. (2002). *Touching feeling: Affect, pedagogy, performativity.* University of California Press.
Setoodeh, R. (2020, June 30). Director Kenny Ortega on the queer aesthetic of his movies from "Hocus Pocus" to "High School Musical." *Variety.* http://variety.com/2020/film/news/director-kenny-ortega-pride-high-school-musical-1234694033/.
Steinmetz, K. (2014, May 29). The transgender tipping point. *TIME.* http://time.com/135480/transgender-tipping-point/.

Exploring Disney's Portrayal of Jessica Jones and She-Hulk as Complex Women Characters

NEWLY PAUL *and* GWENDELYN S. NISBETT

Superhero comics have been in existence since the late 1930s, but with the growth of the internet, audience expansion, and diverse distribution models, superheroes today have become "billion-dollar, transmedia, global commodities" (Cocca, 2014, p. 1). Superhero narratives, which were once limited to comic books, have expanded to other media such as movies, video games, and television shows. The rise of transmedia storytelling—which involves stories told across multiple platforms through distinct self-contained narratives (Jenkins, 2008)—has contributed to the expansion of the superhero genre. Both Marvel and DC have built their transmedia storytelling empires by creating a single universe from which several interconnected stories arise. These stories play out in various platforms and formats such as podcasts, streaming series, books, and merchandise, among others, giving audiences varied entry points into the universe and a variety of viewing experiences. As a result, fan communities have expanded. Fans of the genre, once comprised primarily of White, male, heterosexual populations centered around suburban comic bookstores, are now more diverse (Cocca, 2014) and meet online in fan communities where members communicate and connect with one another, discuss their favorite characters, and use these interactions to build mediated relationships with other fans (Cohen, 2014).

Despite the rising popularity of the superhero genre among a diverse audience, the content itself greatly underrepresents women and people of color. Most superhero movies feature White male leads and White male ensemble casts (Cocca, 2014). Among the superhero films made between 2000 and 2015, only a third pass all three measures of the Bechdel-Wallace test that measures the representation of women in fiction by evaluating whether there are at least two named female characters who talk to each other about something other than a man (Cocca, 2014).

Against this backdrop, Disney+ shows such as *Jessica Jones*, *Ms. Marvel*, and *She-Hulk: Attorney at Law* stand out as unique because they feature female superheroes in lead roles and non-stereotypical characterizations. While the latter two superhero shows debuted on Disney+ in 2022, *Jessica Jones* debuted on Netflix in 2015, along with other Marvel character–based shows *Luke Cage* and *Daredevil*. *Jessica Jones* was rated R for sexual assault themes, violence, and adult language, which is why when it was added to Disney+, the channel received criticism from parents, including the Parents Television Council. In a letter to the company, the council wrote that Disney's "foray into TV-MA-rated fare will forever tarnish its family friendly crown," (PTC, 2022) and that "[t]he mere presence of MA- and R-rated content violates the trust of families and may well turn them off entirely." *She-Hulk*, on the other hand, was rated TV-14. While its content did not raise specific objections from parents, the two shows were perceived as further proof of Disney's desire to expand beyond PG-13 offerings and add programming for adult viewers (Webb, 2022).

Despite this criticism, Disney stands to gain a wider audience by developing shows featuring female characters such as Jessica Jones and She-Hulk, both complex women representing a diversity of roles and identities (Stevens, 2020). On one level, these programs add to the value of Disney+ as a streaming platform. They increase its appeal among subscribers in a competitive market where platforms such as Netflix and HBO Max already offer a variety of streaming options for adults. In a survey conducted in November 2021 among nearly 700 respondents, 63 percent agreed that they would be more likely to watch Disney+ if it offered adult content (Stoll, 2022).

In this essay we apply a theoretical framework known as the social construction of gender (Lorber, 2005) to the narratives of *Jessica Jones* and *She-Hulk* on Disney+. While existing research has documented how female superheroes play feminist roles in comic books and movies (see for example Cocca, 2020; Taylor and Glitsos, 2021; Stevens, 2020), few have examined how the versions released on streaming platforms measure up (see Green, 2019; Rayborn & Keyes, 2018; Trott, 2018 for examples of exceptions). Scholars who are interested in the application of social constructivism and gender examine sources of gender inequality in the "practices and processes of gendering in everyday life" (Lorber, 1994, p. 241).

Theorists who subscribe to the social construction of gender posit that gendered performance is so ubiquitous and commonplace that "we all collude in maintaining the unequal gendered social order, most of the time without even realizing we are 'doing gender'" (Lorber, p. 261). As Butler (1988) explains, gender is not a stable identity, rather it is "an identity instituted through a stylized repetition of acts" (p. 519). In this sense, performance of gender includes external signifiers such as clothes and jewelry, as well as bodily gestures and movements. Though gender lacks an essence, people who fail to perform their gender correctly stand the risk of getting criticized. Their character, motives, and predispositions are questioned (West & Zimmerman, 1987). For example, in the modern workplace, women who are assertive receive lower evaluations, and men who express vulnerability are perceived as under-confident and incompetent (Mayer, 2018). According to Lorber (1994) genders are ascribed traits, and social roles are allotted that relate to these traits. For instance, women are perceived as emotional and nurturing, and considered experts in caregiving functions, while men are perceived as tough and naturally suited to leadership tasks (Huddy & Terkildsen, 1993). People's life experiences, roles and responsibilities are thus a consequence of belonging to a particular gender category, and society maintains strict distinctions among the genders by institutions such as religion, law, and societal values. Mass mediated texts replicate these narratives, thus helping social institutions to reinforce and maintain gendered norms. We use these assumptions of social construction of gender theory to examine the extent to which Jessica Jones and She-Hulk negotiate with gendered tropes typically present in superhero culture.

Situating Women Within the Superhero Genre

In the post–World War II period, superhero comic books primarily portrayed women as secondary characters (with some notable exceptions such as Wonder Woman) and focused on contrasting their femininity with the masculine form and function of male superheroes (e.g., Supergirl and Batgirl were created as less powerful versions of the male version of these characters). Most women appeared as damsels in distress or as one-dimensional characters (e.g., the Fantastic Four's Invisible Girl had the power to disappear, but the energy required for this transformation often caused her to faint and require assistance), and even when women characters were portrayed as multi-dimensional, they appeared marginalized, because of the focus on their bodies (Wheeling, 2017). Violent women characters were shown to be subservient to male characters, though their tactics resembled the masculine acts of violence displayed by the male characters (e.g., Supergirl was depicted as having the same strength as her cousin Superman, but she was shown as lacking confidence and being under his control). In addition, women characters were often killed off before the ending of the narrative (e.g., Batgirl, Aquagirl), which further reinforced gender stereotypes and the marginalized position of female superheroines (Kilkenny, 2017).

These gender-stereotype portrayals of female superheroes have been challenged in the last few decades by a growth in the number of female showrunners such as Melissa Rosenberg, Jac Schaeffer, Jessica Gao and Kat Coiro, female fans of the superhero genre, and the popularity of female superhero characters such as Captain Marvel, Black Widow and Wonder Woman (Ndalianis, 2020). The changing audience demographics of the twenty-first century as well as Third Wave Feminism, which sought to actively subvert, co-opt, and overturn sexist images and symbols, have also been credited with this transformation in popular culture content. In addition, online movements such as the Hawkeye Initiative (Scott, 2010) have consistently protested the over-sexualized portrayals of female superhero characters. The Hawkeye Initiative is a Tumblr site that houses re-drawn versions of hyper-sexualized female comic book characters such as Sara Pezzini from the *Witchblade* series, and Psylocke from *X-Men*. When readers encounter female superheroes in comic book panels where they are shown holding impossible and sexualized postures, readers re-draw these images by replacing the female character with the male character of Hawkeye, a Marvel character. The resulting juxtaposition exposes the double standards of female representation where sexualized poses that appear acceptable and normal for women tend to appear jarring for male characters.

As a result of these changes, scholarship examining female superhero-oriented shows in the 2000s onward have found incremental changes in the genre. For example, Cocca's (2016) analysis of superheroes over the ages found that during the 2000s, women characters such as Buffy, Princess Leia and Ms. Marvel were shown as increasingly having agency and nuanced personalities. Their power was "located not just in their physicality but also in their love, empathy, sisterhood, families, perseverance, and forgiveness" (Cocca, 2016, p. 215).

The television version of *Jessica Jones* is an adaptation of the graphic novel *Alias*, created in November 2001 by Brian Michael Bendis and Michael Gaydos as part of Marvel's MAX comics meant for adult audiences (Whitbrook, 2015). This graphic novel portrays Jones as a superhero-turned-private investigator and documents her adventures in New York and the villains she fights using her superhuman strength. The television series draws its storyline from *Alias*, and employs elements of noir, science fiction, and crime thriller genres. After its debut in November 2015, and through the series finale in 2019, the show won acclaim for its gritty depiction of sexual abuse and trauma through Jones' character, especially in the context of the #MeToo movement. The series has generated positive reviews from critics and viewers as well as active MCU online fan communities.

She-Hulk, a spin-off from the Incredible Hulk, was first released as a Marvel comic book in 1980. It was created by writer David Anthony Kraft and artist Mike Vosburg (with guidance from writer and editor Roy Thomas). The series follows Jennifer Walters as a contentious Los Angeles–based attorney who derives her superhuman powers from her cousin, Bruce Banner (the Hulk) through an accidental blood infusion. The comic book series shows her as a woman who struggles with her identity in a male-dominated profession as well as the hypermasculine superhero world (Stevens, 2020). Though physically powerful, she only enjoys limited agency. The show deals with modern-day issues of sexism in the workplace as well as in women's personal lives, including dating, online trolling, rape culture, and relationships. The show started streaming on Disney+ in August 2022 and had a total of nine episodes. Jessica Gao, who adapted the show for the streaming platform, wanted to mold the comic book material to "fit what's going on in the world, and (bring) in new voices and new perspectives," (Alter, 2022). Gao changed the show's title from the original comic book's title of *She-Hulk* to *She-Hulk: Attorney at Law* to signal to audiences that the show was likely to explore more issues than simply chronicle the adventures of the female version of the Hulk.

Scholarship examining the Disney+ versions of Jessica Jones and She-Hulk has found many instances where the shows divert from the comic book portrayal of the characters. Jessica Jones in the comic series was portrayed as a survivor of the abuse perpetrated by the Purple Man (named Kilgrave in the television series), a villain who has mind-control abilities and used Jones' superpowers to harm other people. This version largely portrayed Jones as a lonely and unsuccessful superhero with no real status within the larger superhero community. While she was shown to subvert gender stereotypic tropes of the comic book genre by not wearing a costume or being portrayed in a sexualized manner, the series ended by showing her embracing domesticity and leaving her superhero work behind via her marriage to Luke Cage, the father of her soon-to-be born child. The Netflix/Disney+ version, on the other hand, portrays Jessica as a more troubled and darker character who struggles with alcoholism and PTSD from her traumatic experiences. Most episodes of the show incorporate dark and gray imagery and depict sensitive portrayals of the struggles of women who have been sexually abused. While Jones learns to heal and cope with her trauma, she remains troubled, and we do not see her forging a romantic relationship.

Similarly, Disney+'s *She-Hulk* pushes against the tropes prevalent in the comic book version of the character. Existing scholarship on the comic book narratives of She-Hulk find that over the decades her character has embraced various forms of feminisms (Stevens, 2020). The 1980s characterization of She Hulk showed her struggling with Second Wave–feminist issues such as balancing her professional identity as a lawyer with her superhero Hulk form. In later years, she was depicted to have moved away from these struggles and embraced her sexuality and materialism, which was more in line with post-feminist ideals. Through all storylines though, we see her monstrous alter-ego in constant conflict with her feminine persona as a lawyer and celebrity. She Hulk's persona was originally created with a desire to fashion a "hero out of a monster" (Lee, 1974, p. 75), and her Hulk form is constantly depicted as struggling to find agency and legitimacy in a hypermasculine society.

Show Analysis

In this essay, we use a lens informed by the social construction of gender theoretical framework to perform a qualitative content analysis examining the portrayal of Jessica Jones and Jennifer Walters/She-Hulk in the shows. Our analysis is based on viewing 39 episodes of *Jessica Jones* between 2015 and 2019, currently available on Disney+, and nine episodes of *She-Hulk* whose first season ran on Disney+ from August to October 2022. After focusing on images, scenes and dialogue we then used a grounded theory approach (Glaser & Strauss, 1967) to discover trends in the representation of female superheroes.

While existing research on gender in superhero comics shows incremental shifts away from sexist to more equitable portrayals, the literature on streaming platforms and gendered representations is still evolving. Our approach using grounded theory allows us to explore the shows by going beyond the categories established by previous research (Tucker-McLaughlin & Campbell, 2012). Our approach yielded three major themes, which we discuss below.

Human and Relatable Superheroes

Both She-Hulk and Jessica Jones are portrayed as twenty-first-century women dealing with modern-day issues, which makes the characters more realistic, contemporary, and relatable to audiences, particularly women. Jessica Jones' (Krysten Ritter) superhero powers are downplayed in the opening episodes—we do not see her violent or superhuman acts; instead, we see an intimate portrayal of her as a person. She appears world-weary, but is shown as a tough private detective, who will do everything she can to help her clients, even the most difficult ones. She is beset with a wide range of human flaws. She is surly and grouchy to everyone she meets. She lives in a filthy apartment. She drinks too much. In a nutshell, she is a mess. But this is where Jessica is a refreshing spin on the traditional superhero. In comparison with female characters such as Captain Marvel (Marvel Comics) or Wonder Woman (DC Comics) who are aspirational, Jessica is arguably more approachable and easier to identify with.

In one of the first scenes of Episode 1 we see Jessica sprawled out in bed, empty alcohol bottles strewn about the room. When the neighbors in the apartment above make noise, Jessica flings a black boot at the ceiling and breaks the plaster. She then picks up her phone only to realize she had forgotten to plug it in. She is both superhuman and all too human. In many ways, she is portrayed as just another girl making her way in the city. She hustles to make a paycheck so that she can pay for her shabby apartment. She has a love/hate relationship with her childhood best friend, Trish Walker (Rachael Taylor). She has annoying and nosy neighbors who show up at inconvenient times. Though she is also given a past story—a family tragedy and a history of abuse—which is shown as the cause of her surly nature, the series does not dwell on it, but focuses more on how she comes to terms with it. Like many people, she expresses a deep sense of isolation and grief at having lost her family, though her trauma is shown as the cause of her ability to bond with other women.

Similarly, we see She-Hulk as an average twenty-first-century woman, dealing with familiar professional and personal problems. In her Hulk embodiment she steps beyond the boundary of gender roles, and in her human persona as Jennifer Walters (Tatiana Maslany) she struggles to find acceptance and respect. She struggles with the idea of being valued at her law firm only as a superhuman creature rather than as a capable attorney. Jen struggles with her family's comments nitpicking her lifestyle. We see her re-evaluating her decisions and second-guessing herself when she gets unwanted attention from men, and as she moves from one failed romantic relationship to the next. When Jen starts a dating profile online, she finds that men are not interested in her human form, but want to date her because she is a Hulk. However, the men she matches with on the app are undesirable and immature, make incorrect assumptions about her, or reject her in her true form. Jen's/She-Hulk's struggles with her dual identity and the need to hide her authentic form are likely to resonate with modern audiences. According to Chappell (2022) Jen's rejection objectifies her explaining, "The world welcomes She-Hulk, but on its own terms, and that often does not include Jen or her desires." As She-Hulk, she is a subject of male fantasy, but men do not want to compromise on their fantasy by accepting her fully.

Jen/She-Hulk tries her best to appease people and live up to their expectations in both her human and Hulk form but fails in her efforts. For example, in the first episode of the show, when the supervillain Titania (Jameela Jamil) wreaks havoc in the courtroom while Jen is arguing a case, her colleagues (who know Jen's secret identity) plead with her to transform into She-Hulk and defend the observers watching the trial. Despite her reluctance to reveal her identity, Jen does this. In the aftermath, she loses her job, and the resulting media attention causes her stress. Jen is forced to take up a new job as an attorney where her boss and colleagues only appreciate her for being a superhero and expect her to show up to work in her Hulk-form, despite her protests. The conflicts with her identity, the desire to please people, and the need to be accepted are common human traits, which are likely to make Jen/She-Hulk's character appear relatable to audiences.

As Brown (2017) explains, traditional American superheroes have always appeared larger-than-life in terms of their actions and the ideals they personify. Characters such as Captain America and Superman "are always honest, fair, fight for the common American good, never put themselves before or above others, and possess a faith in America's ideological principles" (p. 92). They are portrayed as having uncomplicated and simplistic worldviews and clear-cut ideas about morality. Other superheroes, such as The Avengers, are less idealistic, but they portray the strength of teamwork and the ethic of supporting one another through tough situations. These portrayals are in stark contrast to Jessica Jones and She-Hulk who stand apart as solo superheroes, full of contradictions and flaws and very human in their indecisiveness, real-life experiences, and ambivalence toward being a superhero.

Spokespersons of Contemporary Political Issues

Most superheroes in American culture have acted as representatives of American ideals of justice, fairness, and equality. Following 9/11, the figure of the superhero also underwent masculinization to parallel America's response to the attacks and the country's efforts to rebuild its perceptions of global superiority. As time passed, however, superhero narratives grew to address other traumas plaguing American society, such as government-sponsored torture, unlawful surveillance of private citizens, and economic crises (Brown, 2017). She-Hulk and Jessica Jones are embodiments of superheroes who deal with traumas that are prevalent in American society that disproportionately affect women. The shows' narratives also question larger issues in our society including abuse of power and inequality.

Jessica Jones' storyline includes the themes of sexual violence, emotional abuse, post-traumatic stress disorder, addiction, rape culture and consent. Jessica is shown to be a part of a patriarchal society where women are silenced and dismissed at every turn. The show's depiction of the emotions and experiences of sexual violence victims was so realistic and sensitive that it attracted praise from several survivor groups (Rayborn & Keyes, 2018). In Season 1, Episode 8, we hear from Jessica about the abuse she suffered at the hands of Kilgrave (David Tennant). In an emotionally charged scene, she confronts him, saying, "Not only did you physically rape me, but you violated every cell in my body and every thought in my goddamn head." When Kilgrave responds that he did not mean to do that, Jessica replies angrily, "It doesn't matter what you were trying to do. You raped me. Again and again and again!" Yet, the show avoids showing audiences detailed scenes of these acts of abuse. In doing this, it avoids sensationalizing rape, and keeps the focus firmly on the victims. In a departure from the comic book version of *Jessica Jones*, the show uses the word "rape" to describe Kilgrave's actions, which indicates a shift in societal attitudes toward victims.

Thompson (2021) argues that *Jessica Jones*' narratives challenge the tropes of toxic masculinity. Kilgrave's character harkens to the incel movement where he wants to control Jessica as a means of restoring his pride (Thompson, 2021). He gaslights and bullies her, first by inciting a fight between her and her romantic interest, Luke Cage (Mike Colter), and later by taking Jones' friend Trish hostage and threatening to sexually abuse her. Jessica eventually triumphs over Kilgrave and is able to overcome his mind control abilities and kill him. The majority of the show, however, focuses on prioritizing the victims' voice which is often ignored in popular culture.

In addition to questioning society's treatment of sexual abuse victims, the first season of the show also highlights the theme of police brutality and corruption. Though the show avoids direct commentary on these issues, we see several examples of police corruption and brutality toward inmates. In Episode 2 of Season 1, we see Jessica fighting the judicial system to save a young woman, Hope Shlottman (Erin Moriarty), from being sentenced to life in prison for being accused of killing her parents while under Kilgrave's control. During the course of her struggle, we are shown that the law-and-order system is not sophisticated enough to handle complex cases such as Shlottman's, and risks putting an innocent person in prison.

She-Hulk's struggles between her human five-foot, four-inch Jen Walters form, and her six-foot, seven-inch She-Hulk form, embodies the dilemma that women face in reconciling their professional and personal lives. Her experiences underscore the message that women are constantly evaluated according to masculine norms. In the first episode of Season 1, where Jen is shown as coming to terms with her superhuman powers, we see her more famous cousin, Bruce Banner (Mark Ruffalo), cautioning her about controlling her anger. Bruce was referring to his own problematic experiences with his transformation into the Hulk which caused uncontrolled rage and destructive sprees. But She-Hulk responded to his caution by saying, "I do it all the time. When I'm cat-called in the street, when incompetent men explain my own area of expertise to me, I do it pretty much every day because if I don't, I'll get called 'emotional,' or 'difficult,' or might just literally get murdered." This dialogue encapsulates the double bind that many women face in having to maintain a calm, unemotional facade in the face of violence and sexism, lest they be dismissed as too volatile to be competent or trustworthy. The show hammers home this point in the scenes where Bruce is shown trying to help She-Hulk adjust to her new persona. Though he starts helping her under the assumption that her experiences will be exactly the same as his, he soon realizes that they are different people who want different things. While Bruce embraces his superhero persona wholeheartedly and wants to protect the world from evil, Jen wants to resume her normal life and help people through her law practice. We also see that She-Hulk is able to ace all the strength-related tasks that Bruce gives her, equaling his own. Overall, the initial impression of She-Hulk is that of a superhero who is conscientious and in control of her emotions and strength.

Despite this, people who encounter She-Hulk tend to challenge or dismiss her, which is reminiscent of the sexist behavior prevalent in some workplaces today (Parker & Funk, 2017). Interestingly, we also see that She-Hulk's superhuman form gives her the confidence to stand up for herself in life-threatening situations, which she would not have done in her human form. The scenes where she fights men who harass and intimidate her comment on society's patriarchal culture.

In her role as lawyer, She-Hulk grapples with many issues that have contemporary overtones. One of her clients, Wong Sorcerer Supreme (Benedict Wong), wants to ensure that the magical powers of Kamar-Taj sorcerers are copyrighted so that others do not misuse their powers. He approaches Jen for help in controlling the damage done by wayward magician Donny Blaze (Rhys Coiro) who does not have the skills to perform magic responsibly. This case raises the issue of power, as well as public trust and accountability (Francisco, 2022). Since power is not distributed equally in society, people who are more powerful or influential than others should be mindful of how they use it and must be held responsible for their actions. In her attempts to resolve this case, Jen Walters acts as a conduit for challenging the status quo and raises important questions about accountability. Similar to *Jessica Jones*, *She-Hulk* also questions government corruption and overreach. In Episode 2, Jen Walters is asked to represent Emil Blonsky/Abomination (Tim Roth)—a Russian-born solider with the British Royal Marines who was injected with a serum that gave him superhuman strength but left him power-hungry—and plead for his release at his upcoming parole hearing. Through her interactions with Abomination, we learn that his powers were derived from drugs that were administered to him by the military in order to make him a super soldier, raising issues of government overreach and control.

Contrast to Conventional Male Superheroes

Both Jessica Jones and She-Hulk stand out as unconventional superheroes. In many ways, their characterization questions the current genre of male superheroes who embody atypical ideas of masculinity (Brown, 2017). According to Brown (2017), in such depictions, the narrative has a sustained focus on the hero's origin story or his physical transformation from an ordinary human to one with superhuman abilities (e.g., Captain America). Brown adds that this physical transformation valorizes "traditional masculine ideals such as physical strength, resiliency, power, and heterosexual desirability" (p. 39). Superheroes are shown to suffer in their personal lives, usually in their childhood or youth, which shapes their personality, makes them resilient and motivates them to defend others (e.g., Batman). They are also shown to encounter severe physical violence at the hands of villains, which incites pathos among audiences, but they emerge stronger than before from their ordeals, eventually defeating the villain, which further underscores their superior masculinity.

In contrast to these tropes, the violence that Jessica Jones endures is invisible because it is more mental than physical. We rarely see her superhuman strength, quick healing abilities, and ability to fly short distances—and she does not undergo any physical transformation. Though She-Hulk does undergo a transformation, we do not see either show focusing on the lead characters' origin stories. Jessica is said to have gained her superpowers in a car crash where she lost her family, while She-Hulk is shown having inadvertently gained her powers from Bruce Banner.

Part of the appeal of superheroes is their costume, which makes it easier for people to suspend their disbelief, but we see that neither Jessica Jones nor She-Hulk reflect this trope. Madrid (2016) argues that both male and female superheroes are physically idealized, but the differences lie in the details of the idealization. While male superheroes are presented as physically more powerful than women, their clothes tend to cover their bodies, while women superheroes clothes only cover their bodies partially. In contrast to these expectations, we see Jessica wearing mostly black and gray her clothes are always loose-fitting in contrast to the other characters in the series who are always well-dressed, including Kilgrave, who appears mostly in tailored suits. Similarly, She-Hulk does not have a specific costume, and part of the narrative deals with the process of her consulting with a fashion designer, Luke Jacobson (Griffin Matthews), to find professional and superhero clothes that fit. As She-Hulk, she wears the same clothes that Jen Walters wears before the transformation, and other characters constantly remark about their ill-fitting nature and the necessity of finding some more appropriate professional attire. Jacobson designs a few suit jackets and at the end of Episode 5, hands Jen a garment bag that contains a superhero costume he designed. We see She-Hulk wearing this costume for the first time in Episode 8, when she helps rescue Frogman/Eugene Patilio from his attackers. The purple, black, and white jumpsuit resembles sportswear, and She-Hulk pairs it with high-top running shoes. Unlike traditional female superhero costumes, She-Hulk's costume does not reveal her body or sexualize her. By allowing She Hulk to make a conscious choice to wear a costume, the show gives her character agency and choice in how she wants to physically represent herself. In addition, by introducing her costume much later in the series when audience members have already had a chance to watch She-Hulk display her strength while dressed in regular clothes, the show allows viewers a chance to question established norms in the superhero genre. She Hulk is a superhero regardless of the clothes she wears. This challenges the idea that the only legitimate superhero is a costumed superhero.

In addition, the episodes do not center around Jessica or She-Hulk's larger connections to the broader superhero universe, nor do we see them fighting crime consistently or having a number of rivals, which are all typical in superhero series. She-Hulk encounters a few minor villains, but they appear comically incompetent and are no match for her. Though she is shown interacting with the Hulk and with Wong, the Sorcerer Supreme of the Mystic Arts, these characters of the Marvel universe do not feature prominently in Season 1 of the series. Jessica seems reluctant to adopt violence to resolve situations, preferring instead to rely on the police and courts rather than delivering her own version of justice. In this sense, both Jessica and She-Hulk are reluctant superheroes.

Traditionally, female superheroes such as She-Hulk are usually overshadowed by their male counterparts—in this case her cousin, Bruce Banner (Romagnoli & Pagnucci, 2013). In addition, as Moll (2018) notes, many female superheroes are defined in terms of their relationship with a male character. We see both shows questioning these tropes. In Jessica's case, Luke Cage is featured as a bartender, but audiences do not see him using his superhero powers. Similarly, Will Simpson (Wil Traval) is featured as a New York Police Department officer, but not in his superhero form as Nuke, a rival of Captain America. She-Hulk's cousin, Bruce, hardly makes an appearance in the series beyond the first episode when he helps with her transformation. Thus, the shows choose to focus on the two female characters and do a deep dive into their stories. As Lavin (1998) notes, these independent portrayals serve two purposes. First, the female characters are not relegated to the sidelines, which frees them from a male-centric hierarchy system where women tend to be overshadowed by male characters. Second, the female characters do not need to be assisted or validated by other characters. Jen/She-Hulk gets emotional support from her assistant and a handful of co-workers, but they help in their capacities as humans, not superheroes. In addition, neither Jessica nor Jen adopt masculine characteristics or deny their femininity or sexuality in order to be successful as superheroes (Brown, 2004). For example, in Episode 5 of Season 1, Jessica realizes that she cannot stop Kilgrave by herself and needs help from her friends. She seeks help by talking to them about her trauma, and this helps her start the healing process, discover Kilgrave's weakness and use it to overcome him. She also comes to terms with her demons, such as her guilt about killing Luke Cage's wife, Reva Connors, while under Kilgrave's control. Ultimately, Jessica becomes a superhero more by conquering her survivors' guilt and loneliness than by use of her strength.

Implications

In this essay, we used social constructivism to analyze the mediated depiction of two powerful female superheroes, Jessica Jones and Jennifer Walters/She-Hulk, and examined the extent to which various tropes of their shows overlap and challenge traditional tropes in the comic book superhero genre. We found that both characters reject strict gendered roles and question the normative, masculine idea of superheroes. Neither characters dress or behave like traditional male superheroes; instead, they alternate between so-called feminine and masculine qualities. They appear as complex characters—sometimes nurturing and protective, and at other times, fierce, combative and angry. In their actions and words, both characters refuse to perform gender as a necessary part of being superheroes, thus questioning the link between heroism and gender.

The two shows adopt different approaches to tackling some of the most pressing social issues of our times. While *Jessica Jones* is filmed in the noir style with extensive use of dark and gray imagery in keeping with its serious treatment of sexual violence issues, *She-Hulk* uses a sitcom format and a light-hearted approach, with Jen/She-Hulk occasionally breaking the fourth wall, while also throwing a spotlight on sexism and identity-based issues. The shows may differ in tone, but as evident from the themes above, both cater to a contemporary and diverse audience. Indeed, *Jessica Jones* has largely garnered positive responses from audiences. In 2021, the show had 83 percent approval rating on Rotten Tomatoes and 7.9/10 on IMDB. *She-Hulk* has fared slightly worse, even though the show has only had one season so far, with an approval rating of 85 percent on Rotten Tomatoes and 5.2/10 on IMDB.

The success and appeal of these shows is often attributed to the showrunners and writers, who are mostly women. *Jessica Jones*' creator is former *Dexter* (2006–2013) writer Melissa Rosenberg, while Jessica Gao who wrote episodes for shows such as Rick and Morty and Silicon Valley, adapted *She-Hulk* for Disney+. Armstrong (2016) argues, "Having women involved in all the phases of creating heroines makes a big difference, but the writing is particularly important—finally, we're getting superheroines with the kinds of flaws common in the last decade's male superheroes—and anti-heroes." Clearly, the focus has moved from solely young, male audiences to more a diverse viewership.

The representations of female characters on television are important because young women's and men's identities are often shaped by what they observe on screens, and oversexualized women characters teach that women's worth is linked to their sex appeal (Wheeling, 2017). Moreover, media portrayals of characters and issues are important because they negotiate with and question the dominant ideologies related to race, class, gender, and other socio-economic factors in our daily lives (Tisdell & Thompson, 2007). Popular culture depicts characters embracing or questioning power relations and teaches audiences ways of being through the on-screen representations of people and issues. Indeed, with the increasing abundance of streaming platforms and the rise of transmedia communities, understanding the influence of popular culture is more important than ever (Kuijpers and Hakemulder, 2017).

Specifically, the symbolic annihilation (Tuchman, 1979) and stereotypic portrayals of women characters in popular culture are important to study because media depictions have a wide-ranging impact on audiences. The media are instruments through which ideas about gender circulate. By reiterating gender stereotypes of males as "active and heroic subjects" (Cocca, 2014, p. 412), and women as passive sex objects, superhero content contributes to the marginalization of women. These gendered portrayals also signal that the superhero genre are male areas of interest where women are unwelcome. When audiences do not see heroes who look like them, they could be less likely to relate to them. Seeing women objectified repeatedly on screen and cast in stereotypical roles as weak and emotional can cause some viewers to feel low self-esteem and alienation, or create a lack of empathy toward women (Rollero, 2013). There could be other broader implications such as lack of support for women who are in positions of power, or apathy toward victims of trauma and abuse. On the other hand, audience attention and engagement could be increased by showing diverse cast members and characters who subvert stereotypes.

We know that the interpretation of television shows varies depending on the political and cultural context of a given era. The portrayal of women superheroes has changed depending on social roles occupied by women in particular time periods, which is why the messages of *Jessica Jones* and *She-Hulk* resonates with audiences in the context of the Black Lives Matter and #MeToo movements. Given that there are relatively fewer complex and well-written female superheroes, these two shows offer a balance to the disproportionate depictions of women as sexualized and marginalized characters in the superhero genre. *Jessica Jones* and *She-Hulk* not only question the norm of the superhero, but also provide alternative ways of imagining strong and realistic women characters in the male-centric superhero genre. Kaplan (2018) argues that Jessica "makes space for women to be angry, strong, scared, traumatized, determined and weak, showing them as complex human beings rather than the one-dimensional characters you see in other superhero stories" (para. 1). Jennifer Walters/She-Hulk disrupts the norm of the traditional superhero. In the history of female superhero characters, they stand out as anti-heroes. They are relatable yet troubled, fierce yet vulnerable. As nuanced personalities who are willing to tackle contemporary feminist issues and question hidebound traditions, they represent an incremental advancement in the genre of female superheroes.

References

Alter, E. (February 10, 2022). *Game changers: How "Marry Me" and "She-Hulk" director Kat Coiro is challenging Hollywood's "inherent sexism."* Yahoo.com. https://www.yahoo.com/entertainment/kat-coiro-marry-me-jennifer-lopez-she-hulk-marvel-160015023.html.

Armstrong, J. (2016, March 14). *The female superhero is finally here.* BBC. https://www.bbc.com/culture/article/20160311-the-female-superhero-is-finally-here

Brown, J. (2004). Gender, sexuality, and toughness: The bad girls of action film and comic books. In S. Inness (Ed.), *Action chicks: New images of tough women in popular culture* (pp. 47–74). Palgrave MacMillan.

Brown, J. (2017). *The modern superhero in film and television: Popular genre and American culture.* Routledge.

Butler, J. (1988). Performative acts and gender constitution: An essay in phenomenology and feminist theory. *Theatre Journal, 40*(4), 519–531.
Chappell, C. (2022, September 11). She-Hulk highlights the double-edged sword of a dual identity. *Comic Book Resources*. https://www.cbr.com/she-hulk-double-identity-problem-mcu-disney-plus/.
Cocca, C. (2014). The "Broke Back Test": A quantitative and qualitative analysis of portrayals of women in mainstream superhero comics, 1993–2013. *Journal of Graphic Novels and Comics, 5*(4),L 411–428.
Cocca, C. (2016). *Superwomen: Gender, power, and representation*. Bloomsbury.
Cocca, C. (2020). *Wonder Woman and Captain Marvel from comics to film: Superheroes, sisters, and soldiers*. Routledge.
Cohen, J. (2014). Mediated relationships and social life: Current research on fandom, parasocial relationships, and identification. In M. Oliver & A. Raney (Eds.), *Media and social life* (pp. 142–156). Routledge/Taylor & Francis Group.
Francisco, E. (2022, September 1). She-Hulk is the most important marvel show yet for one surprising reason. *Inverse*. https://www.inverse.com/entertainment/she-hulk-episode-4-magic-law-mcu.
Glaser, B.G., & Strauss, A.L. (1967). *The discovery of grounded theory: Strategies for qualitative research*. Aldine.
Green, S. (2019). Fantasy, gender and power in Jessica Jones. *Continuum, 33(2)*, 173–184.
Huddy, L., & Terkildsen, N. (1993). Gender stereotypes and the perception of male and female candidates. *American Journal of Political Science, 37*(1), 119–147.
Jenkins, H. (2008). *Convergence culture: Where old and new media collide*. New York University Press.
Kaplan, I. (2018, March 21). Jessica Jones and the complex power of female rage. *The Independent*. https://www.independent.co.uk/arts-entertainment/tv/features/jessica-jones-krysten-ritter-netflix-superhero-metoo-sexism-a8264216.html.
Kilkenny, K. (2017, June 14). Can an action heroine be too masculine? *Pacific Standard Magazine*. https://psmag.com/social-justice/can-an-action-heroine-be-too-masculine
Kuipers, M., & Hakemulder, F. (2017). Narrative absorption: Introduction and overview. In F. Hakemulder, M. Kuijpers, E. Tan, K. Balint, & M. Doicaru (Eds.), *Narrative absorption* (pp. 1–7). John Benjamins Publishing Company.
Lavin, M. (1998). Women in comic books. *Serials Review, 24*(2), 93–100.
Lee, S. (1974). *Origins of Marvel Comics*. Simon & Schuster.
Lorber, J. (1994). *Paradoxes of gender*. Yale University Press.
Lorber, J. (2005). *Gender inequality: Feminist theories and politics*. Roxbury.
Madrid, M. (2016). *The supergirls: Feminism, fantasy, and the history of comic book heroines*. Exterminating Angel Press.
Mayer, D. (2018, October 8). How men get penalized for straying from masculine norms. *Harvard Business Review*. https://hbr.org/2018/10/how-men-get-penalized-for-straying-from-masculine-norms.
Moll, N.W. (2018). Elite and famous: Subverting gender in the Marvel universe with *Jessica Jones*. In T. Raybon & A. Keyes (Eds.), *Jessica Jones, Scarred Superhero: Essays on Gender, Trauma and Addiction in the Netflix Series* (pp. 28–43). McFarland.
Ndalianis, A. (2020). Female fans, female creators, and female superheroes: The semiotics of changing gender dynamics. In F. Aldama (Ed.), *The Routledge companion to gender and sexuality in comic book studies* (pp. 310–328). Routledge.
Parents Television and Media Council (2022, March 10). *PTC to Disney: Better online parental controls are good, but TV-MA-rated content destroys your brand*. https://www.parentstv.org/press-releases/ptc-to-disney-better-online-parental-controls-are-good-but-tv-ma-rated-content-destroys-your-brand.
Parker, K., & Funk, C. (2017). *Gender discrimination comes in many forms for today's working women*. Pew Research Center. Available at https://www.pewresearch.org/fact-tank/2017/12/14/gender-discrimination-comes-in-many-forms-for-todays-working-women/.

Rayborn, T., & Keyes, A. (Eds.). (2018). *Jessica Jones, scarred superhero: Essays on gender, trauma and addiction in the Netflix series*. McFarland.
Rollero, C. (2013). Men and women facing objectification: The effects of media models on well-being, self-esteem and ambivalent sexism. *International Journal of Social Psychology, 28*(3), 373–382.
Romagnoli, A.S., & Pagnucci, G.S. (2013). *Enter the superheroes: American values, culture, and the canon of superhero literature*. Scarecrow Press.
Scott, S. (2010). The Hawkeye initiative: Pinning down transformative feminisms in comic-book culture through superhero crossplay fan art. *Cinema Journal*, 55(1), 150–160.
Stevens, J. (2020). Exploring the monstrous feminist frame: Marvel's She-Hulk as male-centric postfeminist discourse. In S. Langsdale & E. Rae Coody (Eds.), *Monstrous women in comics* (pp. 31–50). University of Mississippi Press.
Stoll, J. (2022, April 7). *Share of viewers that would watch more Disney Plus if it offered more adult content in the United States as of November 2021*. Statista. https://www.statista.com/statistics/1280646/share-viewers-more-disney-plus-adult-content-us/.
Taylor, J., & Glitsos, L. (2021). Having it both ways: Containing the champions of feminism in female-led origin and solo superhero films. *Feminist Media Studies*, 1–15.
Thompson, M. (2021). Challenging typical ideas of heroism and toxic masculinity in *Alias* and *Jessica Jones*. In L. Piatti-Farnell (Ed.), *The superhero multiverse: Readapting comic book icons in twenty-first-century film and popular media* (pp. 147–162). Lexington.
Tisdell, E., & Thompson, P. (2007). "Seeing from a different angle": The role of pop culture in teaching for diversity and critical media literacy in adult education. *International Journal of Lifelong Education, 26*(6), 651–673.
Trott, V. (2018). "Let's start with a smile": Rape culture in Marvel's Jessica Jones. In W. Haslem, E. MacFarlane & S. Richardson (Eds.), *Superhero bodies: Identity, materiality, transformation* (pp. 47–58). Routledge.
Tuchman, G. (1979). Women's depiction by the mass media. *Signs: Journal of Women in Culture and Society, 4*(3), 528–542.
Tucker-McLaughlin, M., & Campbell, K. (2012). A grounded theory analysis: Hillary Clinton represented as innovator and voiceless in TV news. *Electronic News, 6*(1), 3–19.
Webb, K. (2022, July 22). *Disney Plus is finally fixing one of its key drawbacks by adding R-rated movies—here's what the move means for subscribers*. Business Insider. https://www.businessinsider.com/guides/streaming/disney-plus-r-rated-movies-shows
West, C., & Zimmerman, D. (1987). Doing gender. *Gender and Society, 1*(2), 125–151.
Wheeling, K. (2017, June 14). Female superheroes are not necessarily feminist heroes. https://psmag.com/social-justice/female-superheroes-are-not-necessarilyfeminist-heroes.
Whitbrook, J. (2015, October 5). *Everything you need to know about Jessica Jones, Marvel's most badass detective*. Gizmodo. https://io9.gizmodo.com/everything-you-need to-know-about-jessica-jones-marvel-1734716668.

Is Marvel a Transnational Revisionist Actor?

Interpreting Change in the MCU Post-Blip "Real World"

Pablo A. Sánchez-Rodríguez

When *Iron Man* was released in cinemas in 2008, it was the beginning of the now well-established Marvel Cinematic Universe (MCU). Through 30 movies and 20 series (as of early 2023), Marvel developed an unparalleled cosmos of characters, realities, and narratives, adopting a hegemonic position in contemporary content creation. In other words, the MCU has dominated the media landscape for 15 years, becoming a model for other audiovisual studios and, at the same time, updating their stories to remain socially and culturally relevant. In 2009, Marvel Studios was purchased by The Walt Disney Company, and in September 2018 it was reported that several Marvel series would be developed for the new Disney+ streaming service launched in 2019.

Before this time, all MCU television series had been produced by Marvel Television, with ABC network shows like Marvel's *Agents of S.H.I.E.L.D.* (2013–2020) and *Agent Carter* (2015–2016). However, Disney's interest in developing its streaming platform, required a change of strategy: all new Marvel shows would be created by Marvel Studios and tied to the larger MCU. From January 2021 to early 2023, eight series have been exclusively released in Disney+, introducing new heroes, villains and conflicts in the MCU.

These programs (produced by Marvel Studios) coincided with the need to reinvent the MCU after the conclusion of "Infinity Saga," which began in 2008. The MCU Phase Four (2021–2022), the first part in the current "Multiverse Saga" (projected to end with Phase Six in 2026), marked a turning point for superhero storytelling, introducing progressive themes in the various season streamed on Disney+. This innovative content is critical to understand the current MCU due to the interconnection between the new movies and television programming on Disney+.

This essay analyzes the representation of the "real world" in the MCU Phase Four series to explain Marvel's evolution within its superhero narratives. "Real world" is used in this context as an opposition to the narrative introducing the multiverse and the existence of multiple realities. Therefore, this essay will focus on the Phase Four shows *The Falcon and the Winter Soldier* (2021), *Hawkeye* (2021), *Moon Knight* (2022), *Ms. Marvel* (2022), and *She-Hulk: Attorney at Law* (2022).

First, the connection with the "Infinity Saga" and "the Blip" as a milestone in the MCU will be examined to understand how these Phase Four series pertain to a new fictional order. Next, the original themes introduced in these series will be analyzed: the construction of a new world order post–Blip, the introduction of second-generation heroes, the importance of mental health, the incorporation of racial and cultural subalternity discourses, and the adoption of a more feminist approach to storytelling. Finally, the repercussions on the political and social reality of this narrative shift in the MCU will be assessed. By introducing these progressive topics, I will argue Marvel is changing its traditional role in the global society and giving voice to underrepresented groups.

The Blip as a Turning Point: The End of the Infinity Saga

The MCU "Infinity Saga" spanned eleven years from 2008 until *Avengers: Infinity War* (2018) and *Avengers: Endgame* (2019). These two movies are built on a continuous storyline: Thanos' ambition to obtain the six Infinity Stones to erase half the population of the universe through a finger snap in *Avengers: Infinity War*, causing heroes like Bucky Barnes (the Winter Soldier), T'Challa (Black Panther), Wanda Maximoff, Sam Wilson (the Falcon), Peter Parker (Spider-Man), and Dr. Stephen Strange to turn to ash.

After this fictional vanishment in 2018, *Avengers: Endgame* focused on the remaining Avengers' strategy to undo Thanos' action. The reversal finally occurs five years later in 2023, but the solution (time travel) would also cause a final battle with Thanos, where all Avengers reappear, along with Asgardians, Wakandans, and various other characters features in Phase Four films. In this Battle of Earth, Tony Stark (Iron Man) sacrifices himself to defeat Thanos and his army. This iconic scene is now included in the opening of every Marvel movie and television show, as a tribute to the fallen Avenger and his sacrifice for the greater good.

While *Avengers: Infinity War* and *Avengers: Endgame* would become two of the ten highest-grossing movies in cinema history (as of early 2023), both films also had huge repercussions on the MCU narrative. Thanos' snap, also known as "the Blip," eliminated half of the universe's population, but then returned five years later as if nothing had happened. On Earth, this situation created a new division in society between those who had mourned for those missing, and those returning to their lives without understanding what had happened. This event forced the Phase Four MCU to face the challenge of building a post–Blip social reality that explained life during this struggle.

The Blip was also a defining moment for the Avengers. Apart from Tony Stark's and Natasha Romanoff's (Black Widow) sacrifices, Steve Rogers (Captain America) decides to remain in the past with his beloved Peggy Carter, Thor cedes the rule of New Asgard and joins the Guardians of the Galaxy, Sam Wilson (the Falcon) receives Captain America's shield from Rogers, Wanda Maximoff exiles herself in Westview (New Jersey), and Bruce Banner (The Hulk) goes off the grid in Mexico.

The societal and individual effects of the Blip made it a milestone in the overall MCU storyline. Until then, plots were mainly dominated by four key elements: (1) the characteristics of a hero, (2) the mission and ambition of a superhero, (3) the dilemma of the hero between two realities, opting for struggle or reconciliation, and (4) the never-ending battle between good and evil. With the beginning of the "Multiverse Saga," Marvel now had the opportunity to introduce new superheroes and narratives in the post–Blip MCU on Disney+.

New Narratives Introduced in the MCU Phase Four Series

This section is dedicated to the analysis of the five series of the MCU Phase Four that focused their attention on the "real world" storylines. As explained earlier, the "real world" in Phase Four refers to the representation of post–Blip societal values in the MCU as reflected in the Disney+ shows *The Falcon and the Winter Soldier*, *Hawkeye*, *Moon Knight*, *Ms. Marvel*, and *She-Hulk: Attorney at Law*. *The Falcon and the Winter Soldier* focuses on Sam Wilson and Bucky Barnes (the Winter Soldier) trying to find their place in a world without Captain America's Steve Rogers, struggling with a new Captain America, John Walker (Wyatt Russell), and fighting a rebel movement that tries to reinstate the world that existed during the Blip. *Hawkeye* centers on Clint Barton (Jeremy Renner) and Kate Bishop (Hailee Steinfeld), an admirer that discovers Barton's past as the vindictive Ronin and becomes his partner, fighting Yelena (Florence Pugh) and the Tracksuit Mafia. *Moon Knight* tells the story of Marc Spector (Oscar Isaac), a mercenary with dissociative identity disorder serving as the Egyptian god Khonshu's avatar in his eternal struggle against the goddess Ammit and her devoted follower Arthur Harrow (Ethan Hawke). *Ms. Marvel* introduces Kamala Khan (Iman Vellani), a Pakistani-American teenager and fangirl of Carol Danvers (Captain Marvel), who gains powers due to a magical bangle, but also deals with her family's history. Finally, *She-Hulk: Attorney at Law* presents Jennifer Walters (Tatiana Maslany), Bruce Banner's cousin, who, after developing Hulk's powers by accident, seeks to find stability in her dual roles as superhero and attorney. In these shows, five themes are consistently introduced and represent a turn in the MCU narrative: a new world order with different rules, the construction of the second-generation superheroes, the importance of mental health, the introduction of subaltern racial and cultural discourses, and a more feminist approach in superhero storylines.

A Whole New World: The Blip and Its Everlasting Effects on Social History

As the first series of Phase Four dealing with the "real world" after *WandaVision* (2021), *The Falcon and the Winter Soldier* examines life was after the five-year gap caused by the Blip. This new world is described by Sam Wilson (the Falcon) as a "crazy place [where] nobody's stable. Allies are now enemies. Alliances are all torn apart. The world's broken" (Episode 1), while Bucky Barnes (the Winter Soldier) defines it as "upside down" (Episode 3).

Half of the population (Sam and Bucky included) was Blipped, and their reappearance provoked dramatic changes in a system that needs to accommodate those who once vanished. The end of the Blip brought many societal challenges that were assigned to the Global Repatriation Council (GRC), like "reactivating citizenship, social security, healthcare, [and] managing resources for the refugees who were displaced by the return" (Episode 2). The GRC tries to get back to the way things were before the Blip (Episode 3), but, as Thanos predicted, the Blip also brought benefits for those remaining, as Sam explains:

> For five years, people have been welcomed into countries that had kept them out using barbed wire. There were houses and jobs. Folks were happy to have people around to help them rebuild. It wasn't just one community coming together, it was the entire world coming together. And then, boom, just like that, it goes right back to the way it used to be [Episode 4].

The series also depicts a GRC vote for the Patch Act, which "would seek to restore traditional border regulations and fast-track the return to normalcy" (Episode 4) by "[moving] upwards of twenty million refugees back home to their countries of origin" (Episode 5), as refugee settlements can no longer be sustained by governments after the Blip.

On the opposite side, the rebel movement, Flag Smashers, promotes a world unified without borders, as it was during the Blip, under the motto "One World, One People" (Episode 4). They believe "the GRC cares more about the people who came back than the ones who never left" (Episode 2) when ignoring their supply promises in the camps (Episode 4). Therefore, relying only on themselves, they initially steal medicines, vaccines (Episode 2) and other basic supplies from GRC supply depots, which created loyalty with displaced people (Episode 3), but also the group views violence as a legitimate tool for their cause (Episode 3).

Karli Morgenthau (Erin Kellyman), the leader of the Flag Smashers, claims to fight to gain recognition as "citizens in this goddamn planet" (Episode 5), blaming "corporations and the beasts who run them [for kicking] them out of their new houses and onto the street" (Episode 4). During the series, the Flag Smashers are labelled as "freedom fighters" (Episode 2), "terrorists" (Episode 6) and "revolutionaries" (Episode 4). Karli believes their fight is bigger than themselves, and thus she does not fear death, as "the movement is strong enough to continue without us" (Episode 6).

In this confrontation between the GRC and the Flag Smashers, Sam and Bucky try to stop Karli from resorting to violence, although Sam consistently asserts that the Flag Smashers are helping people in the absence of real GRC actions. In the finale (Episode 6), Sam delivers a powerful speech to GRC representatives stating that the Blip has given elites the chance to understand the consequences of their decisions. Sam suggests involving ordinary people in the decision-making process, inviting the GRC to use its power to do better and find compromises, as they do eventually when pursuing "changes in their overall policies of repatriation and resettlements" (Episode 7).

The only other series dealing with the consequences of the Blip, but from a more individual perspective, is *Hawkeye*. For Clint, losing his family during the Blip was "devastating" and therefore he became the vigilante Ronin, because "everybody dealt with the Blip in their own way" (Episode 4). In the case of Yelena (Florence Pugh), she vanished in 2018 and, after reappearing, began to investigate what happened to her sister, Natasha Romanoff (aka Black Widow) (Episode 5).

In short, Phase Four introduces the new world order set after the Blip, highlighting individual and societal challenges. On one side, those remaining lost their family and friends for five years, while those who vanished, and then returned, lost that time as well. Additionally, the decreased population during the Blip presented a more idealistic societal reality without borders or competition between countries for resources. However, the reappearance of the "vanished" presents the dilemma of re-establishing the status quo ante, that is, the world that existed before the Blip. As will be discussed below, this tension reflects the struggle between conservative and progressive ideologies, worsened due to the massive effects of the Blip.

After Iron Man and Captain America: The Construction of Second-Generation Heroes

One of the most defining aspects of Phase Four has been the inclusion of several new characters that did not appear in the "Infinity Saga," but this did not mean a break with the past. The gap left by the Blip played an important role in the construction of new superhero personalities with the Avengers as role models for Sam Wilson, Kamala Khan and Kate Bishop, or examples to be avoided, as it is initially with Jennifer Walters.

In *Ms. Marvel*, Kamala Khan, who is obsessed with the Avengers (especially Captain Marvel), attends the first AvengerCon (Episode 1) dressed as her favorite superhero. Through the use of a magical bangle, a family heirloom, she gains the ability to create hard light forms and soon commits to the Avengers' values of saving lives and fighting for the greater good (Episodes 2, 3, 4, and 6). However, being a teenage superhero, she also uses these powers to defy what is "normal," while also struggling with her individual and cultural identity (Episode 6).

In *The Falcon and the Winter Soldier*, Sam Wilson's past as an Avenger qualifies him for a more complex storyline in Phase Four, especially after having received Captain America's shield and mantle from Rogers. However, at the beginning of the series, Sam shares he was feeling the shield was someone else's (Episode 1), and, thus, decides to return it to the United States government. Later, Bucky accuses Sam of not having respected Steve's wishes when giving the shield up, stating he had "no right" to do it (Episodes 2 and 4). Yet, both rethink the shield's legacy and symbolism in relation to the admiration they have for Rogers (Episode 3). However, the Flag Smashers believe the shield should be destroyed, as it is a "monument to a bygone era" (Episode 4).

In the end, Sam reconciles with the shield and its "complicated legacy" (Episode 5), holding it after the new Captain America, John Walker, fails to be a worthy successor to Rogers. Nevertheless, the first time Sam calls himself Captain America (and is recognized by others as such) he makes clear he is "trying something different" (Episode 6). Sam's turn is mainly caused by three factors: (1) his vision of the Stars and Stripes as a Black man, (2) his criticism over Walker's Captain America not representing Roger's values, and (3) his belief that the Flag Smashers were doing some good. Consequently, he decides not to fight back against Karli (Episode 6) and even defends her cause in front of GRC representatives. Sam now feels comfortable embracing the title and legacy of Captain America, and in the series finale, the title credits change to *Captain America and the Winter Soldier.*

Another challenging second-generation hero is Kate Bishop in *Hawkeye*, who honors the past, but also strives to find her place in the world. On one side, she is not initially recognized as a superhero by Clint or herself (Episode 5), but she still admires the Avengers' for "choosing to spend [their] life trying to help people" (Episode 6). Kate confesses her admiration for Clint since the Battle of New York when he proves "being a hero isn't just for people who can fly or shoot lasers out of their hands, it's for anyone who is brave enough to do what's right, no matter the cost" (Episode 6). With this powerful message, she commits to becoming a hero using her archery skills, and helps Clint fight against the Tracksuit Mafia, even at the cost of assisting in the arrest of her own mother.

The only example of a MCU second-generation hero not relying on the past when developing her superhero abilities occurs in *She-Hulk: Attorney at Law.* After developing Hulk powers through blood contamination after a car accident, Jen Walters discovers she can transform to and from She-Hulk at will. Even with this control she states, "the idea of becoming a superhero is not appealing" (Episode 1), a choice her cousin Bruce, the Hulk, never had. Jen wants to keep working as an attorney despite her new powers and she refuses to be called a "superhero or vigilante [because] that is for billionaires, narcissists, and adult orphans" (Episode 2). However, Jen is suddenly forced to use her super strength during a jury trial, fired because of her actions, and then hired by a prestigious law firm only for being a Hulk.

She-Hulk's split with other Disney+ Marvel shows, and the standard conventions over superhero narratives, is also evidenced by Jen breaking the fourth wall and talking to the audience as comedy relief. This innovation culminates in the final episode, when she literally climbs through Disney+ app, shows up at the real Marvel Studios, and demands changes to the Marvel crew and K.E.V.I.N. (Knowledge Enhanced Visual Interconnectivity Nexus), a clear reference to Kevin Feige, President of Marvel Studios.

When talking to K.E.V.I.N., Jen challenges the traditional Marvel formula, which normally "throw a bunch of plots, and flash, a whole blood thing that seems super suspiciously close to Super Soldier Serum at the audience in the climax" (Episode 9). She suggests another approach, reinforcing the story of her life "falling apart when [she] was learning to be both Jen and She-Hulk." K.E.V.I.N. eventually agrees to these demands and Jen, satisfied with this change, states, "that's what Hulks do. We smash things. Bruce smashed buildings. I smash forth walls and bad endings" (Episode 9). In the series finale, Jen breaks with previous superhero narratives, as she accepts her dual nature as superhero and attorney, deciding to pursue criminals both in, and outside, of court.

Through these four series, the narrative of second-generation heroes gives Marvel the chance to emphasize the values of the MCU's original heroes, like Captain America's altruism or Hawkeye's bravery. At the same time, this past also inspires the "Multiverse Saga" to challenge predictable endings and stagnant hero profiles. In short, these shows act as a bridge between MCU phases, connecting the legacy of the original Avengers with revolutionary forces of change occurring post–Blip.

Mental Health Can Also Be "Super": The Introduction of Broken Characters

Although the "Infinity Saga" showed Tony Stark's post-traumatic stress disorder (PTSD) after the Battle of New York, and Sam Wilson's group therapy for veterans, the psychological dimension of the heroes had never received much attention before Phase Four. However, in these five series, the inner struggle of the heroes holds an important role in the storylines, serving as another innovative element in the post–Blip narrative.

The theme of mental health is best exemplified in *Moon Knight*, where the main character, Marc Spector, is depicted as having dissociative identity disorder (DID) that makes him "switch" into a different person, Steven Grant, without any memory of his actions. The cause of this disorder is the trauma caused by the abuses Marc received as a child when blamed for his brother Randall's death. Both this "core" personality and the "alter" are incredibly different: Marc is a ruthless American mercenary, while Steven is a gentle British gift-shop employee with extensive knowledge of ancient Egypt.

In this case, Oscar Isaac's acting skills take the viewer within Marc's fractured mind, which finds its climax in Episode 5, set in a psychiatric hospital. There both Marc and Steven explore together the former's blocked memories, like Marc unknowingly creating Steven to cope with his mother's abuse, and Marc's acceptance to become Khonshu's avatar on the verge of death. This realization serves as Marc's and Steven's reconciliation, and, eventually, Marc asks the Egyptian Moon god Khonshu to release himself (and Grant) from his service. When granted, Marc liberates himself from these bonds to start a new life and "save the world" (Episode 6). However, a mid-credits scene during the series finale introduces another of Spector's personalities, the second "alter" Jake Lockley, still under Khonshu's control, because of "how troubled Marc really is" (Episode 6).

Other references to mental health are also in *The Falcon and the Winter Soldier.* Bucky has court-mandated therapy as a condition for his full pardon. When talking to his therapist, Bucky admits feeling lost with his new freedom after going from one fight to another for 90 years (Episode 1) and annoyed with Sam for throwing away Steve's legacy (Episode 2). Later Bucky explains the shield was "the closest thing [he's] got left to a family" (Episode 5) and that Sam's action to return it made him question everything. To solve this identity crisis, Sam encourages Bucky to find his way apart from other peoples' opinions, including Steve's, and change his approach, focusing on making people feel better through closure, instead of apologizing to find comfort (Episode 5).

Because Bucky defines himself as "crazy," he also believes something was wrong with the new Captain America, John Walker (Episode 4). Walker slowly exhibits anxiety over his new role as a superhero until the death of his friend and sidekick, Lemar Hoskins. After this, driven by anger, Walker brutally kills a Flag Smasher in public and stands over him with Captain America's shield covered in blood (Episode 4). During Senate hearings about the incident, Walker starts yelling he had always lived according to government mandates and did what he was trained for (Episode 5), explaining they cannot understand what it takes to be Captain America. When saying this, he gives the impression this "title" of Captain America is a burden, adding that the loss of Lemar caused a mental breakdown that led to killing the Flag Smasher.

Finally, in *She-Hulk: Attorney at Law,* Jen Walters' internal struggle is also addressed through group therapy. After a heartbreak, Jen is questioning everything about herself in her dual role as superhero and lawyer, but the other therapy members encourage Jen to focus on self-care, spending more time with herself, and "stop using She-Hulk as a protective shield" (Episode 7). This reassurance from strangers helps Jen embrace her two realities, going home with a sincere smile while Dua Lipa's song "IDGAF" is playing (Episode 7). Later, after a meltdown that leads to her detention, she even asks for a "mental health break," clarifying she is not running away from her problems (Episode 9).

Marvel's focus on the psychological traits of these Phase Four characters acknowledges recognition of mental health as equally important to physical health. Portraying broken heroes (like Marc Spector) and heroes using therapy to handle their emotional needs (like Bucky and Jen) helps normalize psychological conditions and mental disorders. With this narrative, the MCU takes a step forward, breaking the stereotype of the perfect hero and providing more nuance in the evolution of the heroes introduced in Phase Four.

The Battle of Subalternity: Black and Non-Anglo-Saxon Superheroes Matter

Before the "Multiverse Saga" the MCU had been criticized for the ethnocentric perspective dominating this fictional universe. Contrary to the "melting pot" narrative, superheroes have "reflected and offered fictional evidence of America's romantic self-image as a hypermasculine Anglo-Saxon hero" (Brown, 2021, p. 6). Despite the late inclusion in the MCU of heroes like Black Panther, Falcon and Captain Marvel, subaltern discourses have not been traditionally considered in the MCU stereotypical image of heroes, both racially and culturally.

The term "subaltern" is used as originally formulated by the Italian sociologist and linguist Antonio Gramsci in 1973, when referring to any "low rank" person or group of people in a particular society suffering under hegemonic domination of a ruling elite class that denies them the basic rights of participation in the making of local history and culture as active individuals of the same nation (Louai, 2012, p. 5). The endurance of these subalternities in popular culture reinforces the hegemonic narrative, as it serves for the construction of a societal imaginary in which subaltern actors remain silent or ignored, with the potential effect of disregarding these groups' voices in the real world. Nevertheless, this secondary role has changed in the MCU Phase Four series when including narratives that deflect the classic, or stereotypical, superhero model.

First, racial subalternity receives significant attention in *The Falcon and the Winter Soldier*. The series introduces Isaiah Bradley, a Black soldier who received the Super Soldier serum in the aftermath of World War II, but was never publicly recognized. He was imprisoned for 30 years by the U.S. government for testing purposes to recreate the serum after Steve Rogers had disappeared in 1945 (Episodes 2 and 5). Isaiah explains to Sam Wilson he could not become the next Captain America being Black, as he was not "the great White hope [with] blonde hair, blue eyes, stars and stripes the entire world's been chasing since [Steve] first got dosed with that serum" (Episode 5).

Isaiah's mistreatment by the U.S. government becomes the tipping point for Sam as he questions the legacy of Captain America and the treatment of Black citizens such as himself. Other examples of racial inequity are present throughout the series, such as the police misconduct over Sam until he is recognized as an Avenger (Episode 2), or when he is called the Black Falcon because of his skin color (Episodes 2 and 6). Additionally, as a Black man generally underrecognized in society, Sam easily identifies with the Flag Smashers' goal of fighting for resources against the elites (Episodes 1 and 2) and struggling for real equality. Sam is empathic with the Flag Smashers' cause, because, as Sam's sister Sarah admits, they believe "[their] world does not matter to America" (Episode 4).

In Isaiah's view, every Black man understands the U.S. Stars and Stripes are not symbols to be identified with, because they have been erasing Black history for 500 years. Thus, he believes, "they will never let a Black man be Captain America and, even if they did, no self-respecting Black man would ever wanna be" (Episode 5). Sam eventually realizes all of Isaiah's pain and sacrifice would be meaningless if he is not willing to stand up and keep fighting (Episode 5). He accepts becoming Captain America with the "hate of millions of people [when being] a Black man carrying the Stars and Stripes" (Episode 6), but "we built this country, bled for it, [so] I'm not gonna let anybody tell me I can't fight for it" (Episode 6). In the series finale, a monument is built to honor Isaiah, so that Americans "never forget what [he] did for this country" (Episode 6).

Next, the MCU Phase Four series include subaltern discourses from a cultural standpoint, defying Western ethnocentrism. *Moon Knight* is grounded in Egyptian mythology, especially with the involvement of the Egyptian gods Khonshu (god of the Moon), Ammit (Devourer of the Dead), Taweret (goddess of fertility), Osiris (god of the afterlife), and Ra (god of the Sun). This mythology is also explored in the journey Marc and Steven perform after their death, through the Duat, or "Realm of the Dead," guided by Taweret to weigh their hearts on the Scales of Justice and see if they can enter the Field of Reeds, the Egyptian heavenly paradise. Therefore, the series provides information about an ancient civilization that does not conform with traditional superhero stereotypes. Likewise, the transformation of Layla El-Faouly, Marc's wife, into Taweret's avatar, introduces a female Egyptian superhero who speaks Arabic (Episode 6), a first in the MCU.

Ms. Marvel offers a very interesting window into Pakistani culture. Being the first openly Muslim hero in the MCU, and a teenager in New Jersey, the series depicts Kamala Khan performing common Muslim practices, like visiting the mosque to pray or celebrating Eid, the end of the Ramadan fasting (Episode 2). She and her friends even talk about wearing the hijab as something that gives a purpose when "either being too White for some people and too ethnic for others" (Episode 2). The community role in Muslim culture is also evident when people defend Kamala from being attacked and consider her "their own superhero," which makes them "part of history" (Episode 6). Also, Nakia Bahadir, Kamala's close friend, defies the stereotypical conservative male-dominated conception of Islam by running for the Mosque Board, and gets elected because of her fresh ideas and proposals for change.

During the series, Kamala explores her family's history during the Partition of India in 1947, which led to the creation of Pakistan (Episode 2), an event that plays a key narrative role in the show. The reconstruction of Indian history from 1942 to 1947 from the perspective of Kamala's great-grandparents (Episode 5) serves as a turning point in the storyline, reaffirming Kamala's identity and bonding with her family. Additionally, the involvement of mythological Djinns from Arab culture (Episode 3), the vast touristic walk Kamala takes around Karachi (Episode 4), and the divided reality of Kamala's grandmother holding a Pakistani passport but having Indian roots, allow viewers to explore Pakistani history and culture in a unique way.

These subaltern discourses included in Phase Four reflect the evolving MCU global position. The inclusion of non–Western historical and mythological elements also provides a more inclusive narrative way of giving voice to subaltern actors, and thus solving one of the criticisms in the "Infinity Saga": white skin, blue eyes, and blonde hair no longer define heroes.

Fighting Patriarchy: The Ultimate Battle for Contemporary Female Superheroes

Another criticism of the "Infinity Saga" was the male-dominated universe, as over the course of 23 movies only four main superheroes were female (Black Widow, Wanda, Gamora and Captain Marvel), with all other female characters reduced to secondary roles in the MCU. It took a decade before the release of the MCU's first solo, female-centric film, *Captain Marvel* (2019), at the end of Phase Three. Prior to the release of *Captain Marvel*, only Marvel Television had introduced complex female heroes like Peggy Carter or Quake. The legacy of those characters seems to have influenced Marvel to create powerful female heroes in the five Phase Four "real world" shows.

Kamala Khan and Nakia Bahadir in *Ms. Marvel*, and Layla El-Foualy in *Moon Knight*, are female role models missing in the MCU and examples of empowered women in traditionally male-dominated environments. Also, Kate Bishop in *Hawkeye* is a role model as a female superhero without superpowers, and even Karli Morgenthau in *The Falcon and the Winter Soldier* could be considered a female role model due to her initial idealistic intentions before radicalization and acceptance of violence. Finally, Jen

Walters in *She-Hulk* is the paradigm of this feminist breach against the patriarchy that had ruled the MCU, a subject which will be discussed later.

As new female leading characters, it is also significant that Kamala, Nakia, and Kate are young girls discovering their own identities. While Kate's dilemma in *Hawkeye* has much more to do with being a superhero, in Ms. Marvel, gender plays a relevant role. For example, Nakia recognizes that with the hijab and her physical development, her parents "can barely make eye contact with [her] anymore" (Episode 2). The hijab makes her "feel herself" and she runs for the Mosque Board because "maybe a woman for the Mosque Board actually makes some changes around [there]" (Episode 2).

Conversely, Kamala has overprotective parents, as exhibited when she asks for permission to attend AvengerCon (Episode 1). After her mother asks whether going to "a party, at night" is a joke, her parents state they do not trust "strange boys roaming around at night, thinking God knows what and drinking God knows what." They also forbid her to cosplay Captain Marvel because she is not wearing a "very tight suit" like "all those other girls in skimpy outfits." When Kamala argues they treat her brother differently and she only wants to do a "single normal teenage thing," her father replies, "Come on, beta, you're not normal." Considering Kamala has not yet developed her hard-light powers, her father explains the difference between Kamala and her brother based on gender.

However, the most feminist character in the MCU so far is Jennifer Walters in *She-Hulk: Attorney at Law*. Three consistent themes are evident in this show: (1) her life as an ordinary woman, (2) her life as a female superhero, and (3) sexist behaviors women endure every day. First, it is interesting how Jen's extraordinary ability to control her Hulk powers is linked to her being a woman in a patriarchal society. Her cousin, Bruce, explains her new Hulk powers require checking "her ability to tolerate stress and regulate her emotions, especially her anger." After showing her skills, Jen, in a remarkable speech, replies:

> Here's the thing, Bruce. I'm great at controlling my anger. I do it all the time. When I'm catcalled in the street, when incompetent men explain my own area of expertise to me. I do it pretty much every day because if I don't, I will get called emotional, or difficult, or might just literally get murdered. So, I'm an expert at controlling my anger because I do it infinitely more than you [Episode 1].

Apart from this lack of freedom to express emotions, the series also portrays other difficult moments women encounter. Some of them are the fear of "walking home with headphones" on (Episode 5), men believing they can always do better (Episode 5), ageism (Episode 6), and being called "slut" or slut-shamed (for example, when Jen's private sex tape is released on social media) (Episode 8). On a professional level, the series also portrays how women have to prove "their value to a parade of underwhelming men" while earning less (Episode 5) or are questioned about flirting with their bosses to justify their corporate rank (Episode 9). In a memorable moment, when asked by a male host at the Female Lawyer of the Year gala what it is like being a female lawyer, Mallory, Jen's partner in the law firm, replies, "Twice the work, half the recognition, and you're constantly being asked what it's like being a female lawyer" (Episode 7).

Next, when her Hulk powers are publicly discovered, Jen experiences challenges no male superhero had to endure before in the MCU. First, is her superhero name, given to her by the media, suggesting she "can't even exist without being a derivative of the Hulk" (Episode 2). She is also called a "specimen" on a date (Episode 4) and accused of stealing all the attention as She-Hulk during a wedding (Episode 6). Moreover, despite being a highly qualified lawyer, her new law firm only hires Jen because they want a Hulk in the Superhuman Law Division (Episode 2).

The series also underlines the public misogynistic hate on social media that Jen must endure as She-Hulk. Comments such as "Why are you turning every superhero into a girl? No one asked for that!" and "So we have a #MeToo movement and now all the male heroes are gone?" (Episode 3) are, in fact, based on real social media comments when *She-Hulk* was announced in 2019 (Ankers-Range, 2022). Later in the series, the dark-web group Intelligencia, responsible for this movement against She-Hulk online, posts death threats toward Jen under the hashtag #CancelShe-Hulk (Episode 6) and then leaks information from her private life stating, "she does not deserve your praise, she does not deserve the power she stole from the Hulk" (Episode 7). A conversation among members of Intelligencia provides additional evidence of misogyny toward a female superhero:

> Why does there even need to be a She-Hulk? It's not like there's a He-Hulk. And Lady Thor?—[...] she just sucks, okay? I'm not saying that because she's a female. I would have the exact same criticism if she was a man.—No one's allowed to make jokes anymore. [...]—Is the She-Hulk better than the Hulk? No. Is she as strong as him? Is she as smart as him? No. She wouldn't even have her powers without him, right? So, what do we have to act like she earned everything? [Episode 9].

Finally, *She-Hulk* also consistently shows specific men's sexist behavior, undermining women and treating them as inferior. For example, after Jen is attacked by four men on her way home but is unharmed after transforming into She-Hulk, Jen's father shows up at her place to protect her (Episode 4). This need to protect the superhero had never been seen before in the MCU with male heroes and it reinforces the traditional notion of women needing protection from men, such as when male heroes show up to "take care" of their female partners. A similar moment during the season finale is when K.E.V.I.N.'s projected plot relies on "Bruce swooping down from literal outer space to save the day in [Jen's] story" (Episode 9).

Another example of misogyny in *She-Hulk* is Todd, a billionaire who is an important client of Jen's law firm. At one point, he uses a request for her legal services as an excuse to physically assault her stating, "Listen, babe. Let's just drop the whole city thing cuz I don't play games, okay? And I can feel it, and I can tell that we're both feeling it" (Episode 8), although She-Hulk is fortunately strong enough to stop him. Considering Todd's similar misogynistic profile to that of Tony Stark early in the MCU, it is interesting to see how in *She-Hulk* the situation is reversed, as Todd is revealed to be the creator of Intelligencia and the villain who has targeted Jen to obtain her blood and get Hulk powers.

The series also shows male characters underestimating women in their professional lives. Two examples are a man not taking no for an answer when trying to invite Jen and her friend Nikki for drinks while they are working (Episode 4), and the male host presenting the Female Lawyer of the Year award, stating, "Educated. Accomplished. Beautiful. And doing everything regular lawyers do, except backwards and in high heels." (Episode 8). In the series finale a reporter even asks She-Hulk, "And tell our viewers, who are you wearing today?" with an exasperated Jen leaving the scene after this question. The reporter then says back into the camera, "The Difficult Diva of Law herself" (Episode 9).

All these examples support how feminist narratives and sexist behaviors experienced by women are new elements in the MCU storylines. The stereotypical male superhero saving the day has been replaced in these Phase Four shows with empowered female characters like Kate, Layla, Kamala, Nakia, and Jen. This new feminist approach towards the superhero narrative also means the cult of misogynistic attitudes like Tony Stark in the first *Iron Man* is, hopefully, over in the MCU. This quest for real gender equality in the MCU and breaking with past sexist stereotypes was Marvel's ultimate battle and, so far, the good (feminist) guys are winning.

Conclusion

When a transnational media corporation like Marvel Studios launches new content, it should follow a certain strategy designed to increase its revenue. In this case, Marvel has challenged the classic formula that brought the studio major box office successes to present more complex, integrative, and socially conscious narratives, defending progressive values after the Blip. Far from being innocuous or irrelevant, the transitional nature of this narrative shift offers a very different perspective on the MCU, because its global reach and dominant role in the media landscape can give these changes the power to transform the collective imagination worldwide. Therefore, this move means that Marvel Studios has adopted a new role in global society in this post–Blip order as a sponsor of revisionist and progressive initiatives.

According to Brown (2021), superheroes "occupy a position as idealized role models for children and as avatars for abstract cultural beliefs about justice and the nation" (pp. 6–7). In fact, perpetual revision of superhero narratives makes them "symptomatic signifiers of contemporary consciousness and [...] embodiments of specific needs in a given time" (Schlegel & Haberman, 2011, pp. 33–34). Therefore, how Marvel Phase Four heroes are presented is not arbitrary and may validate the self-image of under-represented communities in popular culture, giving these subaltern groups a space in the public debate (Brown, 2021, p. 149).

The introduction of role models pursuing progressive attitudes, like feminist She-Hulk, unprejudiced Ms. Marvel, and rebel Captain America provides powerful revolutionary images over the globe. For example, Kamala Khan's image in *Ms. Marvel* comics was used by numerous protesters against Trump's rhetoric toward immigrants and ethnic groups (Brown, 2021, p. 141). But as Berger (1972, p. 232, as cited in McSweeney, 2018) argues, "there is a fairly close relationship, generally, between a society and its heroes; if a hero does not espouse values that are meaningful to his readers, there seems little likelihood that he will be popular" (p. 36). Therefore, those post–Blip changes can be linked to the resistant and transformative role fandom, and especially fangirls, is playing in current popular culture (Scott, 2019, pp. 33–40). However, as Gray (2019, pp. 32–33) warns, this may also cause toxic fandom, disliking Marvel for embracing this underrepresented, post-racial, post-feminist world.

Despite this potential negative reaction, Marvel keeps using existing progressive values to cement its position as a contemporary factory of images, heroes, and symbols. And, with this decision, Marvel is helping to inspire change within society thanks to the creation of popular culture icons in the global reformist effort. For example, a woman in India can be empowered by the feminist discourse in *She-Hulk*; a Black U.S. citizen can become the new Captain America and make peace with the Stars and Stripes while defending Black Lives Matter; an individual in South Korea with dissociative identity disorder can find more public acceptance thanks to *Moon Knight*; a second-generation Pakistani teenager in the United Kingdom can relate with Kamala's problems in *Ms. Marvel*; and a citizen in Libya can believe a hero needs no powers to do the right thing like in *Hawkeye*.

Through its Phase Four shows *The Falcon and the Winter Soldier, Hawkeye, Moon Knight, Ms. Marvel*, and *She-Hulk: Attorney at Law* streaming on Disney+, Marvel continues to provide heroes "the world still needs" (Brown, 2021, p. 143). As a major content creator, Marvel Studios is promoting progressive societal values around the globe and redefining heroism after the Blip. Marvel keeps demonstrating that the heroes our world needs today are the ones willing to fight for the end of sexual, racial, religious, and mental prejudices in a global reality that leaves borders and labels behind. Inequality and subalternities pertain to the past, because, as Kamala Khan says, "Whatever it is, it's just gonna be another label" (Episode 6).

References

Ali, B.K. (Writer), & Feige, K., D'Esposito, L., Alonso, V., Winderbaum, B., Amanat, S., Adil & Bilall & Ali, B.K. (Executive Producers). (June 8–July 13, 2022). *Ms. Marvel* [Television series]. Marvel Studios.

Ankers-Range, A. (2022, September 2). She-Hulk episode 3's misogynistic comments were based on real Instagram comments about the show. IGN. https://www.ign.com/articles/she-hulk-episode-3-misogynistic-comments-based-on-real-instagram-criticism-of-show.

Berger, A.A. (1972). Comics and American culture. In G. Lewis (Ed.), *Side-saddle on the Golden Calf: Social structure and popular culture in America* (pp. 227–235). Goodyear.

Brown, J.A. (2021). *Panthers, Hulk and Ironhearts: Marvel, diversity and the 21st century superhero*. Rutgers University Press.

Gao, J. (Writer), & Feige, K., D'Esposito, L., Alonso, V., Winderbaum, B., Coiro, K., Gao, J. & Jacobson, W. (Executive Producers). (August 18–October 13, 2022). *She-Hulk: Attorney at Law* [Television series]. Marvel Studios.

Gramsci, A. (1971). *Selections from the prison notebooks* (Q. Hoare & G.N. Smith, ed. and trans.). Lawrence & Wishart.

Gray, J. (2019). How do I dislike thee? Let me count the ways. In M.A. Click (Ed.), Anti-fandom: Dislike and hate in the digital age (pp. 25–41). New York University Press.

Igla, J. (Writer), & Feige, K., D'Esposito, L., Alonso, V., Tran, T., Winderbaum, B., Thomas, R. & Igla, J. (Executive Producers). (November 24-December 22, 2021). *Hawkeye* [Television series]. Marvel Studios.

Louai, El H. (2012). Retracing the concept of the subaltern from Gramsci to Spivak: Historical developments and new applications. *African Journal of History and Culture, 4*(1), 4–8.

McSweeney, Terence (2018). *Avengers assemble! Critical perspectives on the Marvel Cinematic Universe*. Wallflower Press.

Russo, A. & J. (Directors). (2018). *Avengers: Infinity War* [Film]. Marvel Studios.

Russo, A. & J. (Directors). (2019). *Avengers: Endgame* [Film]. Marvel Studios.

Schleger, J. & Haberman, F. (2011). "You took my advice about theatricality a bit … literally": Theatricality and cybernetics of good and evil in Batman Begins, The Dark Knight, Spider-Man and X-Men. In R.J. Gray & B. Kaklamanidou (Eds.), *The 21st century superhero: Essays on gender, genre and globalization in film*. McFarland.

Slater, J. (Writer), & Feige, K., D'Esposito, L., Alonso, V., Winderbaum, B., Curtis, G., Isaac, O., Diab, M. & Slater, J. (Executive Producers). (March 30–May 4, 2022). *Moon Knight* [Television series]. Marvel Studios.

Spellman, M. (Writer), & Feige, K., D'Esposito, L., Alonso, V., Moore, N., Skogland, K. & Spellman, M. (Executive Producers). (March 19–April 23, 2021). *The Falcon and the Winter Soldier* [Television series]. Marvel Studios.

"This is the Way."

Reimagining Star Wars *in the Revisionism of* The Mandalorian

RAYMOND BLANTON

A Long Time Ago...

I am a child of *Star Wars*. I was a year old when the original film *Star Wars: A New Hope* (1977) (the subtitle *A New Hope* was added in 1981) debuted in theaters. My capacities for imagination have been shaped by the *Star Wars* mythos. Empire. Rebellion. Fear. Hope. I reminisce that many of my early relational dynamics with people, from parents to bullies, were creatively played out in hand-to-hand action figure conflict scenarios, complete with effusive sound effects—the "PHEW" of a blaster and the "VRMM" hum of a light saber.

In hindsight, it is both clear and compelling to me how these stories served and supplied me with a sense of personal hope and triumph. Imaginatively overcoming the maniacal laugh and diabolical plot of Emperor Palpatine meant in some small way that I might possibly overcome the various power struggles of my relationships. Beyond my childhood experience, additional prequels, sequels, and storylines spanning almost five decades have passed similar experiences on to my children and countless others. We have all become part of a *Star Wars* mythology, from the films to an array of animated series, video and board gaming, theme parks and resorts, merchandising, and more. It is an ideological galaxy animated by a treasure trove of artifacts that comprise many of our adolescent and adult identities. And because of Disney's acquisition of Lucasfilm in 2012, much of this mythos is archived on the Disney+ platform. As such, it has become a creative catalyst for much of the future of Disney programming. This is merely one of many reasons the Disney+ platform is apt for analysis.

Critical Methodology

Some believe Disney content and culture contributes to the restructuring of identities by shaping our ideas about representation that often rely on worn-out tropes and reductionistic archetypes. Thus, the central question of this project considers whether or not the original programming of Disney+ is effectively addressing these criticisms. Plus, or minus? Critically, I contend for the plus aspects of Disney+ by reimagining *Star Wars* through the revisionism of *The Mandalorian* (2019–), a space Western created by Jon Favreau. Put differently, staying close to the Latin root, *revidere,* to see again, I demonstrate how *The Mandalorian* helps us see *Star Wars* again, from a new perspective. More playfully, in the spirit of the original *Star Wars* subtitle, *The Mandalorian* offers some "new hope" for the *Star Wars* mythos.

From the outset, I want to be clear that I am a rhetorical scholar invested in the civic dimensions of mythology and popular culture. In this, I align with the work of literary and rhetorical critic, Kenneth Burke, who believed our myths, i.e., our proverbs, literature, and the like, function as equipment for living, as "admonition, solace, vengeance, foretelling, instruction, charting, all for the direct bearing that such acts have upon matters of welfare" (Burke, 1973, p. 296). From a different angle, Burke also believed that myths (i.e., not illusory) are social tools and psychological bridges useful for working together with others (Burke, 1989, p. 267); "strategic" and "stylized" answers to the questions posed by our situations (Burke, 1973, p. 1). In other words, *The Mandalorian*, drawing upon an elaborate *Star Wars* mythos, is much more than mere entertainment. Rather, it embodies strategic and stylized answers to the queries of our times. To this end, I look at the series through two particular critical lenses: a close-up and a wide-angle.

In the close-up approach, I zoom in on two central themes. First, I explore the central theme of the creed, "This Is the Way," in the story and its characters through some specific scene analyses. Second, I demonstrate how this theme is bolstered by a diverse team of creators and collaborators that enhance the story through their use of mythology and the narrative structure of the series. Altogether, these two dimensions work together to help illustrate precisely *how* the series works to reimagine and revise the *Star Wars* mythos.

In the wide-angle approach, I step back and consider *why* these methods work so effectively by exploring an ideological progression: reminiscence, reimagination, reappropriation, representation, and revision. Put differently, I argue this progression helps us see the larger framework of the *Star Wars* mythos at work in *The Mandalorian* to reclaim old stories that lend to the retelling of new stories, moving the story and the Disney+ platform forward.

Collectively, by utilizing Burke's notion of a representative anecdote, which is essentially an inductive case study method, I demonstrate how the *Star Wars* mythos animates both the creative and ideological processes at work in *The Mandalorian* and functions as equipment for living. Altogether, both of these angles are essential for understanding the layered dimensions of meaning at work and help position analysis of the plus aspects of this Disney+ original program.

Disney and Star Wars

In this section, I consider how *The Mandalorian* reimagines and revises the *Star Wars* mythos through a close analysis of the story, with a particular focus on the creed, imbued in the phrase, "This is the Way," and then explore how the design process utilizes mythology to shape its effects.

Close-Up: Take One—Story, Characters, and Scenes

As a disclaimer, my intention is to offer critical insights while at the same time cloaking certain plot developments to ensure the story is experienced as it was intended. Specifically, I focus on select scenes that foreground the backstory of *The Mandalorian* series with a particular focus on the Mandalorian character and creed. I contend these are central to the story and function as an exemplary model for many of the social issues that we face as a global society.

Additionally, I also consider, more briefly, select scenes from Seasons 2 and 3 as well as the related Disney+ series *The Book of Boba Fett* (2021) to denote how the creed remains central even as the story expands. Herein, I look closely at three developments in the story and its characters: The Mandalorian, Mandalorians, and Mandalore.

The Mandalorian

Taking place approximately five years after the events of *The Return of the Jedi* (1983) and the defeat of the Galactic Empire, *The Mandalorian* series begins and focuses on a mysterious figure—The Mandalorian, or at this time, simply, Mando. Stepping back for a moment, the earliest indications of Mandalorians comes from the original *Star Wars* trilogy and the character Boba Fett, an armored bounty hunter employed by the Galactic Empire who never removes his helmet. He first appeared in the *Star Wars*

Holiday Special (1978) and then *The Empire Strikes Back* (1980) and *Return of the Jedi* (1983).

Interestingly, it is worth noting that the Mandalorian character Boba Fett has minimal dialogue and appears for just over six minutes across the entire original trilogy (Winkie, 2022). In hindsight, although he feels like a mere stylized extra, I can attest how for many *Star Wars* fans his mysteriousness and style made him a fan favorite. For instance, for reasons that seem more instinctive than rational, he was one of my favorite action figures and characters from the series, despite his limited role. While his incomplete role was expanded in the prequel trilogy through the character Jango Fett, *The Mandalorian* series satisfied the imagination of fans who have longed for years for more cinematic backstory with the Mandalorian storyline. Moreover, this gratification coincides with new generations of fans that make the series ideal for reconsideration and revision.

This is the sentiment many *Star Wars* fans come to *The Mandalorian* series with. So, when we are introduced to Mando in *The Mandalorian,* suited in battered and variegated armor in a Mandalorian helmet, in pursuit of a bounty, reminiscent of our childhood obsession, Boba Fett, you should imagine masses of nostalgic laden adults leaping from their crumbed couch cushions with intrigue and excitement. Specifically, *The Mandalorian* series presents Mando as a man caught between competing allegiances to a professional code as a bounty hunter and a personal creed as a Mandalorian. When tasked with collecting an elusive but lucrative bounty, Mando experiences a crisis of conscience that sets the story, and the series, in motion.

We learn of his code from some of the earliest scenes in the series, but we do not learn of his creed until Episode 3 from the first season, though there are some indications of the importance of Mandalorians as a people prior to this. I have organized my analysis into two parts. First, I consider two brief scenes that provide some historical cues on Mandalorians. Second, I assess three flashback sequences that provide some backstory on Mando and his creed.

Reputation. In Season 1, Episode 1, "The Mandalorian," Mando seeks a lucrative bounty with a mysterious figure, The Client, who entices him with a bar of pure Beskar steel, which is significant because of its origins on the planet of Mandalore and for its incomparable durability (e.g., it can withstand a lightsaber). Furthermore, upon delivery of the asset, Mando is promised a camtono (a cylindrical container used to store valuables in the *Star Wars* mythos) of Beskar. Based on his reaction, the value of this bounty is highly significant to our protagonist. After Mando agrees, The Client remarks, "the Beskar belongs back into the hands of a Mandalorian. It is good to restore the natural order of things after a period of such disarray" (Favreau, 2019a). At this point, we do not know about the disarray, its origin, or duration, but we are supplied with sufficient intrigue.

Two episodes later, after Mando delivers the asset, simply referred to as The Child, an adorable childlike character who has the appearance of another fan favorite character, Yoda, from the original trilogy, we begin to see visual cues in Mando's body language that indicate a crisis of conscience. We come to learn that the crisis is influenced in part by Mando's own backstory as it coincides with that of The Child's story. Episode 3 is titled "The Sin" for a reason. As the asset is being taken away, the crisis of conscience is revealed in the form of a question when Mando asks what The Client's plans are for The Child. In so doing, he violates the Guild code:

> How uncharacteristic of one of your reputation. You have taken both commission and payment. Is it not the Code of the Guild that these events are now forgotten? That Beskar is enough to make a handsome replacement for your armor. Unfortunately, finding a Mandalorian in these trying times is more difficult than finding the steel [Favreau, 2019b].

Altogether, these scenes serve two functions. The first is the plotting of backstory with regards to the Mandalorians as well as Mando. The second illustrates why Mando risks his livelihood as a bounty hunter to rescue The Child. In essence, from one Foundling (an orphaned child taken in and adopted by Mandalorians) to another, Mando chooses to honor the Mandalorian creed over his Guild code. His creed is his way of life. And the particulars of this creed are revealed in progressive parts in Episodes 1, 3, and 8, through a series of flashbacks to Mando's childhood.

Flashbacks and Foundlings. On both occasions, after accepting the bounty and the Beskar, Mando meanders through the city of Nevarro and descends into an intricate underground tunnel system where we learn of the existence of a covert of other Mandalorians. Throughout Season 1, there are three distinct flashback sequences that provide a progressive account of a traumatic event in the life of Mando—the death of his parents. Of note, the first flashback sequence, in Episode 1, as well as the second, in Episode 3, are interspersed with sequences of an Armorer forging armor for the Mandalorian. Rich with symbolism, these sequences juxtapose the traumatic backstory of Mando, alongside the refining process of melting steel being shaped into indestructible armor. While it may seem casually cinematic, I argue it is the essence of our central character, his creed, and the series—a literal forging process that parallels a more substantive and figurative process of character forging in Mando.

In his various accounts with the Armorer, we learn of the Great Purge, which was the annihilation of the Mandalorian people and the destruction of their planet, and the importance of Foundlings (i.e., children) in

Mandalorian culture, with the latter serving a central role as it relates to the creed. But more importantly, it is a moment that reveals Mando's backstory as a Foundling, which occurs in Episode 1 and again in Episode 3.

In the first sequence, through a series of interspersed flashbacks and the forging process, we see quick-cutting fragments of a backstory, less than half a second each, totaling less than half a minute, featuring a boy and his parents running for cover through the streets with explosions all around them. This montage sequence concludes with the armorer placing the newly forged armor on his shoulder.

In Season 1, Episode 3, "The Sin," the second flashback sequence is set in motion. Mando returns to the Armorer, who fashions him a new cuirass of armor, but not before he is confronted by one of the covert Mandalorians who reveals more about the Great Purge at the hands of the Empire, which has resulted in Mandalorians having to live in hiding. But the Armorer frames the creed as a choice to "walk the Way of the Mandalore," which means to abide by the values and standards of the creed above all else, even at great personal expense (Favreau, 2019b). In a unique ritual of authentication, living the creed is conditional upon never removing your helmet. And with this, the entire Mandalorian covert recites, for the first time, "This is the Way."

It is then that the second flashback sequence convenes, again during the forging of the armor. This time, the quick cuts are a smidge longer, with the duration doubling that of the previous at just under a minute, giving us a more complete, yet still incomplete, picture of his backstory. Again, he requests that some Beskar be reserved for the Foundlings, with the Armorer declaring, "As it should always be. The Foundlings are the future," with the Mandalorian covert again echoing, "This is the Way" (Favreau, 2019b).

In Season 1, Episode 8, "Redemption," we encounter the final flashback sequence while Mando is cornered in a cantina by a mysterious Imperial leader and his squadron of storm troopers, who states:

> Your astute panic suggests that you understand your situation. I encourage a moment of consideration. Or perhaps the decommissioned Mandalorian hunter, Din Djarin, has heard the songs of the Siege of Mandalore, when gunships outfitted with similar ordinance laid waste to fields of Mandalorian recruits in The Night of a Thousand Tears [Favreau, 2019c].

Convinced he knows the identity of the mysterious Imperial leader, Mando details his theory and reveals that Mandalorians are not actually a race of people, but a creed. This initiates our third and final flashback sequence. This time, rather than the flashback being interspersed, it is an extended and complete scene of more than three minutes, revealing that

Mando's real name is Din Djarin, and was rescued by the Mandalorians, raised by the Fighting Corps, and sworn to the creed when he came of age. While there is a brief reference in Season 1, Episode 4, "Sanctuary," to the Mandalorians taking him in as a Foundling after his parents were killed, this scene provides a complete picture of the account.

In the subsequent scene, Mando encounters the Armorer one final time, this time with The Child. The Armorer alludes to songs of eons past that spoke of battles between Mandalore the Great and an order of sorcerers called Jedi. It is then that the Armorer tasks Mando with a mission by creed:

> Armorer: This is the Way. You must go. A foundling is in your care. By Creed, until it is of age or reunited with its own kind, you are as its father. This is the Way. You are a clan of two [Favreau, 2019c].

MANDALORIANS

In Season 1, the story centers on the identity of Mando and his creed in relationship to The Child, setting Season 2 in motion with Mando on a mission to reunite The Child with his kind. In particular, there are two scenes that continue to advance our story, slowly expanding beyond Mando, Din Djarin, and The Child, to a much larger story related to all Mandalorians.

In Season 2, Episode 3, "The Heiress," we learn that Mando is actually part of a faction of Mandalorians. While on a ship at sea, Mando comes into trouble and is rescued by three Mandalorians suited in blue armor: Bo-Katan Kryze (Katee Sackhoff), the leader, Koska Reeves (Mercedes Varnado), and Axe Woves (Simon Kassianides). Having accomplished his mission in search for more of his kind in order to return The Child to its kind, Mando's gratitude is cut short when the Mandalorians remove their helmets.

> MANDO: You do not cover your face. You are not Mandalorian [...]
> BO-KATAN KRYZE: You are a Child of the Watch.
> MANDO: The Watch?
> BO-KATAN KRYZE: Children of the Watch are a cult of religious zealots that broke away from Mandalorian society. Their goal was to reestablish the ancient way.
> MANDO: There is only one way. The Way of the Mandalore [Favreau, 2020].

The second scene in consideration actually comes from a related *Star Wars* series, *The Book of Boba Fett* (2021), which overlaps with *The Mandalorian*. In it we again encounter the Armorer, who is providing care and shelter to Mando. In this exchange, we learn more details about the Mandalorians—their 10,000-year history, which includes a legendary figure,

Tarre Vizsla, who was both Mandalorian and Jedi, as well as the cautionary tale of Bo-Katan Kryze and a mysterious weapon related to Mandalorian rule, their contentious history with the Empire and the loss of millions of their kind, and most especially, the creed.

Again, referencing Mandalorian songs of eons past, the Armorer speaks of the legend of the Mythosaur (i.e., a mythological creature that is symbolically important to Mandalorian culture) rising up to herald a new age of Mandalore, our first indication that the story and series is continuing to expand. At length, Mando and the Armorer speak of an underlying tension amongst Mandalorians related to Bo-Katan Kryze and the destruction of Mandalore. While alluding to their sect being cloistered on the moon of Concordia, we get our first glimpse of Mandalore during the Great Purge on the Night of a Thousand Tears as a flashback. And herein lies both the inherent tension of the Mandalorians and the essence of the creed. The Armorer explains:

> Those born of Mandalore strayed away from the path [...] Only those that walked the way escaped the curse prophesized in the Creed. Though our numbers were scattered to the winds, our adherence to the way has preserved our legacy for the generations until we may someday return to our home world [Favreau, 2022].

Again, the most ardent feature of this episode comes when Mando reveals the essence of the Mandalorian creed in contrast to the way of the Jedi, who forgo all attachment, "That is the opposite of our creed. Loyalty and solidarity are the Way" (Favreau, 2022).

Mandalore

The first season centered on Mando and The Child. The second season centered on Mando's quest to return The Child to its kind and broadened the story to include all Mandalorians. The third season continues this expansion and centers on the story of the Mandalorians coming together to explore and possibly retake their home planet, Mandalore. I briefly consider three scenes to again foreground the creed.

In Season 3, Episode 1, "Apostate," we witness two unique rituals of the Mandalorian covert. The first is the forging of Mandalorian armor, a helmet in this case. The second is a ceremony for a child of the covert, who is committing himself to the creed. Standing before the covert, the Armorer leads the service and a recitation:

> I swear on my name, and the names of the ancestors, that I shall walk the Way of the Mandalore. And the words of the Creed shall be forever forged in my heart. This is the Way. From this moment on, I shall never remove my helmet [Favreau, 2023a].

Moreover, with the creed again centered in the ever-expanding story, its relationship to Foundlings is emphasized once more in Season 3, Episode 4, "The Foundling," where we learn that the highest honor of the Creed is saving a Foundling. This harkens back to the relationship of Mando and The Child throughout the first two seasons, while at the same time advancing this idea to Bo-Katan Kryze and all Mandalorians who choose to walk the Way and live the creed.

Finally, in Season 3, Episode 7, "The Spies," we get further indication of the creed in an exchange between Bo-Katan and Mando. In this sequence, quite a fitting parallel to our own divisive world, Bo-Katan seeks to unite the Mandalorians, stating, "Our people have suffered time and again from division and squabbling factions. Mandalore has been too powerful for any enemy to defeat. It is always our own division that destroys us" (Favreau, 2023b). In a deeply empathetic and genial exchange between them, Bo-Katan acknowledges how her selfishness wrought destruction, while Mando recognizes both his misunderstanding of her and other Mandalorians as well as his commitment to embody the creed, which is about honor, loyalty, and character. Mando remarks that for thousands of years, Mandalorians have been on the verge of extinction and yet, survived, while Bo-Katan acknowledges the animosity among the Mandalorians and her doubt about being able to unify them.

In sum, the scenes work collectively to demonstrate the centrality of the Mandalorian creed—a way of life bound by honor, loyalty, character, and solidarity. To demonstrate the essential nature of the creed, consider one of the final scenes from Season 3, and the fact that "This is the Way" is recited seven different times by the Armorer, Mando, and the Mandalorians. From beginning to almost end (with Season 4 in development), the creed is at the heart of our story and also has immense value as an exemplary model for living. Indeed, over the course of three seasons, what is becoming clearer is the creed is not merely an individuated practice. It is communal. Stronger together has become one of the core ideals of the story and the characters.

Close-Up: Take Two—Designers and Design

Having spent considerable time and space assessing the story and characters to foreground the Mandalorian creed, another close-up consideration concerns how the diverse creators and collaborators use mythology and aesthetics to deepen these connections.

Creators and Collaborators

Keeping the centrality and communal nature of the creed in mind, series creator Jon Favreau has noted, "I think part of what's fun about the experience of making *The Mandalorian* is that it's a team. It's a team of creative people working together" (Bestenheider & Covington, 2020). I believe communality is central to all effective storytelling. Herein, as well, the beauty of the story lies in its communal threads. The same is true of the design team, with each bringing an affinity for the *Star Wars* mythos and advancing it for future creators and collaborators. One of the series directors, Rick Famuyiwa, has affirmed this:

> The spirit of *Star Wars* has always been about these young dreamers, and so.... What I feel is so great about the team that's coming together is that everyone is coming with their own experiences to a universe in a galaxy that can support it. And I think Jon wants to see that, and everyone's going to have their own different point of view of what makes *Star Wars* special to them. But I think that's exactly why the show is so exciting, because they can hold all of that, because the galaxy has always been that big [Bestenheider & Covington, 2020].

With this in mind, I argue that *The Mandalorian* design team has advanced the Disney+ platform in two distinct ways as it pertains to representation, both in front of and behind the camera: race and gender.

Race. *The Mandalorian* reimagines representation. For instance, with regards to casting, traditionally, the series is vastly White in its representation—for example, consider the band of Luke Skywalker and Princess Leia Organa, Han Solo and Obi-Wan Kenobi. Yet, with *The Mandalorian,* representation is expanded and diverse. For instance, the series lead Pedro Pascal is Chilean; there is an indigenous Polynesian Māori director (Taika Waititi) and actors (Taika Waititi and Temuera Morrison); African American actor and director Carl Weathers (Greef Karga); Giancarlo Giuseppe Alessandro Esposito (Moff Gideon), born in Denmark to an Italian father and an African American mother; Iranian actor Omid Abtahi (Dr. Pershing); director Deborah Chow, a Canadian woman of Asian descent; Latino writer and director Robert Rodriguez; Nigerian American writer and director Rick Famuyiwa; iconic German filmmaker and actor Werner Herzog (The Client); Leilani Shiu (Jawa); and performance artists like Misty Rosas (Kuiil; Frog Lady). Altogether, while this does not undo or necessarily satisfy pertinent issues with representation, it is nonetheless one of the ways the series is reimagined and revised.

Gender. While gender is alluded to indirectly in the previous subsection on race, it is worth reiterating here. I contend *The Mandalorian* design team has expanded on the *Star Wars* mythos, again, both in front of and behind the camera, with broader gender representation. Similar to the ethnic expansion, the series features producer Kathleen Kennedy; director Deborah Chow; director Bryce Dallas Howard; and live-action motion capture actresses Leilani Shiu and Misty Rosas. Furthermore, as it relates to characters, consider the ways gender is revised. In the original *Star*

Wars, female leads were limited to Princess Leia. Whereas in *The Mandalorian,* prominent characters include Fennec Shand (Ming-Na Wen), Cara Dune (Gina Carano), Peli Motto (Amy Sedaris), the Armorer (Emily Swallow), Bo-Katan Kryze (Katee Scakhoff), and Ahsoka Tano (Rosario Dawson). And while some could argue that these characters play marginal roles, that cursory perception would belie the development of the larger story across three seasons and additional related series such as *The Book of Boba Fett* and *Ahsoka* (2023–). Altogether, the diverse creators and collaborators of the series serve as examples for how the *Star Wars* mythos is being reimagined and revised.

Mythology

I contend there are two particular ways the creators and collaborators of the series coalesce the larger themes of the Mandalorian creed through their utilization of mythology and aesthetics. To be clear, by mythology I intend the etymological sense of *mythos* as essential story, i.e., the stories that seemingly all stories are about—belonging, journeys, and hope, for instance. In other words, mythology is the lifeblood of the *Star Wars* mythos, and makes it possible for the series to build on this with *The Mandalorian.* For instance, actor Carl Weathers, who directs Episode 5 in Season 2 of *The Mandalorian*, notes:

> As I became more of a student of filmmaking, I really began to appreciate the brilliance of *Star Wars*, and what Lucas had created. And then, I, of course, started to read more. Joseph Campbell's *The Hero with a Thousand Faces* [Bestenheider & Covington, 2020].

More precisely, Weathers is grounding his creative work in mythology—in an essential or archetypal story that lends perspective beyond the screen to underlying implications for humanity. Relatedly, I believe Kenneth Burke's conception of the idea is keen for my purposes:

> Myths may be wrong, or they may be used to bad ends, but they cannot be dispensed with [...] they are our basic psychological tools for working together. A hammer is a carpenter's tool; a wrench is a mechanic's tool; and a "myth" is the social tool for welding the sense of interrelationships [...]. In this sense a myth that works well is as real as food, tools, and shelter are. They are not "illusions," since they perform a very real and necessary social function in the organizing of the mind [Burke, 1989, p. 267–268].

Simply put, Burke marks myth as that which performs real and necessary social functions. It is equipment for living.

Star Wars Mythos. Altogether, the design team's use of mythology, both draws from and builds on the *Star Wars* mythos. It is an ideological universe. The Millennium Falcon. Chewbacca. Yoda. Dagobah system.

Darth Vader. Luke Skywalker. These are the mythological means by which George Lucas imagined his stories. From the beginning, Lucas has always brought in collaborators to expand the possibilities of the story. This has also been true of the production of *The Mandalorian*. For instance, director Rick Famuyiwa notes:

> I really love *Star Wars* and obsessed over it in many different ways. And what was always cool about Star Wars was that it was a galaxy, and therefore, as a kid growing up, I always felt that there were stories within that galaxy that I could be a part of, and was a part of telling, even if it was just me and my friends, or me by myself with my action figures [Leon, 2020b].

Additionally, series lead Pedro Pascal shares in this:

> It's fascinating to experience that as a child. You know, to have your imagination so enriched by these stories. There are such universal themes in the Star Wars stories, and ironically, I think people feel that despite being fantasy, it reflects the world we actually live in, and its inclusiveness and diversity and conflict [Leon, 2020b].

In sum, mythology plays more than an inspiration role for developing plot points. It is the very means by which the creators and collaborators cultivate our imagination and our hopes about what is possible in a world stricken by disorder.

Wide-Angle: Ideology at Play

With previously listed close-up perspectives in mind, I step back and provide a wide-angle approach to *The Mandalorian* to rouse the underlying ideas that contribute to the meaning making process. In short, I am widening our view to enhance the depth of field and improve deep focus on why *The Mandalorian* is such an impactful series. While the close-up analysis provides perspective on how the story is developed, what is happening and who is responsible, the wide-angle analysis explores the ideological realm to expound upon the underlying *why* of its potential meanings. Specifically, I argue for a particular ideological process at play: reminiscence, reimagination, reappropriation, and representation. Admittedly, while this process does not necessarily have clean lines that separate one progression from the next, it is nonetheless an attempt to delineate precisely how the *Star Wars* mythos moves from its reminiscent inception to its ultimate revision.

Broadly, each of these words stands on the prefix, "re," meaning, again. In other words, this critical analysis is an attempt to consider, by reconsidering. At times, repeated encounters broaden our understanding. This is perhaps one of the essential pluses of Disney+ programming.

It enables us to reconsider our considerations in a new light. Sometimes there is change. Other times not. But it is worth reconsidering.

Reminiscence

We begin with reminiscence. It means to remember again, which houses another again, remember. Remember means to be mindful, again. In both instances, we are mindfully looking back. It is memory in motion. And our memories are animated by artifacts, sounds, images, and the like. As I write this, for instance, I have a direct line of sight to my original C-3PO action figure on my desk, and am seated adjacent to an entire wall of graphic designed *Star Wars* prints and posters. But memory is reliable only to a point, however. It is not neutral. It is complicated by the imperfections of human perception, selective reflections, and by both individual and social constructions of identity and reality.

Reimagination

Thus, in order to reminisce, we must reimagine. We resummon an image. Literally, it is an act of creation. As we reminisce, we reimage both time and place. Perhaps we reimagine a preferred identity in contrast to an actual identity. This reimaging is mental and thus empirical and emotional. And these mental states become embodied in objects—old drawings, vintage t-shirts, toys, sounds and songs, and these are deified into even more objects—layer upon layer. For instance, the *Star Wars* theme song, written and conducted by John Williams, can become an anthem march in the mind to oppose the perils of the everyday "Empire" of uncertainty and responsibility. More than a nostalgic sentiment, these acts of remembrance and reimaging turn our memories into companions.

Reappropriation

Altogether, reminiscences and reimagining lead us to reappropriate our memories of meaning for a new time and place. We make them over in our image for a new moment. Reappropriating means to take as one's own. Cultural appropriation has a lot of cultural capital in confronting mindless misappropriations of cultural values, rituals, and ideals. But it also embodies value for learning how to take a seemingly innocuous memory, meaning, or moment from our past and enlist it for further regard or a greater purpose. It does not have to be only negative. It does have positive potential as well.

When I reminisce about my *Star Wars* adolescence, for instance, that remembering and reimagining is being reappropriated in the form of *The Mandalorian*. And the reappropriated form is merging (literally) with the formation of the childhood of my children. It becomes a manifestation of my past and yet their future reminiscence. When I take a memory of connection with a character like Luke Skywalker, for example, and his quest for purpose, as I remember and reimagine it through other character like Rey in *Star Wars: The Force Awakens* (2015) or Mando in *The Mandalorian* (2019–), it is being functionally reappropriated into a commemorative moment with my children. It is this sort of emotional and relational mingling that is important as it relates to the potential of *The Mandalorian* for reimagining and revising the *Star Wars* mythos.

Representation and Revision

Reappropriation longs for a new manifestation, a representation, an ideological or actual body. In short, representation is a manifestation of our stories, meaning, literally, to place before. Collectively, this ideological process functions as a means toward revisionism—literally, to see again. In other words, *The Mandalorian* is essentially a means through which we can see *Star Wars* again, anew. However, if we focus our attention only on representation without understanding the other dimensions that contribute to it, then we are likely missing layers and dimensions worth considering. Having outlined a framework for this substantive and ideological process, a wide-angle approach, these subsequent examples explore how each is animated by the series creators and collaborators. They serve as tangible examples of the ideology in consideration.

Ideology in *The Mandalorian*. A unique way to demonstrate this process at play is found in the words of the diverse creators and collaborators of *The Mandalorian*. In essence, it is the original mythology of *Star Wars* that worked on the creators and collaborators at a young age that effectively shaped the series. In other words, only through their own process of reminiscence, reimagination, reappropriation, and representation are they able to realize their revisionism of the series.

For example, it is telling how many of the series cast and crew were inspired by their specific film experiences with *Star Wars* and other creations by George Lucas and Steven Spielberg. In interviews with the creative team, story after story turns to reminiscence—adults remembering what it was like as a child encountering *Star Wars* for the first time and then wanting to recreate that for others. Indeed, the vast majority of creators and collaborators on *The Mandalorian* series turned their nostalgia into a career and a calling. It is reminiscent of a pivotal scene in Pixar's animated film *Ratatouille* (2007), when curmudgeon critic Anton first tastes Remy's specially prepared dish, ratatouille. With that first bite, he is instantaneously transported back in time to his childhood. He remembers the care of his mother serving him a warm meal. It is a nurturing image of comfort. Similarly, *The Mandalorian* uses the *Star Wars* mythos to arouse our reminiscence by reimaging and reappropriating dimensions of these into new representations, and ultimately revising the *Star Wars* mythos for a new generation of fans.

As it relates to *The Mandalorian,* series creator Jon Favreau notes:

> I think there's an interplay with storytellers and the people you're telling the story to. You find that the emotions run deep with *Star Wars.* And peoples' relationship, especially people who grew up with it from a young age, feel a lot of connection to it. I think the one consistent thing I'm feeling is that people care deeply that it's being handled correctly and that it's being handled respectfully. It meant so much and they want to see it continue into the future and feel like it's all connected with consistency [Bestenheider & Covington, 2020].

Similarly, director Peyton Reed, referring to aspects of set design from the original *Star Wars* to *The Mandalorian* storylines, notes, "Everybody has a personal relationship with every frame of those movies" (Bestenheider & Covington, 2020); Richard Bluff, Visual Effects Supervisor, notes, "It looks like we're transported right back to the late 70s or early 80s, doing exactly the same George did, and we have that characteristic. It takes me back to when I was a kid when I wanted it. I want that model. It's pretty spectacular" (Leon, 2020a); and Hal Hickel, Animation Supervisor, notes, "We were all giddy as schoolchildren when we saw the first takes come through (referencing the Star Destroyer)" (Leon, 2020a).

Beyond the creative team behind the camera, reminiscence also applies to those in front of the camera. Series star Pedro Pascal notes, "For it to materialize in such a specific way, in such visually familiar ways, it continues to have this very surreal relationship to the actual child that you were and these movies that you saw in the movie theater" (Bestenheider & Covington, 2020). Director and writer Robert Rodriguez recalls, "I think why it's resonated so deeply with the audience is that it's just the level of surprise that comes. It's all the tropes put together in a completely new way. I think it feels very true" (Bestenheider & Covington, 2020).

Clearly, the *Star Wars* mythos and *The Mandalorian* are ideal for exploring this identification and meaning making process. Consider the nostalgic inspiration for *The Mandalorian* from series creator Jon Favreau:

> I remember seeing *Star Wars* over and over again, and the formula was one that I didn't know yet. I didn't really have a frame of reference for the source material. So that was my entry into all of the things that helped create *Star Wars.* So, through that, I learned about the western. Through that, I learned about samurai films. What I originally pitched when I went in, I said, look, I don't want to be influenced so much by *Star Wars.* You know, we definitely want to be consistent with *Star Wars*, but I want to be influenced by the stuff

> that influenced George, so let's really look at the samurai movies. Let's really look at Kurosawa films. And that kind of led to the whole *Lone Wolf and Cub* thing that also felt like it applied in certain ways [Leon, 2020a].

In other words, his reminiscence for *Star Wars* initiated the ideological process I have outlined. He reminisced and reimagined and began reappropriating the *Star Wars* mythos for his own time and purposes. He then began writing and collaborating with others to form new representations and revise the *Star Wars* mythos.

With an understanding of the significant reach of reminiscence, it becomes important to be attuned to the process that then unfolds. I argue that reminiscence leads to an initial reimagination. For content creators and artists, this eventually moves from an internal realm to an actual creative realm—acting, producing, writing, directing, creating and so forth. In the behind-the-scenes docuseries, *Disney Gallery: The Mandalorian* (2020), the sentiment of the design team is consistently about honoring the legacy of *Star Wars,* from set design to reimagining marginal characters. For instance, a brief scene depicting the skeletal structure of a large creature in the original film is reimagined as an actual foe featured in the opening episode (Episode 1) of Season 2 in *The Mandalorian*. Thus, as we reimagine, we come to a new layer: reappropriation.

With a sense of the relationship of reminiscence to reimagination, this then manifests in reappropriating the mythos of *Star Wars* into story and character development in *The Mandalorian.* In an obvious sense, *The Mandalorian* is a reappropriation of the *Star Wars* mythos. It is inspired by and based on the *Star Wars* galaxy, and yet, it is *original content.* Beyond merely borrowing from *Star Wars,* though, the creative team focused on reappropriating the influences on George Lucas and his intellectual property, i.e., westerns and samurai films.

Series writer and producer Dave Filoni regards *The Mandalorian* as a primer of westerns, with a focus on simplicity and complex characterizations. For instance, from the original films, Han Solo is dressed like a gunslinger. Moreover, for further example, the creators reappropriated a concept drawing of an insect from the original films and built Episode 2 from Season 2 of *The Mandalorian* around this reimagined and reappropriated creature. So, the ideological process at play begins with reminisce and then to reimagination, reappropriation, and representation before ultimately revising the original into something new.

In sum, this wide-angle consideration illustrates the meaning making process imbued into the close-up considerations. For those of us who grew up with the mythos, we are learning to see *Star Wars* again through a revised lens with a more robust representation. In the case of *The Mandalorian,* the *Star Wars* mythos has been reminisced, reimagined, reappropriated, re-represented, and revised. Moreover, this process sets the stage for future iterations of the *Star Wars* universe, such as the series *Ashoka.*

Conclusion

In this essay, I have attempted to delineate a framework for understanding and appreciating the particular ways that *The Mandalorian*, its creators and collaborators, by way of mythology, are advancing the *Star Wars* mythos through an ideological process of reminiscing, reimagining, reappropriating, re-representing, and, ultimately, revising. I believe these processes provide sufficient evidence of the plus aspects of the Disney+ platform and its original programming. Moreover, leaning into the civic and critical dimensions of Kenneth Burke, I also contend that the Mandalorian creed is not only the heart of the story and its central characters, but also an exemplary model for civic engagement.

While some may quickly rebuff this notion as wishful idealism, what are our other options? As I see it, one viable option is to consider how this series and its varied themes and characters contribute to our cultural moment. Just as in the series, *The Mandalorian* is no longer solely about one Mandalorian. It is about all Mandalorians, bound by a creed of honor, loyalty, character, and solidarity. It is about their hope for renewal and the reclamation of their home, Mandalore. These are sentiments any human can stand for. It is my contention, then, and my hope, that *The Mandalorian* is more than just another streaming series. In essence, it is a mythological tool useful for our living together—equipment for our living. Put another way, as Hugh Duncan notes in the introduction to Kenneth Burke's *Permanence and Change:*

> If in the suffering and horror of our time, we can develop a method for the analysis of what symbols do to us in our relations with each other, we may yet learn to lead a better life. Such is Burke's message to our time [Burke, 1984, p. xliii].

Thus, amidst the disarray and divisiveness of our cultural and ceaselessly mediated moment, the Mandalorian creed becomes an embodiment of empathy, to commitment and compassion. It creatively and effectively reimagines and revises the *Star Wars* mythos. Indeed, while there are varied and valued minuses to consider, from hegemonic ideologies and revisionism to blind spots in representation that ignore disempowerments related to race and gender, there are, in my estimation, pluses that effectively confront these criticisms and help propel us forward. We are, as the series promotes, stronger together. "This is the Way."

References

Bestenheider, B., & Covington, B. (Writer), & Baruh, B. (Director). (2020). Making of season 2 [Television series episode]. In Favreau, J. (Producer), *Disney gallery: The Mandalorian.* Los Angeles: Lucasfilm.
Burke, K. (1973). *The philosophy of literary form.* University of California Press.
Burke, K. (1984). *Permanence and change.* University of California Press.
Burke, K. (1989). Revolutionary symbolism in America. In H.W. Simons & S. Melia (Eds.), *The legacy of Kenneth Burke.* University of Wisconsin Press.
Favreau, J. (Writer), & Chow, D. (Director). (2019b, November 22). The sin [Television series episode]. In Favreau, J. (Producer), *The Mandalorian.* Los Angeles: Lucasfilm.
Favreau, J. (Writer), & Famuyiwa, R. (Director). (2023a, March 1). The apostate [Television series episode]. In Favreau, J. (Producer), *The Mandalorian.* Los Angeles: Lucasfilm.
Favreau, J. (Writer), & Famuyiwa, R. (Director). (2023b, April 12). The spies [Television series episode]. In Favreau, J. (Producer), *The Mandalorian.* Los Angeles: Lucasfilm.
Favreau, J. (Writer), & Filoni, D. (Director). (2019a, November 12). The Mandalorian [Television series episode]. In Favreau, J. (Producer), *The Mandalorian.* Los Angeles: Lucasfilm.
Favreau, J. (Writer), & Howard, B.D. (Director) (2020, November 13). The heiress [Television series episode]. In Favreau, J. (Producer), *The Mandalorian.* Los Angeles: Lucasfilm.
Favreau, J. (Writer), & Howard, B.D. (Director). (2022, January 26). Return of the Mandalorian [Television series episode]. In Favreau, J. (Producer), *The Book of Boba Fett.* Los Angeles: Lucasfilm.
Favreau, J. (Writer), & Waititi, T. (Director). (2019c, December 27). Redemption [Television series episode]. In Favreau, J. (Producer), *The Mandalorian.* Los Angeles: Lucasfilm.
Kasdan, J. (Director). (2022). Gang of outsiders [Television series episode]. In Favreau, J. (Producer), *Light & magic.* Los Angeles: Lucasfilm.
Leon, M. (Writer), & Baruh, B. (Director). (2020a). Legacy [Television series episode]. In Favreau, J. (Producer), *Disney gallery: The Mandalorian.* Los Angeles: Lucasfilm.
Leon, M. (Writer), & Baruh, B. (Director). (2020b). Process [Television series episode]. In Favreau, J. (Producer), *Disney gallery: The Mandalorian.* Los Angeles: Lucasfilm.
Winkie, L. (2022, February 2). *How fandom sent Boba Fett from minor character to leading man.* Vox. https://www.vox.com/2022/2/2/22913238/boba-fett-explained-star-wars-disney.

A Great Disturbance...

Andor, *Diversity, and Representation in the* Star Wars *Universe*

JOHN PERLICH *and* TIM BAIRD

Some might say that America in the 1970s was dreadful. Others would say the '70s were painful. Hatmaker (2015) even went on record, calling it "the worst decade ever," providing a list of evidence (Hatmaker, 2015, para. 4):

> 1970: Invasion of Cambodia.
> 1970: Beatles break up.
> 1972: Watergate.
> 1972: 11 Israeli Olympians killed.
> 1972: Tropical Storm Agnes.
> 1973: Gas crisis begins in America, resulting in long lines at gas stations and the even/odd license plate rule.
> 1973: Mobile phone was invented (which eventually turned us all into texting fiends).
> 1977: Elvis Presley dies.
> 1979: Saddam Hussein becomes president of Iraq.
> 1979: Iranian Revolution.
> 1979: Americans held hostage in the U.S. embassy at Tehran.

Let us not forget the fact that President Jimmy Carter gave his "Crisis of Confidence" speech in 1979. Hatmaker's comments resonate with at least one of the authors who wrote this essay; "it was a tough decade!" However, a bright spot emerged on May 25, 1977—the premier of *Star Wars* (or, *Star Wars—A New Hope* [*ANH*] when re-released in 1981).

Star Wars seemingly changed everything—with innovative storytelling, special effects, and captivating characters, this film introduced audiences to a universe unlike anything seen before. The opening crawl, with its iconic text scrolling into space, immediately immersed audiences in a grand adventure. In short, *Star Wars* revolutionized the motion picture industry. The film's immense success led to sequels, prequels, spin-offs, animated series, and an expansive universe of novels, comics, videogames, and merchandise. Unfortunately, while *Star Wars ANH* was credited with changing nearly everything about film and filmmaking, the movie was not well regarded in the representation of diversity and marginalized voices, despite including James Earl Jones' voice (behind a mask).

Unsurprisingly, criticisms about the *Star Wars* universe continued for decades. Covarrubias (2021) explains:

> With the release of "The Force Awakens" in 2015, a study by Variety showed that the amount of dialogue spoken by female characters tripled from the amount that was in [*Star Wars*] "A New Hope." But that still just means that women spoke only 27.8% of the dialogue in "The Force Awakens," despite having a female lead in Rey (Daisy Ridley). That, however, is more than "Rogue One" (2016) can say. That film has only 18.1% of its dialogue spoken by women, again despite having a female lead in Jyn Erso (Felicity Jones). [*Star Wars*] should have room for all kinds of diverse voices and characters, with representation from all corners of the galaxy.

Translation ... *Star Wars ANH* provided a poor representation of diverse populations, and the situation did not immediately improve. Yes, Lando Calrissian (Billy Dee Williams) was offered up by George Lucas as the first unmasked BIPOC (Black, Indigenous and People of Color) character in the *Star Wars* universe, and Lando later doubled as a pansexual in Jonathan Kasdan's writing of *Solo: A Star Wars Story* (2018)—nonetheless, such accolades were dubious in nature. As Moungabio (2018, para. 5) put it, "on reflection, shouldn't we have arrived here sooner? For a galaxy home to a whole swathe of different characters, races and planets—one has to wonder, where's all that diversity at?" Thankfully, there has been a "great disturbance" in the force of hegemonic influence via the Disney+ *Star Wars* series titled *Andor* (2022–).

Disney+ (as a streaming service) allows producers, writers, directors, and an entire corporation the opportunity to reinvent history. In this essay, we argue that the Disney+ series *Andor* has provided an opportunity to revisit, challenge, and rewrite identities that are represented (or invisible) in the canonical *Star Wars* universe. Series creator Tony Gilroy set out to change the history of *Star Wars* with *Andor*, quickly earning critical acclaim. On a percentile scale (with 100 percent representing perfection) the first ten episodes of *Andor* registered 92 percent, 89 percent, 92 percent, 90 percent, 100 percent, 100 percent, 100 percent, 94 percent, 100 percent, and 100 percent respectively—as per Rotten Tomatoes. According to Pye (2023), reviews like this are impressive considering that the series' main characters have been described as "complex, sometimes morally ambiguous, creatures compelled by their own pain and sense of justice to meddle in machinations that would, in less dire circumstances, be too great for them to consider" (para. 4). Although some might argue the representation of diverse identities within the Star Wars cinematic universe has been evolving for years (e.g., *The Book of Boba Fett*, wherein Temura Morrison [who is Māori] plays the title character, and co-lead Ming-Na Wen is Chinese American), we believe Andor represents a new level of ambition in representation of diverse identities. In short, the characters (and actors) in *Andor* reflect the inherent complexity of culture. Our goal in this essay is to explore the representation of diversity in *Andor* within the framework of Bakhtin's heteroglossia.

Theoretical Framing

Our analysis of *Andor* is grounded in cultural studies—an interdisciplinary field that emerged in the late twentieth century, focusing on the analysis of culture, society, and power. Cultural critics seek to understand how meaning is produced, circulated, and consumed within a particular social and historical context. As a process of inquiry, cultural critics explore various forms of media, recognizing that texts do not exist in isolation, but are deeply embedded in cultural, social, and political contexts. Within this framework, cultural critics interpret texts to uncover their underlying meanings and ideological assumptions. One of the most well-known theorists in the world of cultural criticism is Russian literary critic Mikhail Bakhtin, who was writing well before the emergence of cultural studies, but who, nonetheless, has influenced many contemporary cultural critics. Bakhtin argues that the meaning that we give to words or objects is the result of conversations with a multitude of others. Bakhtin (1996) described heteroglossia; the unfolding of language that goes on around any object; "the dialectics of the object are interwoven with the social dialogue surrounding it" (p. 278). Rather than assuming that homogeneity and stability represent the norm; mobility, mixing, political dynamics, and historical embedding are now central concerns in the study of texts. We can see this idea in something as simple as an apple. If we describe an apple, it is a fruit. It has a specific color and flavor when eaten. However, if we look at the heteroglossia and layered meaning of an apple, we see health, knowledge, a gift for the favored teacher, or even original sin. In other words, meaning is both connotative and denotative, and evolves through time.

We—as an authorial team—have identified the 70s (or *Star Wars* era) as a transitional decade that exemplifies an ushering of heteroglossia (positioned between the protest movements of the 60s and the hedonistic 80s); working toward new articulations of power, identity, and discourse. If America in the late 1960s was characterized by revolution and liberation, the 1970s was a hangover. In the wake of race riots, war protests, and a culture crisis, U.S. citizens were dazed and confused about how to move forward. The 70s became a slow adjustment to heteroglossia—an understanding that we are not all the same, we do not share identical experiences, and our differences are more important than our similarities.

Heteroglossia

Before discussing the representation of diversity in *Andor*, it is important to understand Bakhtin's heteroglossia. Heteroglossia refers to the coexistence of multiple voices or discourses within a single text or conversation. According to Bakhtin, language is always in a state of flux, and it is constantly being shaped and reshaped by various cultural, social, and historical forces. This means that a text or conversation is never static, but rather, it is constantly evolving and changing in response to the various voices that are present within it and anticipates future utterances that will reshape its meaning. Even though Bakhtin developed the concept of heteroglossia in his critiques of the novel, the application of the concept to mass mediated entertainment and art is nothing new. Scholars have used the concept to deconstruct popular culture, critique movies, highlight feminist themes in comics, and even understand Afrofuturist transmedia world building (Balinisteanu, 2012; Hassler-Forest, 2017; Hoy, 1992; Kijinski, 1987; Rowe, 2008).

Bakhtin's theory of heteroglossia suggests that symbols are inherently dynamic, diverse, and (inevitably) divergent. Therefore, symbols have important implications for the representation of culture and identity in texts, media, and language. If language and symbols are inherently multifaceted, which we can see in online reactions to any new movie, TV series, or viral scandal, then representations of social groups in media can provide a window into the cultural zeitgeist for every story being told. If we take the meaning of heteroglossia to heart, then the voices of diverse social groups cannot be removed from our lived realities; the omission or sidelining of diversity (even in fictional worlds) must be representative of something larger.

As *Star Wars* comes to terms with its expanding universe, it is experiencing what Appadurai (1996) defines as a rupture in a cultural narrative, or as he puts it, a "break between past and present" (p. 3). While exploring a diverse universe, authors of *Star Wars* (content and programs) are confronting a split between voices that advocate for the status quo and those who advocate for representation of marginalized identities. Appadurai (1996) emphasizes the value of these ruptures in our cultural narratives by highlighting the "work of imagination as a constitutive feature of modern subjectivity" (p. 3). This means that the ongoing narrative shift or "rupture" that reflects tension within a collective imagination—and shapes the *Star Wars* universe—does not exist within one person, or even one group of people's imagination. Rather it is dispersed across the imaginations and shared spaces of anyone who is compelled to contribute. The shared imagination that Appadurai highlights is the context where the work of heteroglossia takes place. The collective imagination is where the voices of the writers, fans, or anyone else who is interested performs a collective, but not necessarily cooperative, task of creation, definition, and editing. Much like the cultural narratives that have shaped our politics, education, and communities over the last few decades, the conversation about diversity, difference, and divergence has taken root in the collective imagination of the *Star Wars* universe, and the heteroglossia of all interested parties within the conversation define a transition between past and present.

Heteroglossia is manifest in the ongoing dialogue amongst *Star Wars* fans, who argue about what "is" or "is not" real (or important, or valuable) in a fictional universe. As Bakhtin (1996) implied, every community has its own language, with "internal differentiation, the stratification characteristic of any national language" (p. 67). Stratification within a fandom is natural and can be drawn along many lines. It does not matter if you think diversity in *Star Wars* is important, or if *Star Wars* canon should dictate the future. Every *Star Wars* fan can find a community (and discussion thread) tailored just for them. As an example, while many believe an intentionally diverse galaxy far, far away (as depicted in *Andor*) represents great strides for the franchise, others (Toto, 2023) lament "Team Disney" as it continues to "push woke storytelling"—"What about a good story, memorable characters and themes that connect to the classic 'Star Wars' trilogy? Seems important, no?" (para. 17). Only time can tell us which narratives in the Disney universe will resonate with contemporary culture and conscience.

When Disney launched its streaming service in 2019, it was forced to confront the stratified heteroglossia amongst most of the fandoms it served (e.g., the Marvel universe). Bakhtin (1981) points out, "any direct word and especially that of the dominant discourse is reflected as something more or less bounded, typical and characteristic of a particular era, aging, dying, ripe for change and renewal" (p. 60). For years, Disney had been one of the main sources of dominant discourse when it came to the realm of entertainment, and the *Star Wars* universe shaped an entire sci-fi genre. But, with its new content, Disney made a choice to lean into the heteroglossia that shaped and surrounded various fandoms. Consequently, this broadened the collective imagination and provided space for traditionally underrepresented or marginalized voices to join the conversation. At the risk of alienating segments of the fandom, Disney made the decision to include new voices, faces, and perspectives within the *Star Wars* universe.

The adage, "this aged poorly," has been colloquially used to represent the process wherein something once considered innocuous has become troublesome. There are many examples of Disney productions and representations that have become problematic with the passage of time. One of the most well-documented artifacts was the 1946 musical film, the *Song of the South* (*SoS*). As a film, *SoS* was in many ways revolutionary, combining live action with animated characters in a manner that would pioneer a variety of future productions. The star of *SoS*, James Baskett, would later be recognized with an honorary Oscar for his performance as Uncle Remus. Despite the accolades that *SoS* received during the late 40s, it has also been dubbed "deeply racist, presenting a false, romanticized version of plantation life in a post–Civil War South" (Silverio, 2022, para. 3). "In January 2023, Splash Mountain at the Magic Kingdom closed as a result of backlash directed toward *SoS*; the closure was framed as Disney taking steps to erase the ride's racist back story" (Tumin, 2023, para. 5). The ride is scheduled to be closed and reinvented at all Disney parks. Additionally, children raised during the Baby Boomer generation are likely troubled to learn that *SoS*, a childhood favorite film, may never leave the Disney vault.

Although *Star Wars ANH* may not draw a strong parallel with *SoS*, it has an equally problematic past. As previously noted, troubling issues regarding representation have been raised about recent *Star Wars* films. However, the Disney+ series *Andor*, with its multifaceted diversity, representation of indigenous voices, and complicated view of the rebellion, is the clear choice to demonstrate how Disney leveraged their streaming platform and heteroglossia to revise cultural narratives. Premiering in September 2022, *Andor* focuses on Cassian Andor (played by Diego Luna) and the beginnings of a rebellion against the Galactic Empire.

Representations of Diversity in Andor

In this section of our essay, we will explore the changing face of representation and diversity within the *Star Wars* universe via *Andor*, the series. As previously noted, representations of diversity in *Star Wars*—with the obvious exception of fictional alien races—are criticized as being tokenistic and superficial. The characters of color have often been relegated to supporting roles, and their stories have not been fully developed. *Andor* seeks to change this by putting diversity at the forefront of the show by featuring a diverse cast of characters, including people of color, women, and LGBTQ+ characters.

Characters of Diverse Representation

Andor serves as a prequel to the events of the film *Rogue One: A Star Wars Story*. The movie features the character of Cassian Andor (heretofore referred to as Cassian), played by Diego Luna, who is a Rebel Alliance intelligence officer. The story takes place during the early days of the Rebellion against the tyrannical rule of the Galactic Empire. Cassian, a skilled spy and soldier, is dedicated to the cause of the Rebellion and is determined to do whatever it takes to bring down the Empire. The *Andor* series delves into Cassian's backstory, exploring his experiences, motivations, and the challenges he faces while working undercover to gather intelligence for the Rebel Alliance.

The plot of *Andor* revolves around Cassian's dangerous missions and covert operations. He forms a team of unlikely allies, including other rebels, spies, and droids, as they navigate through a galaxy filled with Imperial forces, crime syndicates, and various other threats. Throughout the series, viewers witness the complex and morally ambiguous nature of Cassian's character, as he makes difficult choices and sacrifices in the name of the Rebellion. The series explores themes of loyalty, sacrifice, and the personal cost of fighting for a cause.

The story of Cassian reveals much about the nature of Imperial rule—the Galactic Empire is not particularly diverse or inclusive. In fact, Cassian's backstory illustrates the apathy that often characterizes the Imperial agenda. Starwars.com (www.starwars.com/databank/cassian-andor) explains the history of Cassian.

> Although he's long claimed to be from the world of Fest, Cassian was once known as Kassa on Kenari. A lush jungle planet all-but destroyed by a mining accident, Kassa and his sister, Kerri, lived among a tribe of youngsters who survived on the untamed planet. When he was adopted by Maarva and Clem Andor at the age of 9, Cassian left Kenari behind, but could not shake thoughts of his sister [para. 2].

The environmental damage done to Kenari demonstrates an Imperial agenda that is willing to sacrifice the lives of indigenous people. Bacon (2022), contends that the cover of a mining accident was intended to conceal a larger atrocity:

> This seems to be the Empire's go-to excuse for any disaster, a lie told whenever any atrocity was committed. When Jedha was destroyed by the Death Star,

> they claimed it was a planet-scaled mining accident; some tie-ins have suggested the Empire briefly tried to use the same excuse for Alderaan as well. These examples suggest that, although Kenari was used for mining, the official line conceals an intentional atrocity that ravaged the planet [para. 3].

As a series, *Andor* introduces us to a variety of diverse indigenous people who are victims under Imperial duress.

Imperial disparagement toward indigenous people is further exemplified later in the *Andor* series, as explained by Speicher (2022):

> In Episode 6 of *Andor*, entitled, "The Eye," the Dhani tribes of the northern lowlands of Aldhani are in the process of making their pilgrimage to see the holy, atmospheric phenomenon known as, "The Eye of Aldhani" at the walls of the Imperial garrison. Awaiting them is Commandant Jayhold Beehaz (Stanley Townshend) and a collection of high-ranking Imperial officers (including his superior, Colonel Petigar) who view the event not as a spiritual phenomenon, but simply as an Imperial Viewing Festival. Speaking to them, casually, Jayhold describes the Dhani people as, "simple" and "easy to manipulate." He goes on to describe how the Empire's Machiavellian methods for dealing with the Dhani have served them well over the twelve-year occupation of Aldhani.

The *Andor* series quite intentionally puts imperial policy under the microscope, while simultaneously putting a spotlight on a variety of indigenous groups and people. Visibility for previously marginalized groups is a key feature of the series.

Gender and Sexuality

Although some might argue that a same-sex *Star Wars* relationship was seen in the background during a celebratory scene within *The Rise of Skywalker* (2019), others might contend that the characters Orka and Flix are considered a couple in the animated series *Star Wars Resistance* (2018–2020), many believe that *Andor* has provided the most compelling portrait of diversity in the presentation of gender and sexuality. When describing their reaction to *Andor*, Shatto (2022) asserted,

> We finally got the queer characters we've been craving—and they didn't even die. We're of course talking about Vel Sartha (Faye Marsay) and Cinta Kaz (Varada Sethu), leader and member, respectively, of the rebel cell that Andor finds himself embedded in after his escape from his home on Ferrix [para. 1].

Initially, it seemed that Cinta might play the role of love-interest for Cassian. However, another member of the rebel group (Skeen) squashes the potentially heteronormative moment one morning when Cinta emerged from her tent, saying, "She's already sharin' a blanket, if that's what your wonderin." Skeen is clearly "referring to Vel, who also exits the hut, wearing a blanket" (Shatto, 2022, para. 5). In the mind of Shatto (2022, para. 11), Episodes 4, 5, and 6 of *Andor* provide "what fans have been demanding: unambiguous queerness between two characters of import and with actual character development. Best of all, both women seemingly survive the mission—although many of their compatriots don't."

With regard to gender representation, many might contend that the *Star Wars* universe has seen its share of strong female lead characters—Princess Leia Organa, Padme Amidala, and Rey all come to mind. However, one female lead character is reintroduced in *Andor*—Mon Mothma, the Chandrilan politician, senator, and a founding member of the Alliance to Restore the Republic. Credited as being a "bad-ass," Stahl (2022) points out that Mon Mothma would eventually go on to become Chancellor of the New Republic following the Battle of Endor according to canon (para. 1). Mon is allowed to truly perform the "Iron-Willed" female as she finances a rebellion, navigates a tense relationship within her arranged marriage, and attempts to understand her teenage daughter.

Andor is filled with other strong female characters. Dedra Meero (Denise Gough) is an Imperial Security Bureau officer trying to climb the ranks in a male-dominated Empire—she is tasked with bringing in the terrorist, Cassian. Another strong female lead in the series, Bix Caleen, is played by Puerto Rican actress Adria Arjona, who says about Bix, "I think she's fearless and she's bold, yet really deep inside, she's incredibly loyal and compassionate and cares a little too much for the people around her. I think that's sometimes at her own detriment" (Zaid, 2022, para. 13). Zaid (2022) explains why Bix Caleen is a particularly powerful character:

> Perhaps the most empowering bit about Bix is that she brings further inspiration and representation to the diverse world of *Star Wars*. Whilst *Andor* is at its heart a spy-thriller and drama, the [series] does dabble in socio-political issues, particularly the immigrant experience that many People of Color face in their everyday life. And where that storyline is effectively explored through Mexican actor Diego Luna's Cassian, Arjona's Bix is yet another character that young Hispanic children can look up to and see themselves in [para. 15].

The strong female characters depicted in this series will undoubtedly be remembered by *Star Wars* fans. *Andor* intentionally increases representation of marginalized groups.

Disability

In addition to its portrayal of gender and sexuality, *Andor* also addresses issues of disability and mental health. In an interview with *Entertainment Weekly*, Diego Luna revealed Cassian struggles with PTSD as a result of his lived experience. Cassian, or "Kassa," lost his parents as a child. He was adopted by Maarva and Clem Andor, and watched as his new father was killed by an Imperial garrison on the streets of Ferrix. The trauma of his early childhood was only the beginning for Cassian. We see Cassian's ongoing struggle with PTSD unfold through several episodes of *Andor.* Freshly wounded by the loss of his mother, running from accusations of wrongdoing that could arguably be justified as self-defense, Cassian is detained for "moving too quickly" in front of an Imperial soldier (Episode 7, "Announcement"). Due to a "change in guidelines," Cassian is sentenced to six years of labor in a facility on Narkina 5. Diego Luna beautifully captures the anguish of Cassian throughout the episode ("Narkina 5")—as he is shackled, electrocuted, and beaten—his portrayal of mental strife is significant because it represents a departure from the traditional portrayal (and often invisibility) of mental health in the *Star Wars* universe. We see the eventual result of Cassian's mistreatment by the Empire at the start of *Rogue One: A Star Wars Story,* when he kills an ally in order to avoid detainment by Imperial soldiers. In portraying a character who is struggling with PTSD, *Andor* sends a powerful message to its audience.

To their credit, the producers of *Andor* gave some actors permission to develop a backstory for their characters; this allowed for a deeper exploration of mental well-being and strife. One of the most well-known actors in the *Andor* series is Andy Serkis—known for characters in *The Batman* (2022), *Venom* (2021), *Star Wars: The Last Jedi* (2017), and, perhaps best known as Gollum in the *Lord of the Rings* films. Serkis plays the role of prison supervisor Kino Loy. Serkis depicts Loy as having a dispassionate, apathetic, and detached personality (Jirak, 2022, para. 2). When crafting a backstory to justify Loy's demeanor, "Serkis imagined Kino as a shop steward who fought for workers' rights, which labeled him a troublemaker with the empire. 'When he was incarcerated, he then almost sheds any desire to look out for other people apart from himself'" (Jirak, 2022, para. 2). In other words, Serkis imagined Kino Loy as a caring and protective protagonist who was imprisoned for trying to do the right thing by his workers. The resulting victimization provided Serkis with the motivation to create a moving character with one goal in mind: "To try and get out and just survive the sentence, the torture, the desensitization. I think it was that desensitization that made me perhaps have that slightly lost but kind of hardened and toughened shell," Serkis explained (Jirak, 2022, para. 2). To their credit, the artists involved in the creation of *Andor* were allowed to explore complex motivations including PTSD and disassociation.

Intentional Casting

Significantly, *Andor* has a diverse cast of actors, including Diego Luna, Stellan Skarsgård, Adria Arjona, Fiona Shaw, and Genevieve

O'Reilly. The actors come from a variety of different ethnic backgrounds, and this diversity is reflected in their characters, who come from different planets and have different cultural backgrounds. Compare the cast list of *Star Wars ANH* with the cast of *Andor* and you will notice some stark differences. Names like Mark Hamill, Carrie Fisher, Harrison Ford, and Peter Cushing are replaced with Diego Luna (Mexican), Adria Arjona (Puerto Rican), Forest Whitaker, Varada Sethu (Karala-born), Chook Sibtain, Muhannad Bhaier (Arabic), Abhin Galeya, Raymond Anum, Zubin Varla, Gershwyn Eustache Jnr, and Gary Beadle—truly a diverse cast.

In an interview with Hassan (2022), Luna notes:

> I think the beauty of "Andor" is that we have not just the permission, but the responsibility of being different. As "Rogue One" was the stand-alone in the world of the Saga films, we had a beginning and an end that were meant to be different. Same thing with "Andor," in the world of the "Star Wars" original series that they're doing. We have a beginning and an end, and we are meant to be different [para. 17].

Luna elaborated by pointing out the importance of his personal background as an actor portraying such a significant character in the *Star Wars* universe:

> It means a lot to me, it means a lot to people that look like me or sound like me. Coming from Mexico, it's even more important. We are the neighbors of this gigantic machine, this gigantic industry that feeds us. We can't keep up. I grew up watching American films. The music we get comes in English. We read subtitles. Probably the (Latin) music industry fights more back, but the cinema industry just lost the battle basically. It's hard to find a film in our language in Mexico in the cinemas. Normally you have four screens with a superhero, the other four with the big action or drama coming, and the kids' films and all of that comes from the States. So when this industry makes an effort to represent the people speaking Spanish in the world, it means something [Hassan, 2022, para. 19].

Like the *Star Wars* universe, the film industry is cited by Luna as lacking in the representation of diverse characters. Arjona applauds the fact that new voices are being allowed to speak in the *Star Wars* universe noting, "Diego has been doing it for way longer than me but it gives me hope that now a little girl's gonna watch it (*Andor*) and be like 'Oh my god, that girl kind of looks like me and maybe I want to be like her for Halloween!' or whatever that may be. It sort of comes to show how things are sort of shifting and I'm happy that Tony sort of brought me along," smiled Arjona when asked about representing the Hispanic community in the galaxy (Zaid, 2022, para. 16).

Additionally, Season 2 of the series will almost certainly explore the politics and power dynamics of both the Empire and the Rebel Alliance;

delving into the moral complexities of espionage and terrorism. This allows for a more nuanced portrayal of diversity, as the characters are not just defined by their ethnicity or race, but by their beliefs, values, actions, and ideologies.

Polysemous Readings

It is the nature of heteroglossia that multiple readings can unfold within any text or discourse. Although, as previously noted, *Andor* has been applauded for its intentionally diverse representation of culture by Tony Gilroy and other writers, there have been critics of the series, particularly in the "coding" of Jewish ethnicity (Wright, 2022). *Star Wars* has always taken advantage of the semiotic and symbolic power of the Nazi regime as a vehicle to paint a picture of this Evil Empire. Stormtroopers, Darth Vader's Stahlhelm-inspired helmet, and the Nazi stylization of Imperial Officer uniforms are only a few examples. Wright (2022, para. 2) applauds *Andor* for its depiction of dictatorial regimes: "When it's elaborating on the brutal consolidation of power under the Galactic Empire and the complicated struggle to overthrow it, *Andor* handles politics with more verve and nuance than any incarnation of *Star Wars* before it." However, Wright (2022) is critical of *Andor* in one key area.

One of the main characters in *Andor* is Syril Karn (Kyle Soller); his mother, Eedy (Kathryn Hunter) is equally prominent within the series. When Syril loses his job, he turns to the one person who might help him—his mother. When he knocks on the door to her apartment, she opens the door and slaps him across the face (presumably for bringing shame to her family) but follows this action with a hug. As Wright (2022, para. 5–7) notes, Eedy's emotional manipulation worsens. In an extended interaction, she finds Syril eating cereal for dinner and remarks on his posture. "Is that how you present yourself to the world?" she asks. "It explains a lot. You might as well wear an 'I promise to disappoint you' sign. Too bad we didn't see more of each other when you were flourishing. I'd have a better memory." During this moment, Eedy's real point emerges: "I assume you have no future prospects." Despite Syril's reassurances, she is unconvinced, unilaterally deciding to "call in the family favor" from Uncle Harlo. Eedy performs the "Jewish mother trope," belittling, manipulating, and meddling in her son's life. Notably, invoking Uncle Harlo at the end of their conversation raises the specter of conspiratorial Jewish power—a theme revisited in the show. Wright (2022), as a Jewish person, believes the depictions of both Eedy and Syril are problematic, arguing that "while Eedy and Syril are not Jewish—since, presumably, Judaism does not exist in the *Star Wars* galaxy—there are strong indications that they are coded as Jews. As a Jew myself, this coding is striking—Eedy's appearance, accent, intonation, mannerisms and phrasing, as well as the topics of conversation and the dynamic of her relationship with her son" (para. 13).

While Wright (2022) believes that Gilroy and the production team for *Andor* have done a wonderful job documenting the consolidation of power by a Galactic Empire, other facets of the program are troubling—Syril's number one priority is to join and serve an Empire meant to evoke Nazis, likening him to a Jewish conspirator during the Holocaust. Wright contends that he is not alone in this reading, pointing out:

> All of this adds up to create a visceral impression in me, and I am not the only one to feel this way. Both the Jewish author Abraham Josephine Riesman, as well as the right-wing publication Bounding into Comics, share this appraisal of Eedy. While many of the elements of this coding would be fine on their own, their complete saturation of the character forms the context in which plot points like Uncle Harlo are able to take on a more sinister meaning [2022, para. 14].

Although the coding of Eedy and Syril could be seen as representation for another marginalized group, it is not without the potential for polysemous readings.

Implications

Mikhail Bakhtin's concept of heteroglossia can be applied to the *Andor* series on Disney+ by examining the diverse and multifaceted nature of the storytelling and the representation of different voices and perspectives within the *Star Wars* universe. Heteroglossia, as defined by Bakhtin, refers to the coexistence and competition of multiple voices, languages, and discourses within a literary or cultural work. It recognizes that no single voice or perspective can dominate the others indefinitely, and instead, a multitude of voices interact, clash, and influence one another.

The application of Bakhtin's concept of heteroglossia to *Andor* reveals a changing *Star Wars* universe and an evolving base of engaged fans. In the case of *Andor*, heteroglossia can be observed in various aspects. The series showcases a range of characters from different backgrounds, cultures, and species, each with their own unique perspectives and voices. This diversity enriches the narrative and allows for the exploration of new viewpoints within the *Star Wars* universe. Heteroglossia is evident in the exploration of moral ambiguity in the characters' actions and choices. *Andor* delves into the complexities of the Rebellion and the choices made by its members, including Cassian himself, who only finds himself reluctantly joining the rebellion in an effort to outrun a violent turn in his search for his sister. The series presents different voices in the forms of conflicting ideologies, ethical dilemmas, and differing motivations, giving rise to a diversity of moralities and perspectives. Additionally, *Star Wars* has always been known for its linguistic diversity, and the *Andor* series is likely to continue this tradition. Different languages and dialects coexist, code switch, and blend, reflecting the heteroglossic nature of the *Star Wars* universe. This linguistic diversity represents cultural and social differences, reinforcing the idea of multiple voices with multiple perspectives.

By embracing heteroglossia, *Andor* can provide a more nuanced and inclusive portrayal of the *Star Wars* universe. At no point does *Andor* try to erase parts of the already accepted timeline of the Skywalker Saga. Instead, it allows for the exploration of diverse viewpoints, the examination of moral complexities, and the representation of a multitude of voices and experiences. This additive approach enriches the storytelling by acknowledging and privileging the heteroglot of voices that are inherent in any world, real or fictional. The inclusion of previously ignored communities in the *Star Wars* universe fosters a more dynamic, diverse, and engaging narrative that reflects the complex nature of the galaxy far, far away.

As the story of *Andor* unfolds, we can see a rupture in a cultural narrative being centered and confronted. Much as the title character is drawn into a rebellion that he would rather avoid, Disney is being drawn into a cultural conversation that is influencing contemporary storytelling. Disney's choice to bolster the diversity present in the *Star Wars* universe is a purposeful nod to the diverse sets of fans that, up until this point, have not seen themselves represented in a universe that has shaped the sci-fi genre for almost half a century. It has long been the role of Disney and the *Star Wars* franchise to represent a narrative that reflects a dominant discourse when it comes to our cultural narratives. However, by allowing a discourse that highlights the tension between those advocating for the "ostensibly traditional" and those advocating for a "modern society" is a choice that was not made lightly. Disney, in its choice to highlight social issues and represent diversity in one of its most beloved narratives, is leveraging the often underused and dismissed resource of heteroglossia.

While it is easy to dismiss and ignore voices that challenge our understanding of a cherished text, it is in the passion of the voices that surround us where the power of heteroglossia can be found. In the struggle to be present, acknowledged, and respected, those traditionally marginalized, ignored, or erased voices challenge our dominant storylines and enrich our ability to understand our standpoint within the universe. Going back, after the canon has been set, allowed us to meet the diverse people who helped steal the Death Star plans, found the Rebellion, and enable the central story of the Skywalker Saga. The addition of these stories provides depth and nuance to this far, far away galaxy while allowing viewers to question the simplistic view of good versus evil. The complications that heteroglossia introduces to the *Star Wars* universe (and makes some fans uncomfortable) also provides layer upon layer of richness that will fuel the enthusiasm of future generations of *Star Wars* fans who now may see themselves, their struggles, and their communities reflected in the heteroglot that *Andor* has embraced.

References

Appadurai, A. (1996). *Modernity at large: Cultural dimensions of globalization.* University of Minnesota Press.

Ausubel, J. (2015). *Star Wars and Nazi Germany.* Penn Political Review. https://pennpoliticalreview.org/2015/11/star-wars-and-nazi-germany/.

Bacon, T. (September 21, 2022). *Andor explains what happened to Kenari with the Empire's oldest excuse.* Screen Rant. https://screenrant.com/andor-kenari-mining-disaster-empire-excuse/ .

Bakhtin, M.M. (1981). *The dialogic imagination: Four essays.* University of Texas Press.

Balinisteanu, T. (2012). Goddess cults in techno-worlds: Tank Girl and the Borg Queen. *Journal of Feminist Studies in Religion, 28*(1), 5–24. https://doi.org/10.2979/jfemistudreli.28.1.5.

Covarrubias, M. (2021, May 21). Star Wars and the galactic diversity problem. *Inside Fullerton.* https://insidefullerton.fullcoll.edu/2021/05/star-wars-and-the-galactic-diversity-problem/

Hassan, Z. (2022, September 20). "Andor" star Diego Luna says "Stars Wars" universe introduced diverse characters "the right way." *Datebook.* https://datebook.sfchronicle.com/movies-tv/andor-star-diego-luna-says-stars-wars-universe-introduced-diverse-characters-the-right-way.

Hassler-Forest, D. (2017). The politics of world building: Heteroglossia in Janelle Monáe's Afrofuturist WondaLand. In M. Boni (Ed.), *World building* (pp. 377–392). Amsterdam University Press. https://doi.org/10.2307/j.ctt1zkjz0m.24.

Hatmaker, J. (2015, June 23). Was the 70s the worst decade ever? *Penn Live.* https://www.pennlive.com/entertainment/2015/06/was_the_70s_the_worst_decade_e.html.

Hoy, M. (1992). Bakhtin and popular culture. *New Literary History, 23*(3), 765–782. https://doi.org/10.2307/469229.

Jirak, J. (2022, November 3). *Andor*: Andy Serkis reveals he created a backstory for Kino Loy. *Comic Book.* https://comicbook.com/starwars/news/andor-andy-serkis-reveals-he-created-a-backstory-for-kino-loy/#:~:text=Serkis%20imagined%20Kino%20as%20a,other%20people%20apart%20from%20himself.

Kijinski, J L. (1987). Bakhtin and works of mass culture: Heteroglossia in Stand By Me. *Studies in Popular Culture, 10*(2), 67–81.

Mack, K. (2023, January 9). BIPOC, LGBTQ+, and the power and limitations of umbrella terms. MacArthur Foundation. https://www.macfound.org/press/perspectives/bipoc-lgbtq-power-limitations-umbrella-terms#:~:text=While%20the%20term%20Black%2C%20Indigenous,it%20was%20meant%20to%20embrace.

Moungabio, E. (2018, June 5). Diversity: A Star Wars story. *Cultured Vultures.* https://culturedvultures.com/diversity-a-star-wars-story/ .

Pye, J.S. (2022, October 17). According to Rotten Tomatoes, *Andor* is only getting better. *Culture Slate.* https://www.cultureslate.com/explained/according-to-rotten-tomatoes-andor-is-only-getting-better.

Rowe, N. (2008). Centrifugal Bostons and competing imaginaries in Mystic River. *Journal for Cultural Research, 12*(1), 81–97. https://doi.org/10.1080/14797580802090992.
Shatto, R. (2022, October 13). *Andor* finally gave us the queer Star Wars characters we were promised. *Pride.* https://www.pride.com/geek/andor-finally-gave-us-the-queer-star-wars-characters-we-were-promised.
Silverio, B. (2022, August 10). The Song of the South controversies explained. *Slash Film.* https://www.slashfilm.com/960577/the-song-of-the-south-controversies-explained/.
Speicher, J. (2022, October 15*). "Andor" illustrates the empire's casual racism against indigenous people.* Collider. https://collider.com/andor-empire-casual-racism-against-dhani/.
Stahl, S. (2022, October 1). *"Andor": Mon Mothma and the power of iron-willed women in the "Star Wars" universe.* Collider. https://collider.com/andor-mon-mothma-iron-willed-women-star-wars-universe/.
Toto, C. (2023, May 6). "Star Wars'" still pushing woke storytelling in a strategy that seems far, far away from reality. OutKick. https://www.outkick.com/star-wars-still-pushing-woke-storytelling-in-a-strategy-that-seems-far-far-away-from-reality/.
Tumin, R. (2023, January 26). Disney's Splash Mountain closed. Now superfans are selling the water. *New York Times.* https://www.nytimes.com/2023/01/26/us/disney-splash-mountain-closes.html.
Wright, W.E. (2022, November 28). *"Andor" reflects our ugly ambivalence, trafficking in antisemitic tropes while calling out fascism.* Salon. https://www.salon.com/2022/11/28/andor-antisemitism-jewish-coding-eedy-karn/
Zaid, A. (September 29, 2022). *Disney+'s 'Andor' Shines Spotlight On Strong Female Characters, Including Fan Favourite Mon Mothma.* Geek Culture. https://geekculture.co/disney-plus-andor-shines-spotlight-on-strong-female-characters-mon-mothma/.

Behind My Attraction

A Disney World Autoethnography

David Whitt

Introduction

June 1976. I am nine years old and sitting on the living room floor staring at a map of the United States. With pen in hand, I am planning a rather lengthy family road trip the next month in our station wagon, camper in tow, that will take my mom, dad, and younger sisters, Jenny and Robin, from Marquette, Michigan, to Cedar Rapids, Nebraska, to Orlando, Florida, with our ultimate destination being Walt Disney World. The distance between the states does not look vast, but many of the roads take unusual twists and turns, and in frustration I wonder, "Why couldn't they build roads straight from Marquette to Cedar Rapids to Orlando?" Despite the flaws in our nation's highway infrastructure, I am confident the route planned for our journey is the most efficient. On a bookshelf near me is the "Disney Fund" jar where the Whitt children throw our loose change, and the occasional dollar or two from our grandparents. I have no idea how much money is in the jar, but given how full it is I am guessing it will easily pay for our entire trip.

Growing up on Disney animated film in theaters, watching *The Wonderful World of Disney* on television Sunday evenings, and owning Disney stuffed animals and other merchandise (I got a Mickey Mouse watch for my sixth birthday), my sisters and I anxiously counted the days, hours, and highway miles before we could finally walk down Main Street U.S.A., see Cinderella's Castle, and enjoy the classic rides at Florida's version of "The Happiest Place on Earth." Certainly the Whitt children's exposure to, and enthusiasm for, the Disney brand growing up supports Wills' (2017) contention that American culture, and our attitudes toward gender, morality, and consumerism, have been reshaped by Disney through their films, toys, TV channels, and theme parks. Indeed, since that first Disney vacation almost 50 years ago, I have been to the Magic Kingdom six more times, Epcot and MGM/Hollywood Studios twice, and Disneyland and California Adventure in Anaheim, California, twice. While I would not say I have a Disney obsession, I still have my nine-year-old self's enthusiasm and fascination with the park experience, always looking for opportunities to visit. But why? What is it about Disney that keeps the now-57-year-old me wanting to go back to the parks time and time again?

This is not an easy question to answer, as I have experienced some Disney cognitive dissonance over the years. For example, given the rising costs of Disney park tickets, on-site food and beverages, parking, hotels, and merchandise, along with miles of walking, long lines, heat, humidity, and more walking, I would have legitimate reasons to stay at home or spend my money on more affordable vacations. Additionally, I teach Mass Media and each semester we discuss how Disney has been accused of cultural imperialism, opening parks in Tokyo (1983), Paris (1992), Hong Kong (2005) and Shanghai (2016). More recently, in 2022 Disney was denounced for its delayed response to Florida's controversial "Parental Rights in Education Bill," aka "Don't Say Gay" bill, with some Disney workers walking out in protest. Given these commercial, cultural, and socio-political criticisms, again I wondered, why do I continue to support the Disney brand, buying toys and clothes for my niece and nephews, subscribe to Disney+ and, of course, visit their theme parks? I am not alone. According to the TEA/AECOM Global Attractions Attendance Report (2023), in 2022 approximately 116 million guests visited Disney theme parks around the world, with the most, 17.1 million, going to the Magic Kingdom.

Searching for Answers

To help understand my attraction to Disney parks, I conducted an autoethnography about my guest experience at Disney World in Orlando, Florida, visiting the Magic Kingdom for two days, and Epcot for one. According to Ellis, Adams, and Bochner (2011) autoethnography is "an approach to research and writing that seeks to describe and systematically analyze (graphy) personal experience (auto) in order to understand cultural experience (ethno)" (p. 273). They explain autoethnographers embrace subjectivity and emotionality rather than objectivity and neutrality, recognizing the "innumerable ways personal experience influences the research process" (p. 274). Wall (2006) argues that by acknowledging the link between the personal and the cultural, autoethnography makes room for "nontraditional forms of inquiry and expression" (p. 146). Adams, Jones, and Ellis (2015) discuss how autoethnography has been used in disciplines such as anthropology, art and design, business, communication, criminology, education, geography, nursing, psychology, social work, and sociology, with courses on this method of inquiry taught at several schools. As an individual or audience-centered approach, autoethnographic research would also seem welcome in the cultural studies subfield of fan studies, which, according to Mittermeier (2021) is influencing theme park studies. So using this methodology to study my Disney World experience is natural fit.

In terms of subject matter, Goodall (2004) describes how autoethnographers, who he also calls narrative ethnographers, can write about a wide range of personal experiences such as

> the poetics of living; about the communication of beauty and peace and connectedness; articulate the interplays of aesthetic values in everyday life; of the ability humans have to love, to care for, to hope, to teach, as well as our ability to create friendships, communities, and to perform random acts of creative kindness.... Narrative ethnographers, myself among them, also write about peak experiences and fun, about activities humans engage in for personal enjoyment and spiritual profit [p. 188].

Goodall's overview of autoethnographic subjects provides validation for my research, as the mission of a Disney theme park is all about creating peak experiences, fun and activities for personal enjoyment. As Walt Disney himself said during the dedication of Disneyland in Anaheim, California, on July 17, 1955:

> To all who come to this happy place: Welcome. Disneyland is your land. Here, age relives fond memories of the past, and here youth may save the challenge and promise of the future. Disneyland is dedicated to the ideals, the dreams, and the hard facts that have created America, with the hope that it will be a source of joy and inspiration to all the world [*The Imagineering Story*—"The Happiest Place on Earth," 2019].

Years later, on October 25, 1971, Walt's brother, Roy, would read a similar dedication for the opening of Walt Disney World in Orlando, Florida, proclaiming, "May Walt Disney World bring joy and inspiration and new knowledge to all who come to this happy place ... a Magic Kingdom where the young at heart of all ages can laugh and play and learn—together" (Rasmussen, 2011).

The Autoethnographic Process

While there are several different ways to conduct an autoethnography, the orientation I selected was the interpretive-humanistic approach. According to Manning and Adams (2015) this type of autoethnography involves fieldwork as the researcher records their experiences and perspectives called "thick description" (p. 192). This means I would need to take detailed notes during my time at the Magic Kingdom, recording my observations, attitudes, feelings, and what Ellis, Adams, and Bochner (2011) call "epiphanies," moments of unique insight or personal discovery. These notes would allow me to later create a vivid narrative about my time at Disney, and, hopefully, provide insight into what the park experience means to me.

Manning and Adams explain the interpretive-humanistic approach is common for an autoethnography that examines popular culture, which Disney has been generating for decades.

However, because this book is about Disney+ programming, my autoethnography is not simply a narrative discussing my visit to Disney World. It would also be informed and influenced by documentary content on the Disney+ streaming service that focuses specifically upon Disney theme parks. Fortunately, Disney+ has produced several park-centric programs and segments that provided a wealth of valuable information and insight in preparing for my autoethnography. *The Imagineering Story* (2019) is a six-part series, narrated by Angela Bassett, that traces the history of Disney parks from the opening of Disneyland in 1955, to the latest park in Shanghai which opened in 2016. *Behind the Attraction* (2021) is a ten-part series, narrated by Paget Brewster, highlighting classic rides such as the Jungle Cruise, Space Mountain, and "It's a Small World," but also iconic locales such as the various Disney castles and hotels. *One Day at Disney* (2019), narrated by Sterling K. Brown, and *One Day at Disney Shorts* (2019) show a "day in the life" of various Disney cast members (the name for all Disney employees), ranging from candy makers and window decorators on Main Street U.S.A., to steam train engineers and Mark Twain Riverboat pilots. Finally, *Disney Insider* (2020) is a behind the scenes look at Disney films, toys, and music, with some of the theme park segments highlighting the elephants of Animal Kingdom, and the new 4-D ride Remy's Ratatouille Adventure in the France Pavilion at Epcot's World Showcase.

My objective in watching these documentaries was two-fold. First, I have always been interested in the history of Disney theme parks, along with the design of various attractions. Next, and most relevant for my autoethnography, I wanted to see how Disney attempted to tap into nostalgia through these programs, and how viewing them would influence my park experience. According to Jeziński and Wojtkowski (2016), nostalgia is "a psychological approach in which one emotionally glorifies the feeling of positive attitude towards places and people, rooting those phenomena in the past" (p. 97). Burton (2014) describes nostalgia as "sentimentality for the past, typically for a particular period or place with positive associations, but sometimes also for the past in general, 'the old days of yore'" (p. 1). Both definitions comment on the power of nostalgia to generate within the individual memories and emotions of yesteryear. For example, high school reunions are social nostalgic gatherings where classmates share stories and memories of the past, look back fondly on simpler times, and for some, to quote Bruce Springsteen, discuss their "glory days." In this instance, nostalgia can be a deeply personal and emotional experience, as classmates are, for a brief time, transported back to their teenage years, until the reality of the present breaks this powerful spell.

It would not be hyperbole to argue that Disney is in the nostalgia business. Generation after generation has been influenced by Disney films, TV shows, and toys, while visiting Disney World was, at least for me, something of a cultural imperative growing up. According to Menke and Schwarzenegger (2017), "Evoking nostalgia is a common goal and strategy in advertising and marketing concepts" (p. 4). For Disney, nostalgia is undoubtably a central tenet of their cultural identity. One page from Disney's nostalgia playbook was "The Magic Is Calling" campaign (October 2021–March 2023) promoting the 50th Anniversary Celebration of Walt Disney World in Orlando, encouraging children of all ages to visit the park, relive old memories, and make new ones with family and friends.

The purpose of my autoethnography, and consequently this essay, was to explore and describe how Disney uses nostalgia reflected within various Disney+ documentary programs to not only tell the story of Disneyland/World, but importantly, how they sell the park experience to attract guests (i.e., me). To put it another way, I decided to follow the suggestion of Disney CEO Bob Iger who said of Disney parks, "These projects, these places, these attractions ... how it's being made is extremely interesting and might increase the level of appreciation. But what we want people to appreciate is the perfection of it all" (*The Imagineering Story*—"The Happiest Place on Earth," 2019). As I set out on my Disney World adventure, that was exactly what I attempted to do.

My Days at Disney

It is approximately 6:15 a.m. (5:15 a.m. Nebraska time) on Sunday, October 16, 2022, and sunrise in Orlando is still over an hour away. I am walking across the Disney All-Star Sports Resort to catch the 6:30 a.m. bus that will take me to the Magic Kingdom. The park is scheduled to open to the general public at 8:00 a.m., but for those staying at a Disney property, we get early access to attractions beginning 7:30 a.m. (a nice perk). A few minutes after arriving at the bus stop, a family of four from Minnesota joins the queue, and I see their two young boys, each under 10 years old, still looking sleepy. I turn to the mother and father and say, "This is crazy, right?" They both agree, and we discuss the advantages of hitting Disney at the crack of dawn to avoid long lines for the popular rides. The bus doors open, and I find a seat for the short ride to the park which officially marks the first of three long, but thoroughly enjoyable days of walking, waiting in lines, eating, observation, and self-reflection at the Magic Kingdom and Epcot.

The immersion in nostalgia begins immediately as the bus speakers begin playing a medley of classic Disney songs starting with "When You Wish Upon a Star" and soon after "It's a Small World." From property to park Disney creates anticipation for guests as the music, along with signs within the bus for Disney+ and ABC television programming, attempt to distract from noticing early morning Orlando traffic, construction projects, and other non–Disney related locales visible en route. The bus arrives at the Magic Kingdom, and as I walk toward the entrance notice there are already hundreds of other Disney property guests waiting in line at the front gate who also planned to take advantage of the early entry time. Approximately 15 minutes later, with sunrise finally on the horizon, the park officially opens.

I walk down Main Street U.S.A. to the Fantasyland "rope drop," the designated location to enter that section of the park. At 7:29 a.m. a cast member yells something only a few people near the front can hear, and one minute later pulls the rope back. Like a runner out of the starting block, I quickly move toward one of the more popular attractions in Fantasyland with a lengthy wait time, the Seven Dwarfs Mine Train. By 7:40 a.m. I am enjoying the drops and turns of this rollercoaster still thinking, "This is crazy, right?"

Since arriving in Orlando the day before, I have been trying to temper my inner child, excited to be visiting Disney once again, with that of an academic wanting to do serious research. So far, I have been recording observations about my journey from the All-Star Sports Resort to the park. With the Seven Dwarfs now crossed off my list of "Must Do Rides," I move a short distance across Fantasyland to one of Disney's classic attractions, "It's a Small World," and my real work begins.

"I want to go again"

"It's a Small World" is one of the few rides I vaguely remember when my family visited the Magic Kingdom in 1976. I recall hearing the (in)famous song on a constant loop as the boat we were in moved past the various animatronic children in colorful costumes from different countries. The one thing I absolutely do remember was seeing countless quarters, dimes, nickels and pennies in the water below me ("wishes" from guests), my small arm reaching down, unsuccessfully, trying to grab some change. This time the academic in me paid special attention to the animatronic characters after watching *Behind the Attraction*—"It's a Small World," which featured the history and development of this attraction.

Originally created for the 1964–1965 World's Fair in New York, "It's a Small World" features over 300 audio-animatronic (aka animatronics or robot animation) children from dozens of cultures around the world. *Behind the Attraction*—"It's a Small World" highlights the remarkable contributions of artist Mary Blair, who designed the children and locations, and Harriet Burns who fashioned all the hand-crafted clothing. On previous "It's a Small World" rides, I just noticed the obvious, such as what country the children represented based on attire and scenery. However, this time, I looked much more carefully at each set, appreciating the intricate detail in Mary Blair's colorful and intricate apparel. While floating through Spain, I even noticed for the first time two children dressed as knight-errant Don Quixote and his faithful sidekick Sancho Panza from the classic novel *Don Quixote* (1605 and 1615) by Miguel de Cervantes, a literature reference most children, and probably many adults, would not know.

Maybe it was because I was seeing robotic children "singing" which resonated with nine-year-old me which made "It's a Small World" so memorable in 1976. I certainly would not have been familiar with many of the countries the children represented, or how their clothing and customs reflected their respective cultures. Perhaps the song "It's a Small World," written by brothers Robert and Richard Sherman, playing on a non-stop loop, became something of a mnemonic device, later triggering nostalgic memories of the attraction. Regardless, "It's a Small World" will always be on my list of "Must Do Rides" at the Magic Kingdom. Someday, I may even be able to reach some of that loose change resting just below the surface of the water.

Episodes of *Behind the Attraction* (*BtA*) and *The Imagineering Story* (*TIS*) not only increased my appreciation for the animatronics and designs on "It's a Small World," but also other attractions such as the Jungle Cruise (*BtA*: Episode 1), Haunted Mansion (*BtA*: Episode 2), The Hall of Presidents (*BtA*: Episode 10), The Enchanted Tiki Room (*TIS*: Episode 1), Walt Disney's Carousel of Progress (*TIS*: Episode 1), and my favorite ride, Pirates of the Caribbean (*TIS*: Episode 1). Unlike "It's a Small World," I do not remember riding Pirates in 1976. My first memories of the attraction are seven years later in late December 1983, when my dad and I drove from Marquette to Florida to see our beloved Nebraska Cornhuskers play the Miami Hurricanes in the Orange Bowl on January 2, 1984 (they lost 31–30). A few days before the game we visited the Magic Kingdom. The weather in

Orlando at the time was surprisingly cold and rainy, and we had to wear our winter coats to stay warm. However, the advantage of the low temperatures was the park was not particularly crowded during the normally busy holiday season, making wait times for rides shorter than usual.

My dad and I had been on Pirates earlier in the day, but as we walked past the attraction that evening, we noticed the line was virtually non-existent and decided to ride it again. Interestingly, I cannot recall details of the first time we rode Pirates that day, but I clearly remember the second. After once again floating through animatronic scenes of pirate battles, pirate plundering, and pirates trying to escape a prison by coaxing a dog who has the cell keys in his mouth, Pirates of the Caribbean immediately became my favorite Disney ride. Since then, I have always tried to ride Pirates more than once while visiting the Magic Kingdom. For my autoethnography I was able to ride Pirates twice, each time trying to focus on details I may have missed before, such as the movement of the animatronic pirates, townspeople, and animals, as well as the impressive special effects (e.g., faux fires, cannon bursts, etc.). After watching *Behind the Attraction* and *The Imagineering Story*, I also swear I am seeing Mickey ears in the shadows. While the Pirates narrative has changed several times over the years (e.g., adding Captain Jack Sparrow and other characters from Disney's *Pirates of the Caribbean* film franchise, eliminating auctioning women in the town), many of the dark ride elements have remained basically the same.

According to Disney Imagineer and Creative Executive Marty Sklar, when Pirates of the Caribbean opened in Disneyland in 1967, Walt Disney said, "People can come back and go through it again and they'll see something new, and they'll hear something new" (*The Imagineering Story*—"The Happiest Place on Earth," 2019). In this way, Pirates (along with other animatronic and special effects rides such as the Haunted Mansion) generates nostalgia for me that is both classic and evolving. The nostalgia is classic in that I remember what Pirates was like in 1983 while riding with my father, but also evolving as the attraction's updated story and special effects create an experience both old and new. My enduring enthusiasm for Pirates was best captured by a comment from a young child in front of me during my second time on the attraction that day. After our boat came to a complete stop the child turned to his mom and said, "I want to go again."

The Nostalgia of Disappointment and Fulfilment

While our family vacation at the Magic Kingdom in 1976 was memorable for many reasons (thank you, Mom and Dad), for several years after I had some lingering bitterness about not going on one particular ride.

Of all the Disney park attractions, I was most looking forward to 20,000 Leagues Under the Sea, a water-ride based on the 1954 Disney film of the same name. As a young child fascinated by science fiction, I could not wait to board Captain Nemo's submarine, the Nautilus, for an adventure where guests would look out a porthole to see underwater life and, eventually, survive being attacked by a Giant Squid. However, unlike today's theme parks where you can ride a ride as many times as you like, from 1955 to 1982 guests at Disneyland and the Magic Kingdom had to purchase a booklet with several tickets inside. On the top of each ticket was printed "Good for Choice of One," and attraction options were listed in different lands (D23: The Official Disney Fan Club, n.d.). In other words, you had to plan your ride itinerary carefully based on how many tickets remained in your booklet. This ticket strategy becomes even more problematic for families, as children may have different Disney attractions they want to ride, with parents ultimately making the difficult decision of which ride is sacrificed, which will likely make at least one child unhappy.

Case in point, the Whitt family. I am absolutely certain in the months leading up our Magic Kingdom vacation, and several times in the park that day as well, I expressed my desire to go on 20,000 Leagues Under the Sea. However, after a full day of Disney fun, my mom and dad suddenly informed me around dusk we were leaving, and I would not be going on the ride. In fairness to my parents, I do not recall exactly why this decision was made. Perhaps we were out of tickets, my younger sisters were tired, or my parents had enough of the heat, crowds and long lines. Regardless, I was as crushed as a nine-year-old could be, and left the park incredibly upset, feeling as if the entire day, if not the entire trip, was a waste, and would carry this disappointment with me for years. My 10-year-old brother Joe had a similar experience on another family vacation to Disney World in 2001, when he was unable to go on Space Mountain as it was closed most of the day. Despite having a wonderful time that week visiting other theme parks, including Disney's Animal Kingdom and MGM Studios, along with Sea World, Joe would say about that trip for years after, "Yeah, but I didn't get to go on Space Mountain."

During my autoethnography, I walked through the section of Fantasyland where 20,000 Leagues used to be located (the attraction closed in 1994, later becoming the Seven Dwarfs Mine Train ride), and later rode Space Mountain. I thought about the severe disappointment I felt in 1976 not riding in a submarine under the sea, and Joe's in 2001 not riding a rollercoaster rocket in space. I then wondered how many children, both young and old, have had their Disney park experience tarnished, if not ruined, by not being able to go on a specific ride, not seeing/meeting their favorite Disney character, or whatever plans were affected by weather, illness, or other unforeseen factors. No doubt countless other park goers have memorable stories of Disney dreams dashed, reflecting how our nostalgia for events can be impacted by seemingly minor or non-consequential moments. While missing out on a 20-minute ride (20,000 Leagues) or a three-minute one (Space Mountain) compared to everything the Disney World has to offer may seem trivial, for my brother and I it would define our first Disney experiences as memorable, but incomplete. Today, whenever I see an image or video of Space Mountain, as I did while watching *The Imagineering Story*—"What Would Walt Do?" and *Behind the Attraction*—Space Mountain, I am reminded of the similar narrative and emotional arc Joe and I experienced 25 years apart. Fortunately, our respective stories have a Disney happy ending. I would finally ride 20,000 Leagues with my dad in 1983, and I was with Joe when he conquered Space Mountain in 2012. I even took a picture of his smiling face, with two thumbs up, immediately after and framed it as a reminder that his years of longing were now officially over.

"You Are the Magic"

Another memorable experience at the Magic Kingdom during my autoethnography was the evening of Monday, October 17, my second day at the park. I stood amidst a crowd of thousands near Cinderella's Castle to watch the Walt Disney World 50th Anniversary Celebration projection and fireworks show titled "Enchantment." At exactly 8:15 p.m. "Enchantment" begins, and narrator Angela Bassett (who also narrates all six episodes of *The Imagineering Story*) tells the crowd they have gathered at a "most enchanted kingdom, one overflowing with magic. And once upon a time, it all began with a dream." As fireworks burst in the sky, images of the Magic Kingdom's history, including Walt Disney announcement about the park in 1965 and opening day in 1971, are projected on the castle. Moments later, an animated Mickey Mouse appears on the front balcony and tells the audience:

> Some folks like to say that it all started with a dream. But you wanna know what makes this place really special? It's you. Each and every one of you. Anytime you set foot here you leave this place brighter than it was before. Because you are the magic.

The song "You Are the Magic" then begins, and over the course of the program scenes from classic and modern Disney animated films such as *Aladdin*, *Peter Pan*, *Sleeping Beauty*, *Frozen*, *Brave*, *Coco*, *Moana*, *Soul*, *Alice in Wonderland*, and *Dumbo* are projected on the castle's facade. Next, a medley of popular Disney songs is heard including "Be Our Guest,"

"Under the Sea" and "A Whole New World." As images and colors continually change on the castle, fireworks explode overhead, the crowd cheering and clapping throughout. Toward the end of the show, the song "You Are the Magic" is reprised, and Mickey appears again to remind the audience, "You are the magic." After approximately 18 minutes "Enchantment" ends, and the vast crowd begins to disperse. Not surprisingly, "Enchantment" generated a visceral reaction for some in the audience. I certainly felt goosebumps during different parts of the show, and I noticed several people wiping tears from their eyes as they walked away.

Admittedly, this brief summary does not fully describe all the Disney characters, scenes, music, and special effects in "Enchantment." Indeed, a study of these elements, along with the show's narrative arc, could be a conference paper or book chapter unto itself. However, what is most meaningful in relation to my autoethnography was not only the show, but also where it took place, Cinderella's Castle. After Mickey Mouse, the castle is, perhaps, the second most recognizable symbol of Disney. From Sleeping Beauty's Castle in Disneyland, to the Enchanted Storybook Castle in Shanghai Disneyland, the castle is *the* centerpiece of every Disney park. *Behind the Attraction*—The Castles examines the history of Disney castles, their unique designs, and importance to the guest experience. Series narrator Paget Brewster explains the castles are "a symbol that stands for everything that Walt, and the entire Walt Disney company, represents.... It's to the guests, who stand at the foot of these castles, look upwards, and dream." Toward the end of the episode she states, "No matter where you are in the world, when you see this unmistakably recognizable silhouette" (images of different castles around the world appear) you know (transition to Walt Disney's voice) "that when you wish upon a star, your dreams do come true." Several times in the episode fireworks displays are shown at the various parks, along with images of adults and children looking on in enjoyment.

Interestingly, despite multiple visits to the Magic Kingdom, the first time I remember watching the evening fireworks display was in 2016 when visiting the park with my sister and brother-in-law. However, instead of viewing the program, titled "Wishes," out in front of Cinderella's Castle, our vantage point was behind it, in Fantasyland. Surprisingly, toward the end of the show when "When You Wish Upon at Star" was playing, I became a bit misty-eyed. Something about the combination of visuals, music, narration, and my day at Disney clearly had an emotional impact upon me. I remembered that moment six years later during my autoethnography, feeling goosebumps watching "Enchantment," and then seeing tears of joy from others in the audience.

In both instances, I would argue the location of Cinderella's Castle (and, likewise, other Disney castles) adds an essential component to Disney's fireworks programs, bringing the masses together in a specific place, at a specific time, for a specific event. In other words, it is one thing for me to ride the Seven Dwarfs Mine Train or Pirates of the Caribbean by myself anytime during the day, but completely another to stand among a crowd of thousands in the evening watching Disney animated characters projected on Cinderella's Castle, and hearing "When You Wish Upon a Star" and "You Are the Magic" as fireworks explode in the sky. As an avoid concert-goer, I could not help but think of the similarities between the live music and "Enchantment" as the creation of a collective, and certainly nostalgic, audience experience. Including scenes of fireworks displays in *Behind the Attraction*—The Castles is a reminder of these colorful and vibrant end-of-the-day events at Disney.

Behind My Attraction Discussion

In addition to enjoying rides and watching evening fireworks, my time at the Magic Kingdom and Epcot were also filled with a variety of other memorable experiences. I ate at Be Our Guest Restaurant at Beast's Enchanted Castle (I had the filet), did a five-hour Keys to the Kingdom Tour, a "behind the scenes" look at the park and various attractions, and even tested my marksmanship at the Frontierland Shootin' Arcade, something I had not done since visiting Disney when I was nine years old. However, one encounter left the greatest impression upon me while visiting Epcot on Tuesday, October 18, the third day of my autoethnography.

I was having lunch in the food court outside the Living with the Land ride. As I was enjoying my overpriced roast beef sandwich and side of pasta, I noticed a cast member moving through the area, sweeping up bits of trash off the floor. When she finally made it near my table, I said "Hi," she stopped cleaning, and we talked for a few minutes. Her name was Doris, she was in her early 80s, and had worked at Epcot for 21 years. A few moments later another cast member approached telling Doris she could go on break, and we said our goodbyes. As Doris walked away, her coworker told me Doris loves working at the park and has said she "wants to die at Disney."

My brief time with Doris immediately reminded me of *One Day at Disney* (2019) and *One Day at Disney Shorts* (2019–), which highlighted the jobs of various Disney employees. However, many of the Disney park cast members featured in these reality programs were in more high-profile positions, like a candy maker on Main Street U.S.A., or engineer for the steam train that encircles both Disneyland and the Magic Kingdom. No doubt these individuals achieved minor celebrity status after appearing in these shows. However, I wondered about the unsung cast members, like Doris, who spend day after day doing more thankless jobs, like cleaning up after park guests. Perhaps these individuals should also be the subject of a *One Day at Disney* segment for their hard work and dedication to keeping Disney parks looking immaculate. In the season finale of *One Day at Disney Shorts* (Episode 51) an off-screen cast member says he has "never outgrown Disney." Certainly Doris has not, and I hope I never do either.

While my conversation with Doris lasted less time than the average Disney ride, it would lead to what Ellis, Adams and Bochner (2011) have called an autoethnographic "epiphany," a moment of unique insight or personal discovery. After lunch, as I walked outside near the Journey into Imagination with Figment attraction (an area that reminded me of the 1976 sci-fi film *Logan's Run*), I began reflecting upon the comments and conduct of cast members and guests over the past several days, memories and nostalgia of past Disney visits, episodes of *The Imagineering Story, Behind the Attraction, One Day at Disney* and *One Day at Disney Shorts* I watched in preparation for my visit, as well as my own thoughts and feelings in the different parks. While I occasionally heard crying children and parents complaining about outrageous food costs (I had my moments as well), these did not detract from my overwhelmingly positive park experience. In fact, as each day passed, I noticed feeling more tranquil, personable, and for lack of a better word, happier. For example, while waiting in various lines I talked with guests about where they were from, ride experiences, and food recommendations. Walking around Epcot's World Showcase, I even volunteered to take pictures of a couple, and then a family, so they could have a non-selfie photo memory. Usually, because of my introverted personality, I avoid conversations with people I do not know. However, at the Magic Kingdom and Epcot I found myself enjoying connecting with others, if only for a moment. My Disney park experience was, therefore, not negatively impacted by wait times, crowds, and costs, but instead enhanced by the affability and attitude of guests and cast members, reaffirming Walt Disney's original vision of Disney parks being places that create joy, inspiration, and fond memories.

Watching episodes of *The Imagineering Story* and *Behind the Attraction* both before and after my autoethnography also generated feelings of nostalgia about my time at Disney parks over the decades. The obvious examples of personal nostalgia are seeing video and images from some of my favorite rides such as "It's a Small World," Haunted Mansion, Space Mountain, and the underrated Tomorrowland Transit Authority PeopleMover. However, there are also clips of attractions I rode which are no longer in service, such as the Disney Skyway (an aerial lift between

Fantasyland and Tomorrowland) which I rode in 1996 (closed in 1999), as well as scenes of the park lit up in the evening, which is my favorite time of day to experience Disney (*The Imagineering Story*—"The Happiest Place on Earth"). Finally, seeing video of the Magic Kingdom's opening day on October 1, 1971, reminded me of the trip my family would take to Disney World only five short years later.

While I recognize *The Imagineering Story, Behind the Attraction, One Day at Disney* and *One Day at Disney Shorts* are marketing tools for Disney to attract visitors to their parks, these programs are also video albums brimming with nostalgia, showing images of guests throughout the decades on rides, eating food, watching fireworks, and enjoying the "Happiest Place on Earth." However, on those occasions I am feeling nostalgic for Disney, I do not look at pictures in an album or on my computer. Instead, I watch Disney shows on Disney+ about Disney parks. For example, watching *Behind the Attraction*—Jungle Cruise, I cannot help but remember the many times I have been on the ride with family, friends, or by myself. As a nod to the theme of this book, these programs are most definitely a plus, and a vivid reminder of my many Disney visits since 1976. Not only do these shows generate personal nostalgia, but—according to science—also compel me (and countless other guests over the decades), to visit these magic kingdoms again and again. Dr. Erica Hepper, Lecturer in Personality/Social Psychology at the University of Surrey in England, suggests nostalgia-triggering Disney media motivates viewers to want to return to Disney parks to "indulge their nostalgia by immersing themselves in this reliable world filled with familiar colors, characters, smells and music" (Austin, 2023, para. 18).

Imagineer and Creative Executive Tom Morris perhaps best articulates the magical spell Disney has cast over park guests since Disneyland first opened in 1955 stating:

> At the end of the day it's [visiting Disney] an extraordinary experience that happened to you. You're moved by it, like a good movie moves you … you're actually changed or transformed by the end of the film [*The Imagineering Story*—"The Happiest Place on Earth"].

I certainly can attest to the transformation Morris speaks of as I felt it during my autoethnography. The mix of pure escapism, connection with my youth, and shared experiences with family and friends, is a powerful combination, an alchemy that has somehow altered my DNA. This equation generates within me an intense desire to continually return to what Dr. David Ludden, Professor of Psychology at Georgia Gwinnett College, calls the "nostalgic refuge" of Disney theme parks (Austin, 2023, para. 21). With Season 2 of *Behind the Attraction* debuting in November 2023, I look forward to new episodes that feature other rides I enjoy such as Pirates of the Caribbean and Big Thunder Mountain Railroad. And, if Disney+ ever plans more *One Day at Disney Shorts*, Doris should definitely be a featured cast member.

Limitations

Time at the Magic Kingdom and Epcot allowed me to contemplate the meaning of my Disney park experience, but in hindsight there were limitations in my research. As a neophyte autoethnographer, I was focused on what was observable, tangible and memorable. In other words, my strategy was to take notes on what I was seeing, smelling, tasting and touching in relation to my personal Disney history, feelings of nostalgia, and how Disney+ programs like *Behind the Attraction, The Imagineering Story, One Day at Disney* and *One Day at Disney Shorts* were also guiding my inquiry. However, I was not attenuated to park components that were inconspicuous or hidden from view. For example, Disney created the color Go Away Green to hide security cameras, trash cans, utility boxes, and construction areas. The idea is that this hue will blend into the surroundings and your eyes will ignore whatever objects and areas are camouflaged. They also developed the color Blending Blue to meld tall buildings into the skyline (Fowler, 2022). Obviously, these unique colors did their job as I was more intent on walking around each park and thinking about my personal history with a particular attraction than what was being cloaked by color.

Additionally, I was never aware of anyone receiving medical attention or security personnel dealing with difficult guests. Given how Disney carefully controls what guests see at their parks, it would not surprise me if there were instances like these happening daily but handled offstage so as to not break the illusion onstage. I now have another reason to return to the Magic Kingdom and Epcot, to not only further explore what the Disney park experience means to me, but also try and be more aware of those park elements hiding in plain sight. While a program highlighting some of these hidden park elements would be fascinating, Disney may be reticent to develop one as it would further draw back the curtain on the magic they attempt to create.

Conclusion

According to National Public Radio's Deanna Schwartz (2022) a "Disney Adult" is "an adult who loves all things Disney and spends vast amounts of money and time on Disney-related products and experiences" (Schwartz, 2022, para. 4). While I do not consider myself a Disney Adult, I would say I am an adult who simply enjoys Disney. Therefore, watching the Disney+ programs *The Imagineering Story*, *Behind the Attraction*, *One Day at Disney* and *One Day at Disney Shorts* were not only personally enjoyable, but also enhanced my autoethnographic experience at the Magic Kingdom and Epcot. These media texts increased my knowledge and appreciation for all the thought, skill and detail that went into various rides, the essential, yet often times unnoticed, contributions of cast members, and most importantly, helped me better understand my attraction toward Disney parks and the power of nostalgia. In fact, I am already planning future trips to both Disneyland and Disney World. Hopefully, I can one day share these park experiences with my niece and nephews, creating treasured memories with the next generation of Disney enthusiasts.

I have this tradition when I leave the Magic Kingdom to stop at the front of Main Street U.S.A., turn around, look back at Cinderella's Castle, and reflect upon my day. In 2012, my brother Joe joined me for this moment, and we put our arms around each other's shoulders, enjoying the illuminated castle, grateful for our day together. On the second day of my autoethnography in 2022 I left the park around 10 p.m., and, as usual, looked back at the castle, appreciating the ambiance and perfection of it all. As I turned to finally leave, immediately to my left I saw a father taking a picture of his two young sons, their arms around each other shoulders, just like Joe and I did ten years earlier. It was the perfect moment of nostalgia to end my day, and one I hope those brothers look back upon fondly as well. Thanks, Walt.

References

Adams, T.E., Holman Jones, S., & Ellis, C. (2015). *Autoethnography: Understanding qualitative research*. Oxford University Press.

Austin, D. (2023, September 19). The scientific reason why you can't stop going to Disneyland. *Los Angeles Times*. https://www.latimes.com/travel/story/2023-09-19/disneyland-disney-world-addiction-travel-craving-science.

Burton, N. (2014, November 27). The meaning of nostalgia: The psychology and philosophy of nostalgia. *Psychology Today*. https://www.psychologytoday.com/us/blog/hide-and-seek/201411/the-meaning-nostalgia.

Catalena, M. (Writer), & Iwerks, L. (Director). (2019). The Happiest Place on Earth. In L. Iwerks (Executive Producer), *The Imagineering Story*. Disney Media Distribution.

Catalena, M. (Writer), & Iwerks, L. (Director). (2019). What would Walt do? In L. Iwerks (Executive Producer), *The Imagineering Story*. Disney Media Distribution.

Chamberlin, D., & Antinoro, M. (Executive Producers). (2019). One Day at Disney Shorts [TV series]. Disney Media Distribution.

D23: The official Disney fan club. (n.d.). "E" ticket memories: Five favorite facts about ticket books. Retrieved from https://d23.com/e-ticket-memories-five-favorite-facts-about-ticket-books/.

Ellis, C., Adams, T.E., & Bochner, A.P. (2011). Autoethnography: An overview. *Historical Social Research, 36*(4), 273–290.
Fowler, K. (2022, February 2). Viral video shows how Disney apparently "hides buildings in plain sight." *Newsweek.com.* https://www.newsweek.com/disney-hides-buildings-plain-sight-bye-bye-blue-go-away-green-paint-1677230.
Goodall, H.L., Jr. (2004). Narrative ethnography as applied communication research. *Journal of Applied Communication Research, 32*(3), 185–194.
Jeziński, M., & Wojtkowski, L. (2016). Nostalgia commodified: Towards the marketization of the post-communist past through the new media. Media and Time: Communication in the Past and Present. 96–104. Retrieved from https://www.researchgate.net/publication/313744998_Media_Communication_and_Nostalgia
Manning, J. & Adams, T.E. (2015). Popular culture studies and autoethnography: An essay on method. *The Popular Culture Studies Journal, 3*(1&2), 187–222.
Menke, M., & Schwarzenegger, C. (2017). Media, communication, and nostalgia: Finding a better tomorrow in the yesterday? *Media and Time: Communication in the Past and Present*, 2–5. https://www.researchgate.net/publication/313744998_Media_Communication_and_Nostalgia
Mittermeier, S. (2021). *A cultural history of the Disneyland theme parks: Middle class kingdoms.* Intellect.
Mitchell, F. (Director) (2019). One day at Disney [Film]. Disney Publishing Worldwide Endeavor Content.
Rasmussen, N. (2011). Vintage Walt Disney World: A dedication with style at Magic Kingdom Park. Disney Parks Blog. https://disneyparks.disney.go.com/blog/2011/09/vintage-walt-disney-world-a-dedication-with-style-at-magic-kingdom-park/.
Schwartz, D. (2022, June 11). *For some adults who love Disney, it's like a religion*. NPR. Retrieved from https://www.npr.org/2022/06/11/1104056661/disney-adults.
TEA/AECOM (2023). Theme Index and Museum Index 2022: Global Attractions Attendance Report. https://aecom.com/wp-content/uploads/documents/reports/AECOM-Theme-Index-2022.pdf.
Volk-Weiss, B. (Director). (2021a). The Castles. In D. Johnson, et al. (Executive Producers), I. Disney Platform Distribution.
Volk-Weiss, B. (Director). (2021b). Hall of Presidents. In D. Johnson, et al. (Executive Producers), *Behind the Attraction.* Disney Platform Distribution.
Volk-Weiss, B. (Director). (2021c). Haunted Mansion. In D. Johnson, et al. (Executive Producers), *Behind the Attraction.* Disney Platform Distribution.
Volk-Weiss, B. (Director). (2021d). It's a Small World. In D. Johnson, et al. (Executive Producers), *Behind the Attraction.* Disney Platform Distribution.
Volk-Weiss, B. (Director). (2021e). Jungle Cruise. In D. Johnson, et al. (Executive Producers), *Behind the Attraction.* Disney Platform Distribution.
Volk-Weiss, B. (Director). (2021f). Space Mountain. In D. Johnson, et al. (Executive Producers), *Behind the Attraction.* Disney Platform Distribution.
Wall, S. (2006). An autoethnography on learning about autoethnography. *International Journal of Qualitative Methods, 5*(2), 146–160.
Wills, J. (2017). *Disney culture.* Rutgers University Press.

About the Contributors

Tim **Baird** (Ph.D., Ohio University) is an assistant professor of communication studies at Bemidji State University in Bemidji, Minnesota.

Lori **Bindig Yousman** (Ph.D., University of Massachusetts Amherst) is a professor of communication studies and the associate dean in the College of Arts & Science at Sacred Heart University in Fairfield, Connecticut.

Raymond **Blanton** (Ph.D., University of Nebraska-Lincoln) is an associate professor of communication arts at the University of the Incarnate Word in San Antonio, Texas.

Mindy **Burnett** (M.A., California State University, Fullerton) directs marketing and communications for the University of Arizona College of Veterinary Medicine.

Kristi **Gatto** is a doctoral candidate in the College of Media & Communication at Texas Tech University in Lubbock.

Jennessa **Hester** (M.A., University of New Orleans) is a doctoral candidate in English at Texas Tech University in Lubbock.

Gwendelyn S. **Nisbett** (Ph.D., University of Oklahoma) is an associate professor of public relations at the Mayborn School of Journalism, University of North Texas in Denton.

Newly **Paul** (M.A., University of Southern California, and Ph.D., Louisiana State University) is an associate professor of journalism at the University of North Texas in Denton.

John **Perlich** (M.A., Minnesota State University, Mankato, and Ph.D., University of Nebraska-Lincoln) is a professor of communication studies at Bemidji State University in Bemidji, Minnesota.

Pablo A. **Sánchez-Rodríguez** (M.A., Università degli Studi Roma Tre, and Ph.D., Universidad Complutense de Madrid) is an FPU researcher and assistant professor in international relations and global history at Universidad Complutense de Madrid in Spain.

Samantha **Tecson** (M.A., University of California–Los Angeles) is a student in the Annenberg School for Communication and Journalism's Ph.D. program at the University of Southern California in Los Angeles.

Erika M. **Thomas** (Ph.D., Wayne State University) is an associate professor and the co-director of forensics in the Department of Human Communication Studies and queer studies minor affiliated faculty at California State University, Fullerton.

Rhema F. **White** (B.A., University of South Alabama, M.A., University of Alabama) is a doctoral student in the Communication, Culture, and Media Studies program at Howard University in Washington, D.C.

David **Whitt** (M.A. and Ph.D., University of Nebraska–Lincoln) is a professor of communication studies at Nebraska Wesleyan University in Lincoln.

Index

www.ingramcontent.com/pod-product-compliance
Ingram Content Group UK Ltd.
Pitfield, Milton Keynes, MK11 3LW, UK
UKHW041834100926
8556IPUK00018B/963

9 781476 690056